D0571871

ADDITIONAL PRAISE FOR
LANNY DAVIS'S *SCANDAL*

"For those who applauded the demise of the Independent Counsel Statute, Lanny Davis's book is a fitting funereal tribute. It is required reading for anyone who even dares to think such a law would be wise public policy in the future."

—*Joseph E. diGenova, former U.S. Attorney*
for the District of Columbia and
former Independent Counsel

"Lanny's book shows us how the public debate moved from a question of right and wrong to a question of good and bad. It is a call to arms for Americans who want a true debate of ideas for moving our country forward."

—*Governor Bill Richardson, New Mexico*

"Lanny Davis's important new book documents the growing number of Americans who want to take the country back from the ideological purists and haters on the left and right. Davis sees a new center majority of fiscal conservatism, social liberalism, and cultural moderation and toleration—an ideological mix that happens to be where most Americans are and want their leaders to be. This book should be required reading for every presidential candidate from both parties in 2008."

—*Al From, Founder & CEO,*
Democratic Leadership Council

"I am confident that Lanny Davis speaks for most Americans when he decries the coarsening of our political discourse and the dysfunction it has created in Washington. Hopefully, his work will serve as a wake-up call and prompt a better, more productive kind of national political leadership."

—*Senator Evan Bayh (D-IN)*

SCANDAL

HOW
"GOTCHA" POLITICS IS
DESTROYING AMERICA

Lanny Davis

palgrave
macmillan

SCANDAL
Copyright © Lanny J. Davis, 2006.
All rights reserved. No part of this book may be used or reproduced in any
manner whatsoever without written permission except in the case of brief
quotations embodied in critical articles or reviews.

First published in 2006 by
PALGRAVE MACMILLAN™
175 Fifth Avenue, New York, N.Y. 10010 and
Houndmills, Basingstoke, Hampshire, England RG21 6XS.
Companies and representatives throughout the world.

PALGRAVE MACMILLAN is the global academic imprint of the Palgrave
Macmillan division of St. Martin's Press, LLC and of Palgrave Macmillan Ltd.
Macmillan® is a registered trademark in the United States, United Kingdom
and other countries. Palgrave is a registered trademark in the European Union
and other countries.

ISBN-13: 978-1-4039-7495-2
ISBN-10: 1-4039-7495-0

Library of Congress Cataloging-in-Publication Data is available from the
Library of Congress.
Davis, Lanny J.
  Scandal : how gotcha politics is destroying America / by Lanny J. Davis.
    p.   cm.
  Includes bibliographical references and index.
  ISBN 1-4039-7495-0 (alk. paper)
  1. Scandals—United States.   2. Political culture—United States.
3. United States—Politics and government—1945–1989.   4. United States—
Politics and government—1989–   I. Title.
JK2249.D38   2006
973.92—dc22

                                                              2006043605

A catalogue record of the book is available from the British Library.

Design by Letra Libre, Inc.

First edition: September 2006
10 9 8 7 6 5 4 3 2 1
Printed in the United States of America.

HONORARY DEDICATION

To Presidents George H. W. Bush and Bill Clinton, 2005 ABC Network "Persons of the Year," two men who know the difference between the politics of civil disagreement and the politics of personal destruction

"In today's divisive political climates, they have tried to promote tolerance and bipartisanship, leading by example."

—ABC News

"Because you run against each other doesn't mean you're enemies. Politics doesn't have to be uncivil and nasty."

—George H. W. Bush, December 2005

"The so-called politics of personal destruction is a part of a larger trend to force everybody into little boxes. You've got to be liberal or conservative. We're all supposed to be two-dimensional cartoon characters, not flesh and blood people with strengths and weaknesses. We're right and we're wrong."

—Bill Clinton, December 2005

DEDICATION

To my children, Marlo and David, Seth and Melissa, and Jeremy; to my grandchildren, Jake, Sydney, Devon, Zachary and Noah; to Susie Hudson, our family member and friend to us all; to my wife and best friend, Carolyn Atwell-Davis, who has made it all possible and makes my life whole; and finally, to my son, Joshua, who stood by me in the beginning of the writing of this book, throughout the writing of this book, and typed the last words of this book.

"Americans are simply fed up with what they see as the 'gotcha' culture of Washington, D.C.

"'It's hard to know the truth coming out of Washington,' said Stephen Libor of Andover, Minn. 'This guy did this, this guy did that.' It seems there's no love, kindness or understanding of other people. It's just, 'Nail 'em!'"

—Washington Post, *November 6, 2005*

CONTENTS

PART IV

The Revolt of the Center

ACKNOWLEDGMENTS

First, I want to thank my agent, Ron Goldfarb, who worked with me from the earliest days of my idea for this book and was greatly influential in shaping my thinking and approach in writing it.

Second, my thanks to my editor, Toby Wahl, for making my writing better—and for his early understanding of the themes and issues that motivated me to write this book. My special thanks to Palgrave's publisher, Airié Stuart, who made the ultimate judgment—and the act of faith—in supporting the publication of this book. I hope she is proven right; and to Donna Cherry for her help and assistance on final production.

Third, I am extremely grateful to my research assistant, Sarah Siebert. She was always there, 24/7, and I don't know how I could have written this book without her. Her patience, perseverance, and care in not only helping me with sources but in influencing my thinking cannot be understated.

Thanks to my two colleagues at my law firm, Orrick, Herrington & Sutcliffe—Adam Goldberg, who served with me as a White House counsel, and Joshua Galper, a Yale Law School graduate and, more importantly, a Yale *Daily News* alumnus, for their substantive suggestions and careful editing. And to another Orrick colleague, Kimberly Neureiter, for her suggestions and support, and Marti Handman for being there for the crucial final read and edit.

I am grateful to my partners and colleagues at Orrick, Herrington & Sutcliffe—and particularly the bi-partisan group consisting of Chairman Ralph Baxter, Cam Cowan, Ray Mullady, and Ed Woodsome—for allowing me time and space (i.e., weekends and nights) to write this book and for providing the professional support and friendship that has been so important to me.

There are simply no words that can describe how important Maddie Melendez has been to the writing, editing, typing, advising, and inspiring of this book. Aside from the fact that she manages the "hurricane," as she calls me, Maddie's judgment and balance during times of stress as this book was being written—which is to say virtually every day—allowed me to function and do what I do. The universal question everyone asks is, How does she remain her calm, kind, and unflappable self while still having to work for me? No one seems to be able to answer that question very well, certainly not me.

I am grateful to three authors in particular on whose books I relied for several chapters: Suzanne Garment, who wrote the seminal book in 1991, *Scandal: The Crisis of Mistrust in American Politics*; *Washington Post* reporter Bob Woodward, whose book *Shadow: Five Presidents and the Legacy of Watergate* contained inside sources and behind-the-scenes explanations of presidential scandals that, it seems, only Bob Woodward manages to be able to get; and Ron Chernow, whose biography, *Hamilton*, contains by far the most detailed and colorful narrative of the Maria Reynolds affair.

Finally and most importantly, my thanks to and love for my friend and the toughest editor of all: Carolyn Atwell-Davis, my wife of 21 years. (Another universal question is how she's managed to live with the Hurricane for 21 years.) Despite her busy days during her important work as an attorney and legislative affairs director for the National Center for Missing & Exploited Children, she showed her usual patience and forbearance with my work and writing schedule while still caring for our two sons, Joshua and Jeremy, five cats, two dogs, and still was there to offer suggestions, reactions, and criticisms to keep me on track.

PROLOGUE

On June 14, 2004, hundreds of former Clinton Administration members gathered in the sun-filled East Room of the Bush White House. The crowd, buzzing with a mix of excitement and nostalgia, included almost all the former Clinton Cabinet secretaries, senior White House staff, and "Friends of Bill" from Arkansas and elsewhere. Each was there for the unveiling of President Bill Clinton's and First Lady Hillary Clinton's official White House portraits. It also marked the Clintons' first return to the White House since the Bushes moved in on January 20, 2001. As we waited for both the Clintons and Bushes to appear in this energized atmosphere, I was unsure what to expect. I heard several comments expressing contempt, even hatred, for President Bush. Would the Clintonites greet President Bush with coldness or open hostility when he appeared? How would President Bush react? Given his previous harsh words about President Clinton, would he rise to the occasion himself? I sensed other people in the crowd shared my tension. Our answer came soon enough.

The room fell to a hush as the Clinton family entered the room with the President and Mrs. Bush. They walked down the red-carpeted aisle past the packed chairs lined up in the East Room and sat together in the first row in front of the podium. Next, President Bush stood and stepped up to the platform. The two huge portraits of President and Mrs. Clinton were veiled, behind him, on his left and right. He paused and looked out at the audience—somewhat warily, I thought. He looked down at the Clintons and Chelsea, then he smiled warmly and, it seemed to me, authentically and began: "President Clinton and Senator Clinton, welcome home. . . . Over eight years, it was clear that Bill Clinton loved the job of the presidency. He filled this house with energy and joy. . . . My congratulations to you both."[1] The reaction was instantaneous. Everyone jumped to their feet with a thunderous ovation—an unleashing of emotions that seemed to convert the negative feelings in the room toward President Bush into an outpouring of appreciation. After several other comments praising President Clinton's record of bringing peace and prosperity to America during his two terms as

president, President Bush then complimented President Clinton on his in-
stinctive optimism. He said: " . . . you've got to be optimistic to give six
months of your life running the McGovern campaign in Texas." The room
roared with laughter. Sitting a row or two behind President and Mrs. Clinton
and Chelsea, I could see President Clinton double up with laughter.

When President Bush was done, President Clinton rose. He thanked
President Bush and spoke a few minutes about his memories of the privilege
of serving two terms as President and of the achievements of his administration. What he said next had a great effect on me and, I believe, the rest of the
people in the room:

> The President, by his generous words to Hillary and me today, has proved
> once again that, in the end, we are held together by this grand system of
> ours that permits us to debate and struggle and fight for what we believe is
> right. . . . You know, most of the people I've known in this business, Repub-
> licans and Democrats, conservatives and liberals, were good people, honest
> people, and they did what they thought was right. And I hope that I'll live
> long enough to see American politics return to vigorous debates where we
> argue who's right and wrong, not who's good and bad.[2]

There was a thunderous standing ovation. It grew even louder as President
Bush nodded and pointed toward President Clinton with a gesture of affir-
mation and President Clinton pointed back at him.

I must admit I felt a rush—a rush of patriotism and pride in our country. I felt a sense of awe and privilege that I had been there to witness this
brief moment in history when two successive American presidents from
different parties, with very different family backgrounds and political beliefs, had affirmed their mutual commitment to a politics of civil disagreement, not of personal destruction. Since that day, I have thought a lot
about this moment—the graciousness shown by President Bush, the fundamental distinction President Clinton drew between saying someone is
right or wrong versus saying someone is good or bad, and the common
bond and experience these two men share in recognizing the difference. It
prompted me to ask how the politics of personal destruction that has dominated American politics for the last quarter century or so—this cycle of
scandal, attack, and counter-attack, this seemingly endless game of
"gotcha" politics—started. More importantly, how do we stop it? How can
we return to an atmosphere of vigorous debate and healthy partisanship,
where political adversaries clash in the marketplace of ideas and seek to
win arguments and elections rather than to destroy their opponents personally? How can we establish a new politics, dominated by a broad center

drawn from both the left and right and interested in solving problems Americans care about, not one focused solely on destroying the other party and winning the next election?

This book is my best effort at answering these questions, and it owes its genesis to that remarkable spring day.

INTRODUCTION

"Politics as total (and personal) warfare is Washington's way of life now, and this has lowered the esteem of America's governmental institutions and demeaned the people who have come to the Capitol to serve the nation."

—*Carl M. Cannon*, National Journal, *February 13, 1999*

Today's scandal culture and the seemingly endless cycle of gotcha politics practiced by the extremist ideologues of the left and the right in both parties have their roots in the political and culture wars of the 1960s and the Watergate scandal that immediately followed them in the 1970s. This applies as well to the so-called Great Divide between conservative Red state and liberal Blue state America immortalized in the 2000 and 2004 presidential electoral maps.

Scandal has become the chief instrument of mass political destruction for more than 30 years. More and more Democrats and Republicans in an increasingly broader center see the hypocrisies and counter-productive venom coming from their purist bases. More and more people are fed up with the food fight ideologues on both sides and share Shakespeare's sentiment, "a pox on both your houses." Across the spectrum there is a desire to debate the issues on the merits and find solutions—and a disgust with the politics of personal destruction.

The bitter legacy of the 1960s and Watergate materialized over the last 30 years in the form of a scandal machine that has progressively generated a level of viciousness and personally destructive power unlike anything seen in America before. Given the fact that scandal and the sensationalistic journalism covering it is as American as apple pie, going back to the Founders of our Republic, that is really saying something. Since the late 1970s, this scandal machine has been truly different, however, not just in degree but in kind. Over the last three decades, we saw the evolution from traditional partisan backbiting to a criminal cover-up by President Nixon in Watergate to recent instances of corruption in 2006, such as guilty pleas by lobbyist Jack Abramoff to criminal fraud and bribery conspiracy, and Representative Duke Cunningham to taking bribes. But since Watergate and the downfall of Richard Nixon, there has also been a tremendous increase in the number of hyper-partisan politicians on the left and right who use scandal and the criminal justice system to do their political hatchet work. They have also turned to character assassination charges aimed not just at defeating the opposition but destroying it.

The cycle of gotcha politics has become habitual and virtually unstoppable. Food fights masquerading as policy discussions on cable news networks, ravers and haters on talk radio, and the criminalization of political differences through that unaccountable legal monster called the "Independent Counsel" (initially created and abused by the Democrats) all evolved into the public face, and public shame, of modern day American politics.

In the 1970s and 1980s, the rules governing what was appropriate versus inappropriate conduct of the media and politicians changed dramatically, but it was not until the 1990s that the implosion finally occurred. It was then that the seeds of the 1960s culture wars and Watergate, the evolving post–Watergate media rules, the new telecommunication technologies, the increase in noncompetitive, gerrymandered, effectively one-party Congressional districts—a major reason for the hyper-partisanship in Congress by both parties—have combined to create political rot, horrible rot. The cycle of "gotcha" politics—with each side justifying their shock-and-awe attacks based on the other side's last "gotcha"—became endless and systemic. Political parties and their leaders suffered then, and they continue to pay a price today, as do we all.

The result is that more and more Americans are fed up and, to borrow Howard Beale's line in *Network*, are "mad as Hell and not going to take it anymore." And many Americans appear ready to join a growing revolt of the political center to take the country back. Those Americans not blinded by irrational hate toward those who fail to agree with their chosen political views are looking for political leaders who are able to get in front of this revolt, who can rise above the culture of vitriol and hyper-partisanship, who can debate deeply held ideas and political differences with civility, and who will focus on solving problems, not destroying political opponents. A fundamental realignment of the alienated center-left and center-right into a new centrist majority may happen in the 2008 presidential election—and perhaps as early as the 2006 congressional elections. Even if the Democrats manage to take over both houses of Congress in the November 2006 elections, that could present a significant political danger for them. If they yield to the temptation of playing "gotcha" and follow the hyper-partisanship path of the Gingrichites after the 1994 takeover of both Houses of Congress by the Republicans, it could significantly hurt the Democrats.

Now the question is, which party leaders, if any, have the political courage and political will to seize the moment and take a stand against "gotcha" politics, against the scandal culture that has corrupted American politics for far too long? Which, if any, leader will have the courage to lead his or her party to win the presidency in 2008—and then reach across the aisle to form a grand coalition government drawn from both parties, liberals and conservatives, to take a "time out" from partisanship and solve America's most pressing problems at home and abroad?

THE SCANDAL MACHINE

Partisan-driven scandal in American politics is not exactly new. It has ranged from the sexual scandals of Alexander Hamilton and Thomas Jefferson, each of whom attempted to use them to hurt the other politically, and political corruption scandals such as Credit Mobilier in 1872 and Teapot Dome in the 1920s, to Grover Cleveland's illegitimate child, information about which was leaked during his first presidential campaign in 1884, to Warren Harding's famous extra-marital tryst with young Nan Britton in a legendary (reportedly) stand-up position in a White House closet on the ground floor of the residence. And these are just a few examples. Thus, over two centuries, there is a pattern of politicians using the media, and vice versa, in attempts to bring down political adversaries allegedly caught with their hand in the cookie jar—or their pants down.

Today's version of the post–Watergate scandal culture is different, however, in one significant and unprecedented way: *its far greater destructive power.* This unfortunate power is derived from four key changes that occurred post-Watergate in the last quarter of the twentieth century—changes in journalistic, legal, technological, and cultural attitudes and rules of the game that had been previously understood by politicians and the public alike. These changes evolved over this time period separately but then combined in force in the 1990s like a landslide crashing down a mountain slope. Their power joined together for the first time during President Bill Clinton's two terms and imploded with what was the political equivalent of a nuclear detonation.

The first of the four changes were the post–Watergate rules and incentives governing investigative journalism, especially when related to scandals.

These were heavily influenced by the *Washington Post* and the Woodward–
Bernstein coverage of Watergate and its aftermath. Based on how Watergate
had been covered and reported, it became acceptable to engage in "connect-
the-dot" journalism, where events are placed side by side, implying that they
are causally related when there are no facts to show that they are. Over-
reliance on anonymous sources, the credibility of whom could not be independently verified, also became regular practice. But perhaps most damning,
Watergate showed reporters that bringing down a high-profile politician
might lead to financial and professional gain, even if at the end of the day it
results in no final determination or conviction of wrongdoing.

In addition, post–Watergate journalistic rules also led to the undermining of the "gentlemen's agreement" that had existed between the media and
politicians as to what was and was not appropriate for journalists to publish
about a politician's personal and private (read: sexual) conduct. Specifically,
the previous understanding, which lasted at least from George Washington
to John Kennedy, was that private sexual conduct having no impact on public
responsibilities and no impact on national security had long been considered
out of bounds, with rare exceptions throughout U.S. history. That was certainly the case, for example, when it came to the media looking the other way
during the well-known extracurricular (and sometimes reckless) sexual dalliances of President John F. Kennedy.

In retrospect, a key pivot point concerning these rules of the road was
Gary Hart's dare to the press to catch him having an affair in 1987—something
that they immediately proceeded to do. This was followed by salacious testimony during Clarence Thomas's confirmation hearings in 1991 and
Newsweek's decision to publish a story in 1996 about an alleged sexual advance
by President Clinton in which the actual facts were in dispute. And then there
was the Monica incident—after which all previous rules of media restraint
rushed out the window.

Second, an important reaction to Watergate was the enactment of the
Independent Counsel statute in 1978. This law, which started with the noble
idea that a prosecutor needed to be free of conflicts of interest in investigating the president or the Executive Branch, ended up creating an extra-
Constitutional monstrosity, possessed of unaccountable prosecutorial power
misused by politicians to attack and perhaps destroy their opponents. Too
often, it became a reckless excuse for prosecutorial "fishing expeditions" and
overzealousness that caused considerable pain and damage to the reputations
of innocent people. Its end result was the partisan-driven criminalizing of political differences. The Democrats' insistence on the enactment of the Independent Counsel statute in the aftermath (and a result) of Watergate is a

classic example of the old saw, "be careful what you wish for," because it became a double-edged sword. Yes, the Democrats used (and abused) independent counsels to their political advantage during the Reagan and Bush I
years, but then came the ultimate gotcha: Kenneth Starr's team of prosecutors who ended up uncovering no criminal wrongdoing by the Clintons concerning a 20-year-old land deal called Whitewater, but instead settled for a
case about lying about sex during a civil deposition.

The third change that affected American political culture was the
telecommunications revolution that occurred during the late 1980s and early
1990s. First came the new reality of 24-hour cable news television and the
24/7 news cycle. On top of this, the expansion of the Internet, with its wider
and wider accessibility to the general public and global audience, added a
whole new dimension to media communication. The combination of this
revolution, together with the other post–Watergate political, cultural, and
journalistic changes, was deadly. Under the pressures of 24/7 news, the guiding journalistic rule changed to trying to get it first, even if this was sometimes at the expense of getting it right. And once misinformation was
published or broadcast, it traveled around the globe literally in seconds to
millions of readers and lived on forever in the Internet echo chambers of
Google, Yahoo, and other search engines.

Finally, accumulating bit by bit since Watergate as a result of these various changes, came a culture of public cynicism and increased willingness to
accept innuendo and accusation as surrogates for due process and the truth.
With each new slight and transgression of our elected leaders, the public
grew ever more willing to accept politicians—and in the post–Enron era,
top-level corporate executives—as guilty as charged when accused of
wrongdoing in a headline. It may be the fault of having been burned once
too often, but the benefit of the doubt is no longer freely given. For the
American public, the saying "where there's smoke, there's fire" has become a
guiding principle.

THE CYCLE OF GOTCHA POLITICS

Joined together, with geometrically enhanced synergistic power, these
post–Watergate changes in America became weapons of mass political destruction during the last few decades. And any time one party tried using
them to destroy the other, it simply triggered a counter-strike, which triggered still another, and so on.

The difference between today's excessive and destructive "gotcha politics" and the deserved downfall of public figures due to proven corruption

and criminal conduct admittedly can be fuzzy and sometimes subjective. But the difference is real and significant, reminiscent of the late Supreme Court Justice Potter Stewart's definition of obscenity, "I may not be able to define it—but I know it when I see it." Within the pages of this book, gotcha politics is purely and simply about partisanship, not about uncovering genuine corruption; it is about revenge and payback, not about due process and investigations in search of the truth; and ultimately, it is about personal and political destruction, not winning in the marketplace of ideas or defeating your adversary based on the issues at the polls and in the precincts.

As of early 2006, running a Google search of the expression "gotcha politics" results in over 12,000 "hits." So, something widely pervasive and recurrent has seeped into our political system and media culture. As already noted, Watergate and Richard Nixon's downfall served as the touchstone for the scandal machine that followed, particularly the incestuous and mutual dependence of the combined power of investigative journalists, Congressional investigations, and the criminal justice system. But Watergate was about true corruption and criminal conduct. At the end, after Nixon's smoking gun, the CIA cover-up tape, was found, virtually all Congressional Republicans and Democrats would have voted to impeach and convict President Nixon had he not resigned first in August 1974. The same cannot be said about those who have found themselves victim to the new scandal machine of the post–Watergate era.

Probably the first example of this came in 1977—shortly before passage of the Independent Counsel Act. It included all the elements of the scandal culture and the destructive cycle of gotcha politics described above. That year brought the media and political blow-up over then President Carter's Budget Director, Bert Lance. It involved financial and banking transactions when he was president of a Georgia bank before he joined his friend Jimmy Carter in the White House. Dubbed "Lancegate" by the Republicans, the case followed a script that at the time was still new. Vague allegations of "wrongdoing" or "financial improprieties" were first leaked to newspapers, which lead to headlines and hyped-up network newscasts. These prompted Congressional investigations, which led to more leaks and eventually to televised Congressional hearings based on all of the headlines and public attention. This ultimately brought us to the inevitable denouement of the scandal machine, resignation in disgrace—all without a single piece of evidence presented in a courtroom, without an indictment, and certainly without a conviction. It was scary and dangerous, though we did not know how scary and dangerous at the time.

Then, in the 1980s, it was payback time for the Democrats. With the election of conservative Republican President Ronald Reagan came the hounding and persecution of President Reagan's Labor Secretary Raymond Donovan by Democrats, leading to the appointment of an Independent Counsel and two separate investigations that led nowhere. Well, that is not exactly true. It did lead somewhere for Secretary Donovan—his forced resignation and departure in disgrace from Washington. This was followed by an indictment in 1984 by the Bronx District Attorney, a Democrat, on vague charges of corruption. Donovan was acquitted three long years later by a jury that deliberated for little time and insisted on declaring him innocent individually rather than giving the customary collective announcement of a "not guilty" verdict.

What followed was arguably the keystone event that triggered the most vicious subsequent manifestations of the scandal culture and gotcha politics—the defeat of President Reagan's Supreme Court nominee, Robert Bork, in 1987. From the perspective of liberals and many constitutional experts, there were legitimate grounds to oppose Bork's accession to the Supreme Court. These were not only philosophical objections to his overly narrow approach to the Constitution but also serious questions about whether he had a suitable temperament to serve on the Supreme Court (questions that many stand by to this day). But clearly, with the wisdom of hindsight, some of the techniques used by leading liberal groups to bring Bork down were tainted, at least at times, by the modus operandi that became a model for future hyper-partisanship: misuse of innuendo and misinformation combined with leaks and a barrage of negative media coverage. Enigmatically, those were never adequately countered or corrected by Bork or the Reagan White House.

The fury and outrage by conservatives about these tactics against Judge Bork (as well as those used during the confirmation hearings of Clarence Thomas, in which charges regarding his sexual misconduct were allowed to go out on national television without Mr. Thomas having an opportunity to cross-examine the witness nor refute her charges ahead of time) cannot be underestimated. Nor can the Republican right's desire for revenge for what was perceived as Democratic misuse of independent counsels in the 1980s, and of leaks and smears during Congressional hearings and investigations. (Rightly or wrongly, conservatives coined a new verb for the political lexicon—"to Bork"—as a shorthand for creating unfair misinformation and media leaks during Congressional hearings.) The Democrats had taught the lessons of how to use the scandal machine well, and the Republicans had no problem following those lessons along the same destructive path once they gained control over both houses of Congress in 1994.

When the 1980s ended with a backbencher Republican congressman named Newt Gingrich leading a two-year campaign that resulted in the resignation of then Democratic Speaker Jim Wright, it was clear that there was no stopping the gotcha cycle from entering the 1990s with even more destructive power.

The independent counsel stood at the center of this new, more virulent politics of personal destruction spreading through the political process, and was now clearly the first choice as a weapon of mass political destruction. Witness the Iran-Contra scandal during Ronald Reagan's second term that spilled over into the last days of President George H. W. Bush's presidency. Independent counsel Lawrence Walsh made the reckless decision to re-indict former Defense Secretary Casper Weinberger on the Friday before the 1992 presidential election, gratuitously and unnecessarily including in the indictment a reference to President Bush's knowledge of the activities in question. In retrospect it now seems clear that this was the ultimate criminalization of politics that had so outraged President Bush and leading Republicans at the time. No leading Democrat, and certainly no Clinton supporters cheering that final weekend at this very damaging blow to President Bush's reelection chances, complained publicly. (I certainly didn't!)

The essentially bogus Clinton "scandal wars" of the 1990s were next. Shortly after the Republicans surprised the country (and themselves) by taking over both houses of Congress in the November 1994 mid-term elections, the new harshly partisan and self-styled conservative "revolutionary" Speaker Newt Gingrich reportedly passed the word that Republican-controlled House committees would focus their time, public funds, and subpoena powers to investigate the Clinton White House on whatever ground they could find. This crossed every line—from separation of powers to the recognized limits on partisanship between a Congress controlled by one party and a president from the other—that had rarely been crossed even in the most partisan periods of American history. From January 1995 through 1997—prior to the Lewinsky matter—Republican Senate and House committees spent what the U.S. Government's General Accounting Office (GAO) ultimately calculated to be in excess of $20 million in tax dollars investigating the Clinton White House chasing what turned out to be rabbit holes. These investigations generated thousands of pages of headlines and nightly news broadcasts concerning such scandal will o' the wisps as Whitewater, Vincent Foster's suicide, the White House travel office, campaign finance practices, FBI files, and so on. In the end, they caught Democrats engaging in a number of unseemly fundraising practices (not too different than what Republicans were doing, it must be added)—but with no indictments, much less convictions of anyone from the Clinton campaign or senior officials from the national party. By the end of his and his successor's investigations in 2000, even independent counsel Kenneth W. Starr ended up with no indictments of the Clintons on Whitewater or any of the other White House "scandals," such as "Travelgate" or the suicide of Deputy White House Counsel Vincent Foster, that he had been authorized to pursue by the Attorney General.

With roots tracing back to Gary Hart's ordeal ten years earlier, then came the 1998 investigation by Independent Counsel Starr of a private sexual relationship of President Clinton. The end result: an admission by President Clinton in 2000, leading to a civil order to repay the Arkansas Bar Association for legal fees, on the last day of his presidency, that he testified falsely under oath in a civil deposition in a case that was thrown out on Summary Judgment. Sincere people on both sides differed on whether that false testimony was an impeachable offense, but partisans on both sides felt compelled to challenge the motives and integrity of the other on nightly cable shows and in daily war rooms. The fact that the impeachment in the House split on almost entirely partisan lines contrasted to the Nixon impeachment vote in the House Judiciary Committee in 1974. Also disappointing to the House Impeachment managers, many of whom genuinely believed that President Clinton had perjured himself and thus should be impeached, was the fact that they could not convince a majority of Republican Senators, in a Senate controlled by their party by a 55–45 margin, to agree with them. President Clinton was easily acquitted by far short of the constitutionally required two-thirds vote for conviction.

The Republicans, however, did not avoid the dangers of the inevitable gotcha-cycle boomerang effect. In 1997, the bipartisan House Ethics Committee fined Newt Gingrich $300,000 for various ethical violations, just eight years after he helped the same committee bring down Speaker Jim Wright. Then there was Robert Livingston, the chosen replacement for Gingrich as Speaker and another leader in the partisan House impeachment effort. He resigned suddenly on the eve of the impeachment vote when he was forced to admit to an extramarital affair that his sanctimonious religious right-wing friends could not countenance. (So much for relying on your right-wing friends when the going gets tough!) More recently, in the fall of 2005, there was the ironic spectacle of then House Republican Majority Leader Tom DeLay, who, after being indicted for money laundering by a Texas grand jury, rushed to the microphones and—I am not making this up, the same man who repeatedly declared Bill Clinton guilty of crimes and corruption before he ever had his day in court—demanded that he receive the benefit of the presumption of innocence. Mr. DeLay's announcement in spring 2006 that he would resign from Congress in November does not convict him of any crime—but it certainly proves the older saw, "what goes around comes around." Of course, according to the rules of the scandal culture, his political death warrant had already been signed. In January 2006, DeLay was forced out of his position as House Majority Leader and replaced by John Boehner.

Then again, the Democrats could not resist the temptation of reverting to gotcha politics hypocrisy, too. The general rule in Washington, D.C. is that when the opposition is committing political suicide, get out of the way. But the Democrats could not leave well enough alone when Republican scandals started breaking in 2005. With the indictment of I. Lewis "Scooter" Libby, the Vice President's Chief of Staff, for perjury and obstruction, and the guilty pleas of felonies by lobbyist Jack Abramoff and several of his colleagues as well as Representative Duke Cunningham for bribery, the Democrats again prematurely rushed to the microphones (and the Internet) to accuse the Republicans of being guilty of fostering a "culture of corruption." And this comes from the party that used to denounce Republicans for ignoring the presumption of innocence and for using that same phrase about the Clinton White House.

Much of Democratic attacks on President Bush's decision to go to war in Iraq also has the unfortunate aroma of "gotcha" politics. Instead of focusing on objective facts showing that President Bush and his advisers got it "wrong"—such as selective use and misuses of intelligence on weapons of mass destruction in order to justify a preemptive rush to war and the obvious ill-planning and lack of an exit strategy—too many left-wing bloggers and Bush-bashing Democratic partisans have tried to prove that President Bush and senior administration officials "lied." This defied the lesson President Clinton tried to teach during the unveiling of his White House portrait, that we should "argue who's right and wrong, not who's good and bad." More importantly, focusing on proving the "L" word has become a distraction from the much more important issue of how to get out of Iraq—which an overwhelming majority of Americans want a plan to do—without leaving behind a dangerous rogue state and base for terrorism.

Meanwhile, the rantings on both the left and right of the shouters, food fighters, and hate-mongers on talk radio, cable television shows, and, in recent years, countless blogs go on, seemingly caring little about actual facts and truth before broadcasting and blogging accusations—all of which add more reckless negative energy and fuel to the scandal machine and gotcha politics.

THE REVOLT OF THE CENTER:
TAKING THE COUNTRY BACK

Alienated, angry, disgusted—these are not comforting descriptions of the U.S. voter, but it is the growing reality. Increasing numbers of Americans see through the double standards and hypocrisies of the purist left of the Democratic Party and the purist right of the Republican Party. They see Democratic liberals, who profess to believe in small "d" democracy, attempting to override popular sentiment at the state and local legislative levels by using unelected judges to impose public policy on moral and values questions by judicial fiat. They also see Republican conservatives, who profess to believe in fiscal responsibility, borrowing and spending the country into huge deficits, leaving debts for our children and grandchildren to pay and earmarking hidden subsidies for "bridges to nowhere" in the bowels of appropriations bills that no one reads and no one would approve if the lights were turned on and the American people really knew what was going on.

In fact, the now commonly held belief of the divided America split into Republican "Red States" and Democratic "Blue States"—something that seemed so graphic on the presidential electoral maps of 2000 and 2004—may not be so stark and intractable as the colors indicate. In short, the ingredients of a massive and historic revolt of a new "purple" center are in place—perhaps without precedent since Theodore Roosevelt's Bull Moose campaign of 1912. Today there is a good chance of achieving a new governing majority—comprised of a unique coalition of social liberals, fiscal conservatives, cultural moderates, and supporters of a strong national defense, committed to an effective war against terrorism. The social liberals still believe government is a friend, not an enemy, and is needed to solve the people's most important problems—so long as it is limited, focused, and respects and encourages an open and competitive private market. The fiscal conservatives believe in balanced budgets, pay-as-you-go government, and—if the failure or inadequacy of the private market can be demonstrated—the need for new targeted, dedicated taxes to pay for needed social programs. The cultural moderates are tolerant of religious and moral values and generally prefer democratic institutions at the state and local level, rather than the courts, to determine policies and values-based positions. And supporters of a strong and flexible national defense favor strengthening America's military capabilities to proactively attack Al Qaeda and the terrorists wherever they are. They also see the war in Iraq as potentially undermining that focus on the war on terrorism and recognize there must be a near-term exit strategy—not cutting and running but redeploying U.S. forces in the region to prevent a pro-Al Qaeda takeover.

A GRAND COALITION GOVERNMENT

The presidential election of 2008 could become a historic, watershed, re-aligning election. Which party or leader is able to take advantage of this centrist revolt against the scandal culture and the demand for responsible government that solves people's problems remains to be seen. It may well be that the combination of deep-felt concerns over the War against Terror and the growing centrist revolt against the scandal culture and gotcha politics that holds both Republicans and Democrats in its thrall could be the catalyst that produces a historic window for bipartisan government—a Grand Coalition government in which the president and vice president come from opposite parties, a bipartisan Cabinet, and a bipartisan centrist congressional majority. It would be a government that actually focuses on addressing America's most important domestic problems and defeating terrorism rather than figuring out new ways to "stick it" to the opposing party. It may seem like a dream, but it may be closer to reality than we realize. As usual, the American people may be way ahead of the inside-the-Beltway pundits and politicians who undoubtedly would regard such a Grand Coalition government as unrealistic. We shall see.

PART I

IT DIDN'T BEGIN WITH WATERGATE

REVOLUTIONARY VENOM, ITS PROGENY, AND THE GENTLEMEN'S AGREEMENT FROM HARDING TO KENNEDY

A powerful national political leader, one of the most famous in American history, has an extramarital affair that his political opposition finds out about. He success-fully organizes a cover-up that lasts over four years, but his political enemies don't forget. Leaders of the opposition use lower level operatives, so-called elves, whose network for passing along rumors and documents spreads the poison and sets the trap for future disclosure. Then, when the powerful national political leader is at his zenith of power, the gory details are disclosed under the false charge of financial cor-ruption, not sexual misconduct. Instead of retreating to a dark closet, the leader "publishes it all, himself" in detail and—risking the wrath of his wife—admits to the sex but denies the corruption charge. In the end, his loyal wife seems angrier at the vast conspiracy against him by hate-filled political enemies than at his infidelity. Meanwhile, the leader of the opposition, to whom the elves were totally loyal, claims to have been above the fray, although he secretly visits the chief elf at the time of publication and congratulates him. But, just five years later, this same opposition leader finds himself the object of his own sexual scandal—published by the very same chief elf who is now angry with him and has switched parties.

If I told you this story took place during the first 15 years of the founding of our republic, you probably would think I am making this up. But I am not. As Yogi Berra has said: "It's déjà vu all over again." Many people look back at the Revolutionary Era with understandable idealism and romanticism. The overwhelming public impression is that our Founding Fathers had the highest moral standards and were able to maintain civility and mutual respect toward political opponents—in sharp contrast to today's vitriolic scandal cul-ture. Our country in its youth avoided harsh personal attacks and demonizing the political opposition, right? A closer examination of our Founding Fathers reveals that some of them not only had undisciplined libidos that drove them to reckless sexual misconduct but also that many were bitter partisans. They were all too willing to use media leaks, personal attacks, and character assassination—including spreading the rumors of those sexual affairs—not just to defeat but to destroy their political opponents.

To understand how the scandal culture has taken such hold of the country, it is important to remember that our experience with scandals and gotcha politics has a long and notorious history. As a result, we are going to go back to the beginning to see how our Founding Fathers and those who followed dealt with scandal. We will see what insights this can give us into historic precedents for today's scandal culture and what to do when you are a politician in its crosshairs.

By 1792, the last year of President George Washington's first term, there was already a deeply bitter partisan split in American politics. Treasury Secretary Alexander Hamilton led one side, and Secretary of State Thomas Jefferson led the other. At that time, seen by friends and allies as the real power behind George Washington, Alexander Hamilton was not only the far more powerful of the two. He also represented a clearly articulated philosophy of government that evoked passions, pro and con, in what could be described as the first true Blue State versus Red State split in America along mostly regional and ideological lines.

Hamilton stood for a strong central government. He was the primary author of the "Federalist Papers," which eloquently argued in favor of adopting the new U.S. Constitution to replace the Articles of Confederation. At the heart of the Federalist Papers and the argument for adopting the new Constitution was the need for a strong "federal" government. This was in opposition to the system under the Articles, in which a loose confederation of independent state governments could not create political, much less economic, unity to grow and prosper as a nation. But early into the first Washington Administration, it was clear that there was a large group of early Americans, centered in the South and rural areas, which feared too much central power in the "federal government." They believed that concentrating such power could lead to a return to a British-style monarchy. They came to call themselves "Jeffersonians," named after their leader, Thomas Jefferson, and later "Republicans" (though not to be confused with the current Republican Party, which formed much later). Jefferson, famous for drafting the Declaration of Independence, hailed from the state of Virginia, whose critical role in the founding of the Republic led its native sons to resent any rival power, such as a strong national government, that might infringe on its "sovereign" state rights. Jefferson also spoke idealistically of the need to keep America an agriculture-based culture. He feared that the concentration of merchant, commercial, and moneyed interests in a central government would endanger individual freedom more than anything else.

Washington sided with Hamilton for the most part on this argument, and the catalyst for the de facto formation of political parties is usually credited to the lead up and establishment of the first National Bank by the Federalist-controlled Congress in 1791–92.[1] As Ron Chernow writes in his biography of Hamilton: "The sudden emergence of parties set a slashing tone for politics in the 1790s."[2] Slashing tone indeed. It was in the context of this turbulence and bitter partisanship of 1792—"the rise of political parties, the newspaper wars, the furious intramural fights with Jefferson"—that Hamilton should have been on the lookout for threats to his reputation; but he was not. It was during the summer of 1791 that he began an affair with a married woman, Maria Reynolds. He continued to carry on this affair with her and paid hush money to her husband, James Reynolds, and, as a result, became the first victim of the first American political sex scandal five years later.[3]

More than this, it could be argued that this is also the first example of "gotcha" politics in American history. In October 1792, Hamilton planted the first seed about Jefferson's affair with his slave Sally Hemings. Five years later, in the summer of 1797, a fanatical Republican partisan and supporter of Thomas Jefferson publicly disclosed Hamilton's affair with Mrs. Reynolds, having received the information from an underground network of "elves" (an expression used almost exactly 200 years later to describe the secret network of lawyers who bridged the Paula Jones plaintiffs' lawyers and Independent Counsel Kenneth W. Starr's prosecutors in the Clinton Monica Lewinsky case). This surreptitious network of Jeffersonian messengers thrived in the muck of rumor and leaks, with the objective of destroying Alexander Hamilton personally.

And then another five years later, in 1802, charges about Jefferson's affair with his slave and the fathering of her children were first published, fittingly, in an article written by the same man who had outed Hamilton, James Thomson Callender. He was now angry with Jefferson and wanted to get even—so he switched sides and became a Federalist. Notably, Hamilton actually tried to discourage political exploitation of the Jefferson–Hemings charges, but his fellow Federalist partisans had no such reticence. And so, the pattern of partisan gotcha politics and the movement toward the politics of personal destruction in America had its birth.

The contrasting ways in which both Hamilton and Jefferson chose to deal with the publication of these sex scandal allegations also point to two different pathways of handling a scandal crisis once it breaks out by getting the truth out yourself—"tell it all, tell it early" versus "deny, deny, deny"—a strategic split that, to say the least, can be seen in subsequent scandals throughout U.S. history up to the present day.

HAMILTON'S SEXUAL COMPULSIONS

Hamilton's nightmare all began in the summer of 1791. Hamilton was at the zenith of his power. He was George Washington's most trusted adviser, not only on all things economic, which one would expect as Secretary of the Treasury, but also on foreign affairs and most domestic policies as well (and served as his chief, and apparently only, speechwriter). That summer Hamilton was working feverishly on his landmark *Report on Manufacturers*, a vast tract setting out his economic and fiscal polices as well as an accounting that he had promised Congress by year-end. He was fighting—and winning—his battle to win the heart and mind of President George Washington over Jefferson and Madison, and was making progress on his goals of assuming Revolutionary debts and establishing a national system of taxation, commerce, and fiscal policy controlled by the first national bank.

Perhaps it was this string of successes, among other reasons, that led him to his gross misjudgment. As we have seen in many other examples throughout U.S. history, times of peril for many great public men is when they are at their peak, and hubris sets in. And with hubris often comes a sense that the rules of appropriate behavior do not apply to them—or at least, that they are too clever to get caught. And so it was with Hamilton that summer. As he described many years later, his first encounter with the 23-year-old Maria Reynolds, then married to James Reynolds, was when she appeared on his doorstep in Philadelphia, a maiden in distress who pleaded her case. Her husband treated her very poorly, she said, and had left her for another woman, sending her to the poor house. But the meeting came at an "inopportune moment" (i.e., his wife was home), so Hamilton, never missing an opportunity to show his chivalry, decided to visit Mrs. Reynolds at her home later that evening, presumably without mentioning the need to help the poor maiden to his wife, Eliza. To describe what happened next, it seems best to let Hamilton speak for himself:

> In the evening, I put a bank bill in my pocket and went to the house. I inquired for Mrs. Reynolds and was shown upstairs, at the head of which she met me and conducted me into a bedroom. I took out of my pocket and gave it to her. Some conversation ensued from which it was quickly apparent that other than pecuniary consolation would be acceptable.[4]

Let us read the end of that last sentence one more time. The legendary author of the Federalist Papers, true to his skills as a writer, just came up with a euphemism for *doing it* that will, in all likelihood, never be exceeded by any future American leader.

To be fair to Alexander Hamilton, Mrs. Reynolds was not exactly an innocent overwhelmed by the charms of one of America's most famous and powerful political leaders. A Philadelphia merchant who knew her during her marriage to Reynolds wrote that she had told him that her husband "had frequently enjoined and insisted that she insinuate herself on certain high and influential characters—endeavor to make assignations with them and actually prostitute herself to gall money from them."[5] Hamilton eventually discovered that Mr. Reynolds, the husband, was actually aware of his wife's involvement with Hamilton—indeed, had encouraged it. It seems Mr. Reynolds wished some form of compensation in return for sharing the wonders of his beautiful, young wife with the Treasury Secretary. In addition, at least according to Maria, Mr. Reynolds had dabbled in speculating in government securities, while using inside information provided to him from a high-level Treasury Department official, William Duer, who was also an acquaintance of Hamilton's.

The political danger inherent in this combination of sexual misconduct and potential government corruption should have been obvious to such a brilliant man, especially one who was so prideful of protecting his public reputation that it later led to his death during a duel with Aaron Burr. Why Hamilton did not understand this danger and avoid undertaking such a reckless risk, which left him vulnerable to blackmail, remains a complete mystery to this day. Well, maybe not such a complete mystery. World history is replete with instances in which brilliant and powerful men find their mind and prudent judgment overtaken by a certain part of their anatomy, for reasons that even they themselves cannot explain. Hamilton actually rationalized continuing the relationship because he believed Maria was genuinely in love with him. Hamilton suffered, wrote Hamilton biographer Ron Chernow, from a sexual "addiction," was in the grip of a "dark sexual compulsion. . . . [He] seemed to need two different types of love: love of the faithful, domestic kind, and love of the more forbidden, exotic variety."[6] Another Hamilton biographer wrote: "Nor was the affair a passing, if torrid, sexual dalliance between two lonely people. . . . Sexual ardor is a powerful force, especially in a man of great physical energy and strong creative drives."[7] Hamilton seems to have convinced himself to avoid being cruel to poor Maria by forcing her to quit him cold turkey. Or, as Chernow surmised, was it he who had the true addiction, covering up his need for her under the pretense of weaning her off

of his love or at least of his infatuation?[8] Another contemporary Hamilton biographer, however, bluntly rejected the notion of a real romantic relationship
going on here. "A plain statement of the facts is that Mrs. Reynolds was a
whore, her husband was a pimp, and both were blackmailers." And as to
Hamilton—pretty simple: "He was a john and a gull."[9]

HUSH MONEY

Meanwhile, the wounded husband overcame his spousal pride and focused
on more material objectives. On December 15, 1791, at the very moment
when Hamilton was finishing up his *Report on Manufacturers*, Mr. Reynolds
demanded $1,000 from Hamilton (which in 2005 dollars would be the
equivalent in rough calculations of over $1 million). It was demanded as and
understood to be nothing more or less than hush money. And Hamilton
paid it.[10] After doing so, he seemed to resolve to end the affair once and for
all. Yet he continued on with Maria and continued to pay hush money for
several more months in 1792. In fact, Hamilton continued to make payments through the spring of 1793, and, finally, after James Reynolds demanded another $300 that Hamilton resisted, he made his last payment on
June 2 for $50.[11]

THE INEVITABLE LEAK

As when most hush money finally ends, the story eventually seeped out, bit
by bit. The key player in the leak was Jacob Clingman, a friend of James
Reynolds and another lowlife archetype who had served as a clerk to the former respected Speaker of the House, Frederick Muhlenberg of Pennsylvania.
Clingman was a strong supporter of Jefferson and another Hamilton hater.
One afternoon in February or March 1792, Clingman visited the Reynolds
household and discovered Hamilton leaving. Several days later, while he was
with the Reynolds, there was a knock on the door and it was Hamilton again.
Sputtering, Hamilton allegedly explained that he was delivering a message
that he had been "ordered" to give to Mr. Reynolds.[12]

Clingman, who traveled in Republican anti-Hamilton circles, had long
been privy to the Republican-generated rumors that Hamilton had speculated in government securities using inside information obtained as Treasury
Secretary. So this scene, and subsequent conversations with James Reynolds
describing the ongoing payments made by Hamilton, reinforced Clingman's
prior impressions that Hamilton was, in fact, partnering with Reynolds in a
scheme to manipulate government securities using insider information.[13]

When Clingman and Reynolds found themselves in jail in December 1792 for an unrelated criminal charge, and despite the fact that Hamilton helped arrange their release, Clingman was apparently ready to play "gotcha." He went to his old boss, the former Speaker Frederick Muhlenberg, and accused Hamilton of involvement in a scheme to manipulate government securities, with the payments to Reynolds for that purpose. As proof, Clingman gave Muhlenberg a batch of unsigned notes from Hamilton to Maria Reynolds, in Hamilton's handwriting. Muhlenberg sought out advice from his two Republican political colleagues, Representatives Abraham B. Venable and James Monroe (a close friend of Jefferson's and America's future fifth president).[14]

The three, believing they had evidence of Hamilton's governmental corruption, decided to confront him first with a letter summarizing the accusations before presenting the evidence to President Washington. On the December 15, 1792, the three visited Hamilton in his Philadelphia office. Instead of denying everything, as the four expected, Hamilton admitted to the sexual affair and, indeed, described it in prurient detail. He showed them a batch of letters from James and Maria Reynolds, and confessed the affair, the hush money payments, and his fear of his wife learning of the matter: "It was as if Hamilton were both exonerating and flagellating himself" at the same time. His heartfelt confession convinced the men that there was no government corruption or basis for believing that Hamilton had participated in illegal manipulation of government securities. In the end, Muhlenberg even expressed regret and sympathy for putting Hamilton through the humiliation.[15]

Amazingly, the secret of Hamilton's affair held for four and a half years. Sure, there were oblique references to it here and there as whispers and rumors clearly abounded, but it did not go further than that. It remained an ever-present threat to Hamilton's reputation, however, that his enemies kept in their back pockets. Monroe, in the midst of a series of articles attacking Hamilton and defending Jefferson just days after the revelation of the sexual scandal at Hamilton's office, sent Hamilton a warning that he must have read as not too subtle a threat: "[Hamilton should] exhibit himself to the public view, that we might behold him a living monument so that *immaculate purity* to which he pretends and which ought to distinguish so old and arrogant a censor of others."[16] Surely one can imagine Hamilton wincing at the sarcasm. It has even been argued that it was this "Sword of Damocles, perpetually dangling over his head" that prevented Hamilton, one of America's greatest Founders (and many would say *the* greatest given his key role, and that of the Federalist Papers, in the adoption of the U.S. Constitution), from running for president before his untimely death at the hands of Aaron Burr on July 12, 1804.[17]

THE COVER-UP UNRAVELS

Of course, a scandal of this sort cannot stay secret forever. And in many ways, Hamilton's attacks on Jefferson, especially a subtle allusion to the then still very sub-rosa rumors about Jefferson having had an affair with one of his female slaves and fathering some of her children, provoked what followed. In the midst of the intense campaign over the succession to George Washington in the fall of 1796, Hamilton wrote a series of anti-Jefferson essays under the pseudonym "Phocion." One claimed that Jefferson's "simplicity and humility afford but a flimsy veil to the internal evidences of aristocratic splendor, sensuality, and Epicureanism." Obviously, the Jeffersonians could not let a slight such as that stand. Four days later, perhaps not coincidentally, an anonymous writer fired a shot back in a letter to the Jeffersonian newspaper, the *Aurora*, addressed to Secretary of the Treasury Oliver Wolcott, Jr. (who had actually accompanied Monroe and the others when they confronted Hamilton in his office back in December 1792). The letter asked Wolcott whether he had knowledge about "the circumstances of a certain enquiry of a very suspicious aspect, respecting real malconduct on the part of his friend, patron, and predecessor in office." (The anonymous writer is assumed to be John Beckley, a former clerk of the House of Representatives whom Monroe had entrusted to copy the batch of letters to Maria Reynolds—in violation of Monroe's commitment to Hamilton to keep them confidential—that had come from Clingman and that Hamilton had verified four years earlier.)[18]

But it was not until the summer of 1797 that the scandal exploded into the public domain, leading to Hamilton's first crisis of scandal management. Evidence suggests that the source of the leak was the same John Beckley from the earlier letter to the *Aurora*, who was known to hang out with both Jacob Clingman and another Republican partisan and pamphleteer named James Thomas Callender. In June 1797, Callender, described as "an ugly misshapen little man who made a career of spewing venom," published a series of pamphlets, subsequently compiled into a published book entitled *The History of the United States for 1796*.[19] Pamphlets five and six not only contained the detailed account of Hamilton's sexual affair with Maria Reynolds but charged that the money paid to James Reynolds was part of an illegal government securities manipulation scheme in which Hamilton was centrally involved. In fact, to Callender's warped, hate-filled mind, Hamilton's alleged sexual liaison with Maria Reynolds was just a pretext to cover up the true facts concerning Hamilton's involvement in securities fraud conducted in concert with James Reynolds. "So much correspondence could not refer exclusively to wenching," stated Callender. "No man of common sense will believe that it did."[20]

Callender published all of the "letters from Hamilton to Maria Reynolds that Hamilton had entrusted to Muhlenberg, Venable, and Monroe at their December meeting (again, the same letters given to John Beckley for copying). Thus, it is the venerated two-term president James Monroe—who presided over the historically unparalleled and bipartisan "Era of Good Feelings"—who appears to bear at least primary responsibility for exposure of Alexander Hamilton's secret affair.[21] One respected biographer of Hamilton directly accuses Monroe of betraying Hamilton based on pure partisan political motives:

> Monroe, however, did not believe that gentlemanly proprieties transcended the dictates of partisan politics, and he wasted no time before informing Jefferson and the Republican's chief political operator, Clerk of the House John Beckley, of the whole episode. Seeing no practical way to use the information just then, they nonetheless copied the documents for an opportune future occasion.[22]

There were various partisan motives aside from Hamilton's inflammatory reference to Jefferson's flimsy Epicureanism that might have prompted the timing of Callender's exposè: the recall of James Monroe as Ambassador to France because, according to Hamilton and his Federalist followers, he was overly sympathetic to the "Jacobins" of the French Revolution; the retirement of George Washington and the absence of his unifying influence gave Republicans the courage to go after Hamilton and the Federalists with the desire to undercut Hamilton's ability to influence the new president, John Adams, the way he had influenced and dominated George Washington.[23] Of course, there is evidence of another motive—payback time for Hamilton's oblique but threatening references to rumors of Jefferson's affair with a slave woman the previous fall. Whatever the specific reason, the overwhelming motive was partisanship—politics, pure and simple: promote your own party's interests by attempting to destroy the leader of the opposition.

GETTING THE TRUTH OUT: TELL IT ALL, TELL IT YOURSELF

History will never know whether Hamilton would have dignified Callender's pamphlet with a response had it been limited to exposure of just his sexual affair, or what its impact would have been had he chosen to ignore it. His friends urged him to do just that, but that was not Alexander Hamilton's way—certainly not when his public service and official integrity had been falsely challenged and besmirched. Hamilton decided to ignore his friends and respond—early, fully, completely, and personally. He chose, as one historian put it, a "ferocious counterattack, grinding out articles under nine different *noms de plume*, single-handedly taking on hordes of opponents with an energy and skill that inspired awe in his enemies."[24] As distressing as it must have been to decide on complete transparency on the subject of his marital infidelity exposed to the public and especially to his wife, it was Callender's charge that the payments to James Reynolds were part of a corrupt scheme to manipulate government securities that, in his mind, could not be left unanswered—exactly the primary motive leading Hamilton to bare all the details to Muhlenberg, Venable, and Monroe four and a half years before. And so, in mid-July 1797 he holed himself up in a Philadelphia boardinghouse to write his detailed response. He was, in short, "prepared to sacrifice his private reputation for his public honor.[25]

On August 25, 1797, Hamilton published in the *Gazette of the United States* his 95-page booklet titled *"Observations on Certain Documents Contained in No. V & VI of "The History of the United States for the Year 1796," In Which the Charge of Speculation Against Alexander Hamilton, Late Secretary of the Treasury, Is Fully Refuted. Written by Himself"*—37 pages of personal confessions, supplemented by 58 pages of letters and affidavits.[26]

In "picaresque detail," Hamilton constructed an "account that would encompass all known facts and remove any room for misinterpretation." He was not at all subtle about making the important distinction, in his mind at last, between confessing to the personally painful and embarrassing private sexual misconduct, which he knew would hurt his wife greatly versus rebutting and renouncing any inference that such private behavior affected his public performance and integrity. He wrote:

> This confession is not made without a blush. . . . I can never cease to condemn myself for the pang which it may inflict in a bosom eminently entitled to all my gratitude, fidelity, and love. But that bosom will approve that even at so great an expence [*sic*], I should effectually wipe away a more serious stain from a name which it cherishes with no less elevation than tenderness.[27]

His friends were distraught at his "tell it all" strategy. His good friend Noah Webster wondered why a great man like Hamilton would stoop to "publish a history of his private intrigues, degrade himself in the estimation of all good men, and scandalize a family to clear himself of charges which no man believed." Another said the "ill-judged pamphlet has done him inconceivable injury."[28]

However, one correspondent at the time may have articulated best the distinction between private sexual behavior and public performance that perhaps showed more prescience and applicability to a sexual relationship involving a president of the United States some 200 or so years later: "If he fornicates with every female in the cities of New York and Philadelphia, he will rise again, for purity of character . . . is not necessary for public patronage."[29]

His enemies were gleeful. Callender rejoiced at Hamilton's decision to publish all the details. As he wrote to Jefferson, "If you have seen it, no anticipation can equal the infamy of this piece. . . . [The] whole proof rests upon an illusion, 'I am a rake and for that reason I cannot be a swindler.'" The partisan Republican newspaper, *Aurora*, paraphrased Hamilton as saying: "I have been grossly . . . charged with . . . being a *speculator*, whereas I am only *an adulterer*. I have not broken the *eighth* commandment. . . . It is only the *seventh* which I have violated."[30]

Even in those days, there were people who believed in vast right-wing (or left-wing) conspiracies. In this case, their reaction to Hamilton's decision to opt for full transparency at the risk of his personal humiliation and possibly his marriage actually suggested that it was all a ruse to disguise the real truth, that is, that he had engaged in corrupt speculation in treasury securities along with James Reynolds and wanted to divert attention by admitting to adultery. These speculations, and that is all they were, were not only published by Callender at the time but, for some reason, have been repeated by distinguished historians since, even though there is not a shred of historical fact to support the speculation.[31]

And what was his wife Eliza's reaction to all this? Shortly after Callender's pamphlets were published in July, John Barker Church, Hamilton's brother-in-law, wrote in a letter: "Eliza is well. She put into my hand the newspaper with James Thomson Callender's letter to you, but it makes not the least impression on her, only that she considers the whole knot of those opposed to you to be [scoundrels]."[32] Of course, at this point Hamilton had not yet published his full confession of the affair. But, even after Hamilton's published confession, Eliza remained true to her husband, convinced that he remained a patriot due respect from his country and that those who had pursued him in this matter were the real villains.[33] One could argue that Eliza seemed to focus her anger more on her perception of a "vast Republican conspiracy" (if not yet a "right-wing conspiracy") than on her wayward husband.

PAYBACK TIME FOR JEFFERSON

It is hard to believe, but it is true. Five years later Thomas Jefferson got his own "gotcha"—from the same person who exposed Alexander Hamilton, the Honorable James Thomson Callender. Formerly a Jeffersonian Republican par excellence, by this time Callender was the hateful enemy of his former hero. Jefferson was hardly an innocent, although he managed to maintain the pretense of being one, at least to the general public. While ambassador to Paris, Jefferson openly flirted with married women and had affairs of which insiders at the time were well aware. In fact, one of his most blatant overtures was to Alexander Hamilton's sister-in-law, the beautiful Angelica Church. Jefferson had even asked Angelica to travel to America, visit him at his home at Monticello, and offered to travel with her to Niagara Falls. Hamilton himself probably knew about Jefferson's overtures to his sister-in-law.[34]

There were also early rumors about Jefferson's possible affair with one of his young slaves, Sally Hemings, and his fathering of many of her children. Rumors began in 1787 when Jefferson, as ambassador to Paris, welcomed his two daughters, who brought Sally Hemings with them. Called "Dashing Sally" at Monticello, she was described as beautiful, "near white," and with "long straight hair down her back." Hemings was inherited as Jefferson's slave from his wife's family. There was strong speculation that his wife's father was also Hemings' father—that is, that Hemings was his wife's half-sister.

As already noted, Jefferson might have seen Hamilton as opening the scandal wars when he wrote oblique references to Jefferson's "Epicureanism" and "sensuality" in his October 1796 essays under the pen name "Phocion."[35] But Jefferson, as was his way, remained silent and ignored this needling. Then came James Callender, by now a born-again Federalist. It seems Callender had been convicted of violating the Sedition Act for criticizing President Adams. Jefferson and the Republicans were the ones who had championed Callender's published attacks on Adams, but when he was convicted and sentenced to a nine-month jail term and a $200 fine (as much as several thousand in today's dollars) under the Act, they abandoned him—at least in Callender's view. Once out of jail, Callender sought financial help from President Jefferson, but he received only $50 (probably several hundred dollars in today's money) for his efforts. That, apparently, was enough for Callender. The "vengeful" and "heavy-drinking" man accused Jefferson of subsidizing his attacks on Adams and Hamilton while he was vice president and produced some documents backing up payments from Jefferson.[36]

Finally, on September 1, 1802—five years after the publication of Hamilton's detailed confessional and refutation of Callender's pamphlets—the angry Callender delivered his payback to his erstwhile sponsor Jefferson. He wrote a story that he was said to have learned about in jail that Jefferson had bedded his teenage slave, Sally Hemings, and fathered children with her. It is a claim—though never acknowledged by Jefferson during his lifetime—that resonated for nearly two centuries before it was accepted as fact.[37]

Callender wrote in his colorful style that presumably used to delight Jefferson and his pals when the scandal-mongering was aimed at Alexander Hamilton, but not so much appreciated now: "It is well known that the man whom it delighteth the people to honor, keeps and for many years has kept, as his concubine, one of his slaves. Her name is Sally. . . . By this wench Sally, our President has had several children. There is not an individual in the neighborhood of Charlottesville who does not believe the story, and not a few who know it. . . . The African Venus is said to officiate as housekeep at Monticello." He referred to his former Republican Party as the "mulatto party" and he challenged the President to join him in a court of law and debate the truth of the relationship with "the black wench and her mulatto litter."[38]

Incredibly, despite having been exposed and embarrassed with at least the tacit approval, if not complicity, of Jefferson, Hamilton shrank from encouraging the exploitation of the Jefferson–Hemings story by his Federalist and media colleagues. He reportedly told the *New York Evening Post*, a newspaper he helped found and to which he was an early significant contributor, that he was "adverse to all personalities not immediately connected with public considerations."[39] But other more partisan Federalists ignored Hamilton's high-level advice. Gotcha politics was just too pleasurable to resist. Gleeful over the reversal of fortune, Federalists taunted the President in verse, albeit vicious and racist:

> Thy tricks with *sooty* Sal, give o'er
> Indulge thy Body, Tom, no more
> But try to save thy soul.[40]

Ten months later Callender died—drowned in three feet of water in the James River on July 17, 1803. The coroner's jury found he had drowned while drunk. However, given the fierce partisanship of the era, some Federalists were not above questioning whether "Callender had been bludgeoned by vindictive Jeffersonians, then dumped . . . in the river."[41]

So, what did this first foray into gotcha politics teach the young nation? It appears that the wrong lessons were learned—or, perhaps from a purely partisan political standpoint, the right lessons were learned. First, scandal can

hurt, personally and politically. And it certainly can serve as a useful distraction—a change of subject when, perhaps, the issues and policies are not going
your way. Next, it is important to understand what did not happen. Even
though Hamilton had openly admitted to having the affair and having paid
hush money to keep it quiet, there was no call for his resignation by President Washington and no call for his impeachment by the very Jeffersonian
Republicans that were so hateful toward him and so desirous to see his personal and political demise. In other words, this was viewed as about private
conduct, not public corruption or abuse of office. So long as Hamilton insisted that the latter had *not* occurred and there were no facts contradicting
his assertion (then or to this day), then people at the time were able to view it
as a private weakness and not a public problem.

It should not be surprising that during the Clinton impeachment efforts
by House Republicans, as one leading historian has pointed out, the Clinton
defense team actually prepared a detailed paper on the Hamilton–Reynolds
affair. The White House Special Counsel, Gregory Craig, wrote: "Hamilton
paid hush money, destroyed evidence and got (Mr. Reynolds) out of town, it
was considered a personal matter and didn't reflect an abuse of power." Har-
vard Law Professor Alan Dershowitz noted, "Washington and Madison
agreed" with Hamilton defending himself by "saying it was sex."[42] The *St.
Louis Post-Dispatch* agreed, pointing out that "none of the founding fathers
suggested impeachment" though they knew that hush money was paid to
cover up an adulterous relationship. Of course, impeachment-supporting Republicans had the immediate rejoinder that Hamilton may have paid hush
money, but he did not lie under oath—quite the contrary, he told it all himself (after he knew the charges had gone public).[43]

GROVER CLEVELAND MAKES NO APOLOGIES

So as the years progressed in America's first full century, each political party
learned to pounce on leaders or scapegoats from the other party who were
unlucky or careless enough to get ensnared in public scandal. There were
plenty of financial scandals involving the usual litany of bribes, kickbacks, and
official corruption. But even the two most historically famous of these seem
like small potatoes by today's standards. The first, which broke in 1872 during President Ulysses S. Grant's first reelection campaign, was the so-called
Credit Mobilier affair, involving a holding company that skimmed off huge
profits (estimated at the time by some to be as much as $30 million, probably
in excess of $100 million in today's dollars) in the federally subsidized con-
struction of the Union Pacific Railroad. Company officers allegedly paid off

key Republican leaders of Congress in discounted stock to thwart an investigation. But the dollars involved were nominal by today's standards (a few hundred dollars per person) and the charges and proof so insubstantial that one of the Republican congressmen accused of taking the stock was elected President of the United States eight years later—Rep. James A. Garfield of Ohio.[44]

The second, the Whiskey Ring, seemed to involve bigger sums—millions of dollars (equivalent to several hundred million in today's dollars)—and broke late in Grant's second term. Hundreds of distillers and federal officials were suspected of diverting millions in liquor taxes into their own pockets. The conspiracy was uncovered, with much publicity and sanctimonious chest-beating, by Treasury Secretary Benjamin H. Bristow in 1875. President Grant himself vowed to "let no guilty man escape."[45] Grant then discovered that his own personal secretary, Orville E. Babcock, was in on the scheme. Grant interceded on his behalf, but still, 110 conspirators were convicted.

Sex scandals, however, seemed to disappear from the political landscape—at least those the public learned about—after the Hamilton–Jefferson experience. In the 1828 presidential campaign, supporters of President John Quincy Adams accused Andrew Jackson of being an adulterer, but that does not really count as a "sex" scandal because he actually married and loved Rachel Donaldson Robards, only to discover years later that her divorce from her abusive husband was not legally recognized. When she died shortly after Jackson's election in December 1828, Jackson blamed her death on the vicious political attacks. The President-elect angrily said at her funeral: "In the presence of this dear saint, I can and do forgive all my enemies. But those vile wretches who have slandered her must look to God for mercy."[46]

It was nearly 100 years before the next notable political sex scandal hit the headlines: The sudden public disclosure in 1884 that New York Governor Grover Cleveland, then the Democratic candidate for president running in a tight race against Maine Senator James G. Blaine, had fathered an illegitimate child. Cleveland had been a reform-minded sheriff of Erie County, New York, from 1871 to 1873 and was elected mayor of Buffalo in 1882. The next year he won the New York governorship by a landslide. Voters seemed drawn to his honesty and reform-mindedness, which was supported not only by his record as mayor of Buffalo but also by his gruff and authentically candid personality and style. It was in that context that Cleveland faced what seemed like a huge, perhaps even career-ending, sex scandal during the critical closing days of a very close 1884 presidential campaign.

He had *allegedly* fathered the child during a brief tryst with Maria C. Halpin, a native of Jersey City, New Jersey, who left her two children behind at the age of 33 to seek a new life in Buffalo, New York. The word "allegedly" is appropriate because after Ms. Halpin arrived in Buffalo, she dated—and apparently bedded—more than a few distinguished citizens of Buffalo, all of them (other than Grover) married. When she announced she was pregnant, she named Cleveland as the father. While he was unsure (there were no DNA tests then to settle the issue), he accepted responsibility, reasoning that since he was a bachelor, he did not have an offended wife to worry about. (One can appreciate why he was so popular at least among this group of distinguished married citizens of Buffalo.)

The child, a boy born in September 1874, was named Oscar Folsom Cleveland, after another leading citizen of Buffalo and Cleveland's law partner, Oscar Folsom (whose daughter, Frances, Cleveland married while serving as president—he at the age of 49, she at the age of 21). Cleveland quietly, and secretly, fulfilled his responsibilities, paying the child's expenses—$5 per week—at the orphanage after Ms. Halpin turned to drink and was institutionalized in an insane asylum. (The son was ultimately adopted by a prominent New York family and became a doctor.)[47] And there the secret remained—private and of no one else's business, having nothing to do with his public performance or political career, and thus, no reason to ever explode as a public scandal. At least that is what Cleveland thought.

The Democrats' prospects looked promising in 1884. The last two presidential elections had been a virtual 50–50 split in the country, reminiscent of the Red State versus Blue State elections nearly 120 years later. They had come close to electing a president in 1876, when Republican Rutherford Hayes lost the popular vote to Democrat Samuel J. Tilden by 284,000 votes out of more than 8 million cast, or 51 percent–48 percent, but, thanks to a deal within the House that allowed the South to bring an early end to Reconstruction, Hayes was elected President by one electoral vote. 1880 proved another close election, when Democrat and Civil War hero Winfield S. Hancock came within 10,000 votes out of almost 9 million cast of winning the popular vote, losing to James Garfield by one-tenth of one percent, 48.3 percent to 48.2 percent.[48] So when the Democrats nominated the popular New York governor, Grover Cleveland, for president in 1884, they had reason to be optimistic—especially given the reform, clean government image Cleveland was known for.

The campaign still remained close—the country was still as split down the middle as it had been in 1876 and 1880. Democrats supporting Cleveland were not bashful about getting personal and hitting scandal machine hot buttons to rally the electorate against Republican James Blaine. In 1876, when seeking the presidency on the Republican ticket, Blaine had been subject to unproven accusations that he was involved in graft from railroad interests (when the Democrats published the so-called Mulligan letters, which suggested, but did not prove, Blaine's corrupt involvement). Despite the lack of indictments or any hard evidence ever presented against Blaine, the innuendo was enough to doom his chances to get the nomination or the presidency, both of which ultimately went to Rutherford B. Hayes. These accusations lingered in the 1884 election, with Democrats running a scurrilous campaign slogan against Blaine: "Blaine! Blaine! James G. Blaine! Continental liar from the state of Maine."[49]

Then suddenly, on July 21, 1884, the *Buffalo Evening Telegraph* published a banner headline: "A Terrible Tale—Dark Chapter in Public Man's History." After enduring Democratic taunts of corruption against Blaine, Republicans jumped all over the news about Cleveland's illegitimate child. They also must have banked on the hypocrisy rule of the scandal culture—always a good strategy when a political scandal breaks. According to this rule, the scandal itself (especially when it concerns sexual misbehavior, something with which too many people may identify) is less important than the fact that the person accused has sanctimoniously trumpeted his own purity or integrity up to that point. The rule, the Republicans must have reasoned, certainly applied to Cleveland, whose carefully cultivated image of high-mindedness, integrity, and reform were central to his political persona and appeal. Thus Republicans must have anticipated that voters would see through the hypocrisy of Cleveland's clean image once they learned that he secretly fathered a child with an unmarried woman and covered it up for more than ten years.

There was one problem with their plans. Cleveland did not follow the usual instincts a politician has when suddenly caught in a scandal that has some basis in truth—namely, to deny, decline to comment, make excuses, or blame someone else. Instead, when Cleveland's panicky Democratic campaign advisers rushed in to tell him about the *Evening Telegraph* story and ask him what to say, Cleveland gave them a simple instruction: Tell the truth. And they did. So, that was the end of that. Of course, the Republicans refused to give up. Their campaign slogan was artful and deliciously evil: "Ma, Ma, Ma, where's my Pa? Gone to the White House, Ha, Ha, Ha!"[50]

The slogan was cute, clever, and became famous—but there was a fatal flaw. It did not work. Cleveland had inoculated himself by telling the truth, the whole truth, and nothing but the truth, personally and sooner rather than later. He took responsibility and moved on to address the issues of civil service reform and, in the political phrase famous some 108 years later, "it's the economy, stupid."

It also did not help Republican Senator Blaine's chances when he was seen in the closing days of the campaign dining at a sumptuous feast in the company of Republican fat cats John Jacob Astor, Jay Gould, and other tycoons during a time of recession and high unemployment. (Yes, even then wining and dining with fat cats was not unusual in politics!) Nor did Blaine help his cause among New York Catholics—New York being the swing state that would decide the election—when he sat passively at a New York City Republican Party dinner while a bigoted protestant minister, Reverend Samuel D. Burchard, declared, "We are Republicans, and don't propose to . . . identify with the [Democratic] party whose antecedents are Rum, Romanism, and Rebellion."

So Grover Cleveland won, barely, carrying 20 states with 219 electoral votes, including New York, to Blaine's 18 states or 182 electoral votes. The popular vote margin was razor thin—just 62,000 out of more than 10 million votes cast.[51] It is speculative—but still a safe bet—to state that had Cleveland not dealt with the scandal story involving his illegitimate son candidly and openly, he would have lost the presidency.

We have learned from these stories of Alexander Hamilton, Thomas Jefferson, and Grover Cleveland several things about the seeds of today's scandal culture and the destructive gotcha politics that inevitably accompanies it.

First, great men (and some day, hopefully, great women) who lead our country as presidents or as its most powerful political leaders are not immune from petty, devious, and vicious tactics carried out with the objective of not just defeating the opposition but destroying it. Indeed, it could be argued that their greatness may even be related to their willingness to engage in such tactics because, as in the case of Hamilton and Jefferson, their passionate beliefs in the righteousness of their own philosophies and causes seem to justify virtually any means of defending their positions and attacking those who oppose them.

Second, great men, with driving egos and driving passions, seem to have powerful sexual drives that override their political judgment, prudence, and ability to assess risk, although it could be argued that we do not need to look very far back in history to learn that lesson.

Third, and perhaps most importantly, truly great issues divided the country during the first decade of its founding. At stake was the core issue that led to the adoption of the Constitution to replace the Articles of Confederation—the debate between those who believed a strong centralized government was needed to build a great and prosperous nation and those who feared such centralized power, preferring sovereign power to rest mainly with the individual states and the citizens of those states. That great debate, which in many fundamental respects echoes within today's division between Red states and Blue states, led great men to see great reasons to do great harm to their political opposition. And so, way back then, the seeds and the rationale for the scandal culture and its destructive machinery were born.

And the lessons for dealing with the scandal machine when a politician is caught in its cross-hairs? Hamilton chose the gutsy "let it all hang out" tactic. He knew that once Callender had published his charges, he needed to do whatever was necessary to keep his name in history from being forever linked not just with sexual indiscretions but with official corruption—and we know, of course, that Hamilton took more pride in his integrity and reputation than his very life—something he proved without question during his fatal duel with Aaron Burr in 1804.

Jefferson answered that same question by choosing the completely opposite strategy—utterly ignoring the charges Callender published about him. It certainly worked during his lifetime, although it also meant that the charges never went away. For some 200 years, the rumors persisted, investigations continued off and on, and finally, in 1998, they were, in effect, confirmed. As Chernow wrote, "Hamilton offered testimony of his own inexcusable lapses in this area, while the sphinx-like Jefferson was a man of such unshakeable reticence that it took two centuries of sedulous detective work to provide partial corroboration of the story of his sexual liaison with Sally Hemings."[52]

GENTLEMEN'S AGREEMENT

Interestingly, after the Jefferson–Hemings story came and went, while there were certainly some notable scandals that broke out over the next 160 years as we have just seen, in general, Americans and the politicians attempting to lead them had reached a certain understanding as to what was, and was not, acceptable to use as a public accusation in order to win an election. At least that was the case until a bullet killed the young thirty-fifth President of the United States, John Fitzgerald Kennedy.

From Grover Cleveland to John Kennedy, America experienced various outbreaks of financial and political scandals, many of them fanned by one party in the hope of doing serious damage to the other. But none of them did, despite some pretty serious headlines and media hype. The reason is that during those 80 or so years there existed a set of rules much like a "gentleman's agreement"—nothing written down, not even discussed, but pretty much accepted by the political and media establishment and, at least implicitly, by the public.

The essence of the gentleman's agreement was that different types of scandals should not be treated the same way. For scandals involving financial fraud, bribery, and the like, it was okay to use these for political purposes, but with an important caveat: underlings were fair game, but if it involved the leader, then a reporter ready to write better have a smoking gun—or leave it alone. The rules regarding sexual scandal, however, were clear. Don't write at all (unless the publication was a pure scandal sheet)—unless it involved a serious compromise of public performance or national security, such as blackmail.

During the Kennedy years, the manifestation of the gentleman's agreement regarding extracurricular sexual activity was apparent. Despite the open secret surrounding Kennedy's sexual activities, no White House reporter ever wrote about them. And Kennedy's virtually symbiotic relationship with the most influential reporters, such as *Newsweek* editor Ben Bradlee and influential syndicated columnists James Reston and Joseph Alsop, showed that the line between journalists and political leader was so blurry that sometimes there was no discernable separation at all.

PEDESTRIAN SCANDALS

Some of the most notorious financial scandals in the late nineteenth and early twentieth centuries were reminiscent of Shakespeare's famous line—full of sound and fury, at the time, but ultimately, in the long-term world of politics, signifying nothing. That is to say, while the American people read about them, and politicians huffed and puffed about them, they really did not have any lasting effect. The political establishment remained largely untouched. Thus, there was no serious or long-term political damage to either party—consistent with the gentleman's agreement.

Typical was the late-nineteenth-century scandal, Credit Mobilier. There was a lot of media hype and breathless scandal headlines about Credit Mobilier, which is why school children might know that name from history books, a symbolic representative of "gilded age" scandal and corruption in the late nineteenth century. But the actual sums involved were relatively paltry, even when translated into today's dollars. The alleged payments to the congressmen were in some cases as small as a few hundred dollars.[53] And one of the recipients of the discounted stock, Congressman James Garfield of Ohio, went on to be elected President of the United States eight years later. Meanwhile, President Grant had the misfortune of being in office during the scandal and has been tarred with its notoriety, even though he had nothing to do with it. This unfairly contributed to his reputation in U.S. history books as a president who presided over significant scandal.[54] Some things never change.

Another good example of a scandal that created plenty of hype and gnashing of teeth in its day, despite its actually mild nature, was the historically famous Teapot Dome scandal of the early 1920s. Again, like Credit Mobilier, this is one of those scandals that high school students memorize when they are studying for their U.S. history exams—depicted as some big scandal that happened under the presidency of Warren Harding, somehow tainting him as corrupt in the history books. But most people do not remember what the scandal was about, or even what the name Teapot Dome stands for.

Teapot Dome, despite its fame, was not much of a scandal at all in financial terms, at least relatively speaking. Teapot Dome was the name of a rock formation in Wyoming where considerable U.S. government-owned oil reserves were stored. It appears that President Harding's Secretary of the Interior, Albert B. Fall of New Mexico, executed a simple bribery scheme. An arch foe of conservationists (reminding one of a future Secretary of the Interior under President Ronald Reagan), Secretary Fall persuaded Harding to transfer control of federal oil reserves from the Navy Department to his jurisdiction at the Interior. He appears to have had a reason other than the best interests of the American public. Once he had control over those oil reserves, he proceeded to grant dirt-cheap leases to his friend, Harry Sinclair, who ran the Mammoth Oil Company (later Sinclair Oil) to tap into those lucrative reserves. In return, Fall was said to have received a cash payment of about $308,000,[55] the equivalent of at least several million dollars today. He also was accused of accepting another $100,000 from the Pan-American Petroleum and Transport Company for access to oil reserves in Elk Hills, California.

Fall denied wrongdoing, surprisingly enough. He claimed that the payments were not "bribes," but rather, they were "loans." Ultimately, Secretary Fall and his friend Sinclair were found guilty—Fall for accepting a bribe, Sinclair for criminal contempt of court (he hired a detective agency to shadow the jury). They were both tried and convicted in 1929. Fall was fined $100,000 and served ten months of a one-year sentence in 1931 in a New Mexico state prison. Sinclair was also fined $100,000 and received a short sentence for jury tampering.[56]

But despite the notoriety it received and the fact that the name "Teapot Dome" has lived on as an emblem of American political scandal, the scandal itself came and went, and no one really seemed to care much. Not that bribery is anything to be dismissive about, but the point is that it was a contained scandal. Certainly, it did not affect the politics of the time very much, nor did it affect the Coolidge and Hoover Administrations at all while the scandal and Fall and Sinclair's trial and convictions played out.

The greatest effect the scandal ultimately had was on Warren Harding's reputation in history. Harding initially defended the leases and his Interior Secretary when the story first broke, but before he could learn the facts, he died suddenly on August 2, 1923, and was replaced by his Vice President, Calvin Coolidge. When the facts came out, Harding had nothing to do with Fall's actions, and no historian suggests he could or should have known about the alleged bribery scheme. Yet mention the name Harding and most people will vaguely remember from their high school history classes that during his short-lived presidency, he was somehow "soft on corruption"—entirely as a result of Teapot Dome, similar to the exaggerated effect of Credit Mobilier on Grant's legacy.

This would not be the last time, as we shall see, that the word "corruption," through sheer repetition, became associated with a president when that president had little or nothing to do with the corruption that actually occurred during his term of office.

JUST SEX

This is not to say that Harding was entirely an innocent. While his extracurricular activities must have been widely known among many people, according to the gentleman's agreement during those times, it was not reported.

It seems hard to believe that no one within the small community where he presided as editor over the local town newspaper, Marion, Ohio, knew of Harding's womanizing tendencies. Yet there appears to be no published references to these activities in his own newspaper—or in any others, for that matter. Although he was married and a leader of his community, elected to the U.S. Senate from Ohio, Harding had had an affair with Carrie Fulton Phillips, beautiful, ten years younger, and married. When their affair broke off just as World War I was breaking out in Europe, she went to Germany where she became extremely pro-German. In 1917, she actually tried to pressure Senator Harding to vote against the Declaration of War with Germany, with the implicit threat of exposing their affair. To his credit, he refused and called her bluff, and she never went public. It was not until 1963 that the affair was publicly disclosed when love letters written to her by Harding were found and published.

An even better example of the rules regarding how a public figure's sex life is out of bounds for reporters was the affair Warren Harding carried out while he was President of the United States with Nan Britton, 30 years his junior. (As my father would say, God bless him!) Historians describe Britton as a "cute blond from Marion"—which surely could have been a good song title in the 1920s. Britton apparently had a "crush" on Harding dating back to 1910, while he was a U.S. Senator and she a freshman in college. She apparently pined over his campaign posters in her college dormitory.

The affair apparently began in a hotel room in lower Manhattan on July 30, 1917. As one historian put it, perhaps not entirely with tongue in cheek, Harding had found the fair young Nan a job, and she, naturally, "expressed her gratitude" by having sex with him that historic evening in New York City. The affair continued, and, in January 1919, some 17 months later on the blissful and romantic location of a couch in Senator Harding's U.S. Senate office, a child by the name of Elizabeth Ann Christian was conceived. The still married Senator Harding made secret child support payments to support young Nan and baby Elizabeth. A little more than a year later, he was elected President of the United States. The child support payments continued unabated despite his new station in life. Apparently, "trusty Secret Service agents" delivered them. (And there was no grand jury empaneled at the time to subpoena them!)

Once president, did President Harding use all his masculine discipline and good judgment to cut off the affair, given the fishbowl of the White House and the presidency and the possibility of getting caught—if not by his wife, then by the White House press corps? Absolutely not—for the rules were different then. In fact, in one of the legendary sexual acts in White House history, Harding is said to have had sex with the lovely Miss Britton standing up in a White House closet just off the Oval Office in January 1923. Harding died eight months later of a stroke. Had the awesome act in the closet been generally known, some wags might have attributed his fatal stroke at least in part to the acrobatics undertaken in the confines of a small closet.[57]

But that is the point: While the affair may not have been generally known, dozens of people in the White House and dozens of people in the social whirl of small-town Washington, D.C., who were experts on knowing such things, must have been in on the secret. The White House then was no different than White Houses before or after. There were Secret Service agents, butlers, staff, secretaries, and others around and near the president who had the same capabilities and proclivities to know what the President was doing in his private time (and with and to whom). It is also likely that people such as these talked to their friends and these stories were bound to reach the ears of reporters who covered the White House at some point. But still, Warren Harding's sex life remained unreported.

So it remained a secret to the general public—at least until four years after President Harding's death when, in 1927, Nan Britton decided to cash in (I know that today's twenty-first-century readers will be shocked to learn this!) and wrote a book called *The President's Daughter*. She is said to have described the affair in "painstaking detail." She also dedicated the book to "all unwed mothers and to their innocent children whose fathers are usually not known to the world"—a dedication that surely brought tears to the eyes of millions. Well, maybe not millions, but the book—estimated by one historian to be 175,000 words—sold very well. With 90,000 or so copies sold, the book was on the functional equivalent of the "best seller" list for months.[58]

There must have been many Americans who, upon the publication of Nan Britton's book, were genuinely shocked that the President of the United States should have had an affair near the Oval Office with the First Lady living just a few steps away in the residence, and at the poor judgment and lack of discipline that such behavior demonstrated. But what did not seem to shock anyone—and for at least another 50 years, what never seemed to have occurred to anyone, either in the White House press corps, the White House staff, or the general public—was the fact that no one at the time leaked the affair to the press, or that the press having heard about it, never wrote about it. Because it was understood: that was out of bounds.

KENNEDY—THE LAST DAYS OF THE GENTLEMEN'S AGREEMENT

Fast-forward almost exactly four decades. Over those 40 years, there was Franklin Roosevelt's reported affair with Lucy Mercer while he was President; Dwight Eisenhower's reported affair with Kate Summersby while he was supreme commander of Allied Forces in Europe; and most emblematic of all, the active and hardly disguised sexual escapades of the thirty-fifth President of the United States, John F. Kennedy—all not exploited by the political opposition, all not written about by the press corps.

Kennedy's conduct, even by today's standards, seems so reckless and beyond the pale that it is hard to comprehend why no one in the White House press corps broke ranks to write about it. Surely, for the same reasons given above, the affairs had to have been widely known and discussed in the small community of the White House staff and media. Kennedy's reputation as a womanizer was not only well known in Washington; it was also well known by his wife, Jackie, even before she married him, and the entire Kennedy family both before and after he became President.

It is hard to separate rumor from fact when it comes to JFK's sexual exploits while President. At the very least it is well documented by historians that JFK liaised with Judith Campbell Exner, girlfriend of mobster Sam Giancana, many times in the White House starting in May 1961. She was first introduced to Kennedy before his election, in February 1960. The details are not important, although Ms. Exner's memoir published in 1977, *My Story*, has certainly much independent corroboration. What is significant is that during the glory days of Camelot there was surely no one in the White House, in the political establishment of either party, including the most partisan, anti-Kennedy Republicans, who took steps to encourage published reports about Kennedy's private life.

In addition to the usual complicity between the politicians and the Washington press corps to keep quiet regarding sexual peccadilloes, there was also an incestuous relationship between Kennedy and the press to the point where the objectivity that the press usually maintained on policy issues relating to the President became, at least among leading members of the media establishment, almost entirely lost. Probably the most dramatic example of this deterioration of the formal, even adverse, relationship between reporter and President was the close friendship frankly conceded by the former executive editor of the *Washington Post*, Ben Bradlee, in his 1995 memoir, *A Good Life*, between JFK and himself. Bradlee recounted that relationship in ways that seem highly compromising by today's (and even by those of the 1960s') journalistic standards.[59]

Bradlee describes in his memoir one magical scoop that resulted from that friendship while he was *Newsweek*'s Washington bureau chief. Bradlee and Phil Graham, the new owner and publisher of the *Washington Post* as well as of *Newsweek*, attended a White House party in February 1962. Shortly after midnight, he recounts that President Kennedy approached him and asked him if it was too late in the week to change the cover of *Newsweek*. Bradlee said that it was but still encouraged the President to tell him the scoop. "Under the spectacular Peale portrait of Benjamin Franklin," Bradlee writes, the President told him that Francis Gary Powers, the pilot of the CIA's U–2 spy plane that had been shot down by the Russians nine months before, had been swapped for Rudolph Abel, a colonel in the Soviet intelligence agency and the highest-ranking spy ever caught by the United States. Bradlee relayed the scoop to Graham, who said it was not too late to change the front page of that morning's *Post*. Bradlee went to a telephone, sat on the "sill of a large window facing Lafayette Park in the main entrance of the White House," and dictated the story to the *Post*'s managing editor "to the strains of Lester Lanin's dance band." "It was the kind of moment that made Kennedy nervous about me, and me nervous about my relationship with him," Bradlee candidly writes.[60]

It is impossible to know whether Bradlee pulled his punches when writing critical stories about Kennedy's presidency or policies because of the closeness of their relationship, but surely he would not deny that to do so would have put him in a difficult, if not impossible, personal and journalistic position. And did his closeness cause him to be blind to Kennedy's reckless sexual behavior while President? He says that he personally had no knowledge of President Kennedy's private activities, "since most of the 125 conversations I had with him took place with Tony [Bradlee's wife at the time] and Jackie present, [and thus] extracurricular screwing was one of the few subjects that never came up." With laudable candor, however, he adds that "it is now accepted history that Kennedy jumped casually from bed to bed with a wide variety of women." He writes that he is "appalled by the recklessness, by the subterfuge that must have been involved." However, "in those days reporters did not feel compelled to conduct full FBI field investigations about a politician friend."[61]

Clearly dozens of other reporters seduced by the Kennedy charm felt the same way—and chose not to write about Kennedy's sex life. But to repeat: The point is that the prevailing rules were that such stories were out of bounds. The judgment was that his sex life did not affect Kennedy's public performance and, therefore, it was no one's business—regardless of whether such conduct exposed serious character flaws and showed "recklessness . . . [and] subterfuge" by dangerously exposing the president to blackmail by mobsters and others.[62] But it was not just that writing about President Kennedy's sex life was seen as over the line. Leading establishment journalists during this period of U.S. history saw themselves, at least at critical times, as almost a part of the government they covered and thus carrying a special responsibility to protect that government. As Bradlee wrote insightfully in his memoir: "With membership in the establishment went a heightened sense of responsibility." Bradlee also made a candid omission about his own closeness to John Kennedy and the possibility that that closeness had compromised what was now needed, after Watergate, more than ever—a safe distance between journalists and the politicians they covered. Bradlee recounts: ". . . I realize I may be speaking about myself here, although I believe I am speaking about my colleagues too. I had already declined an invitation to join the newspaper establishment's Valhalla, the Gridiron Club. I felt that newspaper people and newsmakers should keep a civil distance from each other."[63]

Therefore, it is no surprise, as Bradlee's analysis correctly describes, that the *New York Times*, after stumbling upon one of the greatest scoops of the newspaper's history—news of the CIA-sponsored invasion of Cuba at the Bay of Pigs in the early spring of 1961, just months into the new Kennedy Administration's term—decided not to run the story after President Kennedy and other senior Kennedy Administration officials reportedly pleaded with

Times columnist James Reston and *Times* editors not to do so. They agreed because they were convinced at the time that publishing the scoop would clearly compromise the operation and risk lives. (Years later, Reston and others would say that compromising the operation would have been a good thing—it might have actually prevented this huge policy fiasco—and that the decision not to publish was a mistake.)

It was that same blurring between journalism and government that occurred at the height of the Cuban missile crisis and that many credit as having helped save the world from nuclear holocaust. As we now know, there was a "back door" proposal sent to both President Kennedy and Premier Khrushchev that ultimately formed the basis to resolve the Cuban missile crisis and avoid a nuclear holocaust: The Soviets would agree to remove the offensive nuclear missiles from Cuba under UN supervision and Cuban leader Fidel Castro would promise never to accept offensive weapons of any kind again from the Soviets. At the same time (the Americans did not want it to be phrased as a quid pro quo), the United States would secretly pledge not to invade Cuba again. In addition, Kennedy made a secret commitment that the United States would remove all Jupiter missiles, capable of carrying nuclear warheads, from Turkey. As we now know from the players involved, the basics of this proposal actually originated with an ABC-TV network journalist, John Scali, and his KGB source, Aleksandr Feklisov (known as Fomin). While there is some dispute to this day as to whether the proposal first came from Scali or Fomin, it is undisputed that they both played a role.[64] Scali conveyed this proposal to President Kennedy and his Executive Committee of the National Security Council, which ultimately led to the dramatic final resolution. To this day there is some controversy over whether Scali's role as a journalist was unacceptably compromised by the role he played as an important go-between, but the fact is, no one really cared then or now if it meant that Scali played an important role in saving the world from nuclear holocaust, which he undoubtedly did.

And then on November 22, 1963, an assassin's bullet did more than kill President Kennedy. It put an end to the establishment's tacit understanding between media, political leaders, and the public as to what news was, and was not, appropriate to print. The gentleman's agreement was over. The wars of the 1960s—Lyndon Johnson's loss of credibility over Vietnam and the political and cultural wars that divided the country by region, race, and class as it had not been divided since the Civil War—replaced it. The seeds of a new kind of politics and journalism sprouted in the 1960s: politics driven not just by disagreements but by personal hatreds, with the goal not just to defeat the political opposition but to destroy it; and journalism driven not just to expose criminal conduct and rid government of corruption but to use scandal to bring down politicians and to increase the prestige (and financial resources) of the investigative journalists responsible for doing so. By the end of the 1960s and early 1970s, American politics and journalism would never be the same.

CHAPTER TWO

SEEDS OF THE
CULTURE WARS:
THE 1960S

On November 3, 1964, I sat in Yale history professor Claude Barfield's living room in a suburb of New Haven, Connecticut, watching the presidential election returns with a group of fellow Yale sophomores. Professor Barfield taught a small discussion group of about 12 students, a course focused on politics and the Populist, Progressive, and the New Deal eras and had invited us to watch the election returns in his home. One of my friends, Victor H. Ashe, now ambassador to Poland and formerly mayor of Knoxville for 16 years, was an active Republican from Tennessee who had predicted weeks before that his party's nominee, Arizona Senator Barry Goldwater, would lose. "Too radical," he said conclusively, and "good riddance for our party." By election night, Ashe and most other political pundits had been proven right. The results should have surprised no one: President Lyndon Johnson, the Democratic nominee who had been John Kennedy's Vice President, had won by a historic landslide, winning 61.1 percent of the vote and 44 states, with a 486 to 52 electoral vote margin.

But I remember today as clearly as if it were last night the reaction of one friend in the class, an activist Republican conservative, which in those days was a rare thing at Yale, and an especially religious person. I looked at him, and his eyes were tearful as he recognized that Johnson would win by a landslide. But it wasn't his tears that shocked me. There was an intense look of hate—his face was literally warped with anger. The intensity of his expression was actually scary. "The evil-doers have won for now," he said. "We'll destroy them some day—you'll see." This was a really nice guy, always quick with a smile, fun to be with, smart in class. Now his Dr. Jekyll had turned into Mr. Hyde. I shall never forget that look. It taught me, then and to this day, what can happen to a human being when righteousness and politics combine.

Five years later, almost to the day, I sat with a good friend named Joseph Lieberman (Connecticut's current U.S. Senator) in the Yale Law School auditorium. It *was for a meeting of a new Connecticut liberal Democratic group, the Conference of Concerned Democrats (CCD), formed in the aftermath of the 1968 presidential campaign. It seemed a straightforward meeting to elect statewide officers. Joe Lieberman had been nominated for the state steering committee. This was partly a reflection of his leadership among supporters of the late Senator Robert F. Kennedy's presidential campaign, before Kennedy had been tragically assassinated in June 1968. Most of the CCD organizers had been active in the campaign of Senator Eugene McCarthy, who had challenged President Lyndon Johnson on an anti-Vietnam War plank late in 1967, when Robert Kennedy had declined to do so. There were still some hard feelings among McCarthy supporters for those who had supported Kennedy over McCarthy. But that seemed so long ago and most of the liberals in the room saw the CCD as a way of uniting the McCarthy and Kennedy liberals and reformers in Connecticut Democratic politics. We needed to prepare for the coming 1970 U.S. Senate race and to find an anti-War candidate to run in the Democratic primary. That candidate appeared to be Reverend Joseph Duffey, a soft-spoken congregationalist minister who had led the Connecticut McCarthy campaign in 1968 along with state campaign coordinator Anne Wexler, a highly regarded anti-War activist. Wexler and Duffey had become the titular leaders of Connecticut's liberal movement after the 1968 presidential campaign. (Duffey would go on to become the Democratic nominee for U.S. Senate in 1970, with Wexler as his campaign manager. He was defeated by Republican Congressman Lowell Weicker—who was ultimately defeated by Joe Lieberman 16 years later.)*

I and most other people in the small group of about 100 people from around the state assumed that the CCD Steering Committee election would not provoke controversy. We certainly thought that Lieberman, Duffey, and Wexler would be elected without contention. But suddenly a well-known liberal activist stood up and delivered a vitriolic speech personally attacking Lieberman, Wexler, and Duffey. This was more than 30 years ago, but I dimly recall him denouncing them for compromising with State Democratic Party leader John Bailey during the negotiations over how many delegates McCarthy supporters would get to go to the 1968 Democratic National Convention. He also criticized Lieberman for refusing to support McCarthy even before Robert Kennedy entered the race. They had negotiated and compromised, he said, as if that was a dirty phrase. We need a new politics that throws out the John Baileys of our party, not cuts deals with them, he said. It was not just the extreme words used that were so patently false and absurd—it was the intense tone of sanctimony and personal attack that horrified me. He was not only convinced he was right. He sounded like he believed that anyone who disagreed with him was morally challenged. I literally felt a shudder of repulsion. This was, I thought, a fellow liberal. With friends like these . . . I wondered. Is this what politics had to be about?

To understand the genesis of the scandal wars that came to dominate American politics in the last quarter of the twentieth century up to the present day, you can draw lines directly back to the 1960s. After the assassination of John Kennedy on November 22, 1963 (and some would say, at least in part, as a result of that assassination), American politics fundamentally changed.[1] New rules emerged regarding how politicians acted toward each other; how the media and politicians interacted with each other; and most importantly, how the political forces on opposing sides of the ideological divide saw and dealt with each other.

On the Republican right, 1964 was the critical turning point. This was the year when a "New Right" grassroots movement took over the national Republican Party and nominated Senator Barry Goldwater of Arizona—the hero of the conservative movement for many years. But these Goldwater "New Right" forces were more than conservatives. They were true believers. They saw liberal Democrats not just as opponents having a different government philosophy or policy but also as cultural enemies who were traitors to American values and who needed to be destroyed.

In the second half of the 1960s, the Democratic Party developed its "New Left" counterpart, ironically similar in approach to the New Right and in the venom that energized them. As in the Republican Party's experience with the Goldwaterites, Democratic liberals found themselves associated with, and at times apologetic about, the extremist edges of the New Left movement that had become radicalized over Vietnam, race, and American culture generally. The New Left lost patience with liberals' commitment to the political process to change Johnson's Vietnam War policy and other domestic policies. They used the language of revolution and, in the case of the more radical groups involved in the civil rights movement, "Black power" and dark threats of racial violence. This scared middle America—and, as we now know in retrospect, turned a lot of Democrats into Republicans. And like the Republican conservative establishment in the face of the extremists of the Goldwater movement, too many mainstream Democratic liberal leaders, rather than confronting the New Left, were prone to enable or even defend them.

The result was that, by the end of the 1960s and the 1972 presidential election, both parties were in danger of domination by ideological purists who had personalized their political differences into hatred and vitriol. A dangerous new symmetry had set into the American political culture. For both the New Left and the New Right, it was not enough to defeat the political opposition and criticize their policies. It was necessary to destroy the opposition and describe their policies as evil.

HATERS ON THE RIGHT

During the early 1960s while John Kennedy was President, the Goldwater conservative movement became a national political force that took over the Republican Party. To some extent, the same basic forces (and the children and grandchildren of its early leaders) dominate the Republican Party today. (President Bush and Karl Rove certainly seem to see things that way over the last six years). For a long time, "true believer" conservatives in the Goldwater mold had been frustrated by the national Republican Party's leadership establishment. Anchored and financed largely in New York and on Wall Street, the GOP establishment had dominated the party and selected its presidential nominees at least since 1948. After Nixon's defeat in 1960, grassroots conservatives were determined not only to nominate Goldwater in 1964 over the "Rockefeller wing" (as in New York moderate Governor Nelson Rockefeller), but also to capture control of the party machinery from the grassroots up. And that is exactly what they did.

In many ways these Goldwaterites resembled religious evangelicals—true believers who genuinely were convinced their cause was both right and righteous and their enemies both wrong and evil. In those days, however, the power of the religious right was not as great over Republican Party leaders as it is today. Indeed, people forget that while Senator Barry Goldwater was a classic political and economic conservative, on religious and cultural issues he was actually quite moderate, even liberal (God forbid he would ever admit the latter word about himself). For example, he was tolerant of homosexuality and in his later years did not subscribe to the "right to life" absolutist approach to abortion.[2]

In fact, Barry Goldwater's brand of conservatism was, first and foremost, a rebellion against the centralized role of government and the policies of economic redistribution implicit in the New Deal. Goldwater's seminal book, *The Conscience of a Conservative*, first published in 1960, was the conservatives' bible; William F. Buckley, Jr., and the *National Review* magazine he founded, had been the intellectual leader of the mainstream conservative movement in the 1950s. Buckley spawned dozens of other conservative writers who, despite seeing themselves as a beleaguered minority even within the Republican Party, made up for numbers with intense and often brilliant intellectual repartee and analysis.

The core principles of Goldwater's conservatism were based on a consistent view that government was the problem, not the solution; that private enterprise and unrestrained capitalism was the solution, not the problem; and that worldwide communism was the greatest threat to humankind and a direct security threat to the United States. As Goldwater wrote in *Conscience of a Conservative:*

> I have little interest in streamlining government or in making it more effi-
> cient, for I mean to reduce its size. I do not undertake to promote welfare,
> for I propose to extend freedom. My aim is not to pass laws, but to repeal
> them. It is not to inaugurate new programs, but to cancel old ones that do
> violence to the Constitution, or that have failed in their purpose, or that im-
> pose on the people an unwarranted financial burden. I will not attempt to
> discover whether legislation is "needed" before I have first determined
> whether it is constitutionally permissible.[3]

And on election eve, 1964, with most of the Republican Party's establishment distancing themselves from the obviously losing Goldwater campaign,
a relatively well-known movie actor and TV show host named Ronald Reagan spoke to a national television audience, and said:

> You and I are told increasingly that we have to choose between a left or
> right, but I would like to suggest that there is no such thing as a left or right.
> There is only an up or down—up to a man's age-old dream, the ultimate in
> individual freedom consistent with law and order—or down to the ant heap
> of totalitarianism, and regardless of their sincerity, their humanitarian mo-
> tives, those who would trade our freedom for security have embarked on
> this downward course.[4]

Little did he know that that speech would launch a political career that
would send him to the governor's mansion in California two years later and,
with the same brand of purist Goldwater conservatism, TV likeability, and
authenticity that made his 1964 election eve speech so powerfully received,
to the White House 16 years later.

Unfortunately for Goldwater, known (like Ronald Reagan) even by his
political adversaries in the Senate as likeable and authentic, he had a political blind spot: stubbornness and defensiveness, even regarding politically
untenable positions. Some would say his intellectual honesty was also a
problem, preventing practical politics to deter his conservative philosophy
from being carried to its most logical extremes. Thus, in the early days before the 1964 Republican nomination, he allowed himself to be depicted as
(and sometimes actually proclaimed himself) opposed to the Social Security
system, unemployment compensation, trade unions, and federal aid to education. On foreign policy, Goldwater and his fellow conservatives' deeply
principled anticommunism and opposition to the threat of the Soviet Union
often led to portrayals of them as apologists for the demagogic, Red-baiting

tactics of Senator Joseph McCarthy. (McCarthy himself had self-destructed when he attacked the United States Army and, implicitly, Republican President Dwight D. Eisenhower for being soft on communism.) In some speeches, his radical right-wing supporters—and sometimes, it seemed, Goldwater himself—talked about nuclear war as a possible option to defeat Soviet communism.

This was not the first time, and certainly would not be the last, that the leader of an essentially ideological movement would be too slow to separate himself from the extreme voices in his base whose provocative positions, though not harmful in obtaining the nomination, became huge liabilities when facing the more centrist electorate of general elections. This inevitably places the "mainstream" leaders of that movement in the conundrum of either denouncing the extremists, defending them, or remaining silent.

There were plenty of such extremist voices within the Goldwater movement. These included Robert Welch and his small but noisy John Birch Society, which opposed the Civil Rights movement, arguing that it was supported by the American Communist Party. These extremists also crusaded against Chief Justice Earl Warren, formerly Republican Governor of California, who they argued should be impeached because of un-American decisions that would lead to race mixing and socialism. These were also the people who warned that the United Nations and their pinko fellow travelers, liberal Democrats, were part of a worldwide conspiracy to impose a "one world government" of communists and atheists.

As the 1964 Republican Convention approached, it was clear that Senator Goldwater's grassroots zealots had captured the National Convention, literally from the ground up. The titular leader of the moderate "establishment" wing of the Republican Party, New York Governor Nelson Rockefeller, as well as other Republican moderates called on Goldwater to support a platform plank at the Republican Convention condemning these extremists and their reckless charges.

During a memorable speech at the 1964 Convention in San Francisco's Cow Palace, Governor Rockefeller, with his finger pointing sternly at the Goldwater-dominated crowd, declared:

> During this year I have crisscrossed this nation, fighting . . . to keep the Republican party the party of all the people . . . and warning of the extremist threat, its danger to the party, and danger to the nation. . . . These extremists feed on fear, hate and terror, [they have] no program for America and the Republican Party . . . [they] operate from dark shadows of secrecy. It is essential that this convention repudiate here and now any doctrinaire, militant minority whether Communist, Ku Klux Klan or Birchers.[5]

I remember watching that speech on TV and, along with others, being shocked by the close-ups of the Goldwaterites on the Convention floor and in the galleries of the Cow Palace. They were shouting profanities at Rockefeller, shaking their fists with faces literally warped with hatred. I remember their eyes, in particular. They were the eyes of the true believer—fanatic and intense. They were so hate-filled that I had to wonder, looking into them, whether they would have taken out a gun and killed Rockefeller on the spot, given the chance, and then justified the murder as saving the country from the enemy.

There is no way to overstate how scary these people seemed up close on the TV screen. My father, a strong FDR liberal Democrat, was watching with me. "I have seen these kinds of faces before," I so clearly remember him telling me. "They are the faces of fascism—the same faces we saw in the 1930s cheering on Hitler. They are the faces of the self-righteous—so convinced that anyone who disagrees with them is evil that they believe that anything goes to destroy the opposition."

Little did I realize how correct my father was in identifying this moment as an important one, an ugly close-up of the future years dominated by the politics of personal destruction that would shape and shake America over the next quarter century.

Of course, it is not unusual that political adversaries hated each other. We have already seen that the level of hatred between Alexander Hamilton and Thomas Jefferson could not have been more intense nor more personal. And there could be no greater hatred engendered by the profound moral, cultural, and ideological split over slavery between the North and South that led to our devastating Civil War. And the Republican business community's and the wealthy's hatred of FDR was fierce as well. As Charles Peters, the near-legendary founder and editor of the influential neo-liberal magazine, *Washington Monthly*, wrote, "Roosevelt was hated by the rich. Country club locker room jokes about Eleanor and Franklin were usually unfunny, always vicious, and as ubiquitous as tennis rackets and golf bags. 'Let's go to the Trans-Lux [a New York movie theater featuring newsreels] and hiss Roosevelt,' a fur-clad matron says to her obviously affluent friend in a classic Peter Arno cartoon."[6]

But two things made the hatred from Goldwater purists an important transformational force in American politics in years to come. First, they were *successful* in taking over the national Republican Party—and the very source of their success was the extremist, "true believer" approach they took to politics. Historically, the more radical boundaries of a political ideology have been either marginalized or, as in the case of the Populists, preempted by the

mainstream of a political party. But here, the purists of the Goldwater movement actually gained control of the party apparatus itself (eventually resulting in Ronald Reagan's 1980 nomination for president). A small core of true
believers, energized and invigorated, turned out and took over, while the
complacent moderates stayed at home only to find that they had lost control.
It was a lesson not easily forgotten. Second, the success of Goldwater's supporters provided a template for the New Left within the Democratic Party.
In the hands of the left, however, the strategy had the opposite effect—
leading to the unraveling of the party's FDR/liberal majority coalition and
forcing it into minority status in presidential elections for at least the next
generation.

But the future success of these Goldwaterites was anything but obvious
in the closing days of the 1964 campaign. The only thing that seemed clear
was that the Republican Party was about to experience a national political
disaster. While the crowd roared, the polls sank. Goldwater went down to a
landslide defeat—buried under the weight of his own extreme positions and
dragged even lower by his unwillingness to separate himself from the purist
and most extreme of his followers. This is a similar reticence that plagued
Democratic liberal leaders in the next decade, leading them to a historic
landslide defeat just eight years later. One of the final moments contributing
to Goldwater's political debacle—certainly not causing it, but which has become an emblem of it—was a TV commercial that the Democrats produced
and ran only once on national television. It is often referred to as the
"Daisy" ad.

TV political ads were still relatively new, with a few having been used in
presidential campaigns as far back as the 1952 Eisenhower–Stevenson race.
But many people believe that this ad remains one of the most successful neg-
ative-attack ads in U.S. history. It is also probably one of the nastiest and
most devastating ever. The anti-Goldwater ad started out with a little girl
standing in a beautiful field counting as she pulls petals off a flower (thus, the
"Daisy" moniker). Her counting is replaced with a man's voice counting to
zero as the camera slowly focuses on the girl's eye, which is suddenly filled by
the mushroom cloud of a nuclear explosion. Johnson's voice is then heard
saying: "These are the stakes: to make a world in which all of God's children
can live or to go into the darkness. We must either love each other or we
must die."

The ad ran just once, during the "Movie of the Week" on September 7,
1964, but its impact was immense. News broadcasts replayed it, political
pundits commented on it, and, using today's parlance, it gained "traction"

in multiple national and local media. There was little doubt then, and no doubt today, that this ad was unfair, inaccurate, and over-the-top. Goldwater did not favor nuclear bombs to fight the Soviet Union. The danger of nuclear war if he had been elected President could not responsibly be suggested as greater than if Lyndon Johnson were reelected, but that is exactly what the ad suggested. While some of his right-wing extremist supporters from the John Birch Society seemed to be willing for America to sustain acceptable losses in a nuclear war as the price to destroy the Soviet Union, Senator Goldwater had certainly never adopted that position. Plus, there was no evidence that he was so reckless as to risk nuclear war. (Just as there was no evidence that Lyndon Johnson would be so reckless as to commit the United States to a massive ground war in Southeast Asia fighting peasant guerillas.)

Never mind that I remember loving the ad, so much as to cheer when I saw it. I remember a group of us around the television in Davenport College at Yale were watching and we all cheered and gave each other high-fives. Sure it was a cheap shot, we knew, but if it was wrong, it was wrong for the right reason. Goldwater did have some hard-line views on the Soviet Union, and he did seem a little too sanguine about the use of nuclear power. So it was fair game, we reasoned. (That was the expression used when someone in the Bush White House decided to out a covert CIA agent, Valerie Plame. Her husband had written a critical op-ed piece for the *New York Times* about the absence of evidence that Saddam Hussein had tried to obtain uranium from the African country of Niger. Supposedly, that made her "fair game.")[7] It is a fact, fair or not, that the reason why the "Daisy" ad was so devastating to Goldwater, even though it only ran once, is that it did identify an underlying public doubt about him. For Goldwater, the image he had created, at times unwittingly but also at times purposely, was that of the Lone Ranger or cowboy from the Southwest, speaking the truth, shooting from the hip, and not giving a damn. So, the "Daisy" ad—as unfair and demagogic as it was in retrospect—had a ready audience of Goldwater doubters set to believe the worst. And Goldwater was responsible for that, not the Democrats.

The ad could have been a key factor in turning an inevitable defeat into one of the greatest landslide defeats in U.S. history. American campaigns would never be the same. In fact, it could be argued that today's gotcha culture, using innuendo-based TV attack ads, began with this ad. We Democrats may have celebrated the ad and rationalized that it resonated because of the public's serious doubts about Goldwater's judgment, but Republican leaders—

and not just Goldwater partisans—also took note, as did their media and political consultants. "Fair game? Well, our turn will come," they must have
thought. There will be payback time, and, as we know, there was.

THE EMERGENCE OF THE
PURIST DEMOCRATIC LEFT

It is nothing short of remarkable that the Democratic Party somehow managed to go from winning in an overwhelming political landslide in the 1964
presidential election to losing the presidency just four years later. It may be
even more remarkable that another four years after that, they not only lost
again, but they also lost by one of the greatest landslides in U.S. history. As
we now know, 1968 was the start of a new Republican conservative majority
that dominated the nation for the next 24 years, winning the presidency by
landslide margins in four out of five presidential elections.[8] With the wisdom of hindsight, we also now know that this unraveling of the Democratic
Party majority coalition was a result of four issues on which the party allowed radical and counter-cultural platforms to dominate, known in the late
1960s as "wedge issues." In their radicalized iteration, these four issues
alienated and peeled off important segments of the FDR coalition that
switched to the Republicans starting in 1968 and stayed there up to the
present.

The first of these wedge issues was Vietnam and national defense, in
which legitimate opposition to the war in Vietnam morphed into radical
voices attacking the military, burning the flag, and the like, which, ultimately, caused many to argue that the Democratic Party had become
overtly anti-patriotic and anti-American. The second issue was the Civil
Rights movement for racial justice, where a broad consensus favoring civil
rights for blacks (the word used back then, as opposed to today's preferred
"African Americans") who continued to suffer from rampant discrimination, especially in the deep South, evolved into liberals feeling they needed
to defend forced racial-based busing and quotas (even when they did not
agree with those policies), thus alienating vast segments of the American
middle class, including many liberal Democrats. Urban problems and
crime were the focus of the third issue. Liberal Democrats, instead of being
the first to condemn rioting and crime as victimizing inner-city blacks
more than anyone else, were seen as "soft" on violence and crime or as
"apologists," while Republicans (under skillful demagoguery by the former
Vice President Richard M. Nixon) became the party of "law and order" and
social stability. Lastly, by 1972, the Democratic Party's acceptance of pro-

gressive changes in American culture for women, minorities, young people, and for individual freedoms regarding sex, contraception, and lifestyle left it open to charges of being part and parcel of the counter-culture. Even Senator George S. McGovern, the Democratic candidate for president in 1972, from the indisputably rural, conservative, middle-American state of South Dakota, and a World War II bombardier and war hero, was successfully associated by the Republicans and President Nixon as favoring the "Three As"—"Acid" (as in LSD); Amnesty (for Vietnam draft dodgers); and Abortion (also associated with promiscuous sex encouraged by the recent invention of the "pill"). These three perceived positions associated with Senator McGovern stuck—as did the "Three As" as a short-hand expression for labeling McGovern a "radical" out of touch with "middle America's" cultural, religious, and family values.

In each instance, what started out as legitimate Democratic Party positions on these issues that could have commanded a broad center of the country morphed into radical positions that alienated middle America. It began the process of peeling off or unraveling the FDR coalition of southern rural whites, blue-collar northern workers, and moderate-to-conservative Democrats as they looked to the Republican Party as closer to their values. This also started the "new conservative majority" realignment that reached its zenith in the election and reelection of Ronald Reagan in 1980 and 1984 by landslide margins. It is also reflected today in the Red State–Blue State divisions that resulted in the election of George W. Bush to two terms with a virtual 50 percent–50 percent ideologically and culturally divided country.

What is important, indeed critical, to understand is that the development of these four wedge issues is significant not just because it explains the unraveling of the FDR Democratic majority coalition and the creation of a new Republican conservative majority. What is significant is that the use of these wedge issues, begun in the Goldwater campaign, *started a process of personalizing and demonizing the political opposition that infected American politics for the remainder of the twentieth century*. The Republican right in 1968 and after did not just disagree with liberal Democrats on Vietnam, Civil Rights, law and order, and cultural issues. They labeled them as evil, unpatriotic, un-American, and even treasonous. The New Left in the Democratic Party did not just criticize Vietnam War policies but attacked fundamental American values and culture. They used the language and, at times, the actual weapons of violence and revolution that fed the effectiveness of the Republican use of these four wedge issues. The era of hate-based politics and the destructive cycle of payback between the ideologues of both parties had begun in earnest.

VIETNAM: FROM ANTI-WAR TO ANTI-MILITARY

The classic pattern of taking a disagreement over policy and transforming it into a way to demonize the opposition and attack their fundamental values is plainly visible in what happened to the anti–Vietnam War movement in the mid- to latter 1960s. By 1967 and 1968, the mainstream of the liberal wing of the Democratic Party had reached the conclusion that the Vietnam War was a policy mistake, and many had decided it was a moral mistake. Most had started out believing John Kennedy's rationale, when he first committed ground forces to Vietnam in 1961. This rationale argued that the Vietnamese communist insurgency, the Viet Cong, were really backed by the North Vietnamese communists and, ultimately, by the Chinese and Soviets, who were testing U.S. resolve on containment in Southeast Asia. Stopping communists in South Vietnam was the key to preventing a worldwide threat to communism moving across the globe. That was certainly my view as late as 1966, when I became chairman of the *Yale Daily News* and wrote editorials sympathetic to President Johnson's effort to obtain a negotiated peace that preserved South Vietnam's integrity. "Unilateral withdrawal" and "cutting and running" were concepts that even many liberal Democrats unhappy with the War did not support.

But, by late 1966 and 1967, the center of Democratic liberalism (where I saw myself) became more ardent in their opposition to the War. By reading history and studying the facts (as well as attending "teach-ins" at universities, where history and political science professors would lecture on the history of Vietnam, a place most of us had not heard of a year or so earlier), more and more liberal Democrats came to oppose the War based on a new understanding of three fundamental issues. First, the Vietnam War was not the beginning of a monolithic advance of communism across the globe, but rather an indigenous nationalist-dominated communist movement. Second, the Vietnamese communists wanted the southern and northern pieces of their country united (which had been divided only as part of partial decolonization by the French after World War II). Third, far from being under Chinese Communist dominance, the Vietnamese people had hated the Chinese (and vice versa) for over two thousand years. They would not easily succumb to Chinese communist domination, any more than they were succumbing to U.S. or, before them, French colonial domination. Meanwhile, the Johnson Administration's often indiscriminate carpet bombing of peasant villages, women, and children, as well as its use of napalm raised serious moral questions, not just for liberal Democrats but for Americans of both parties.

Then, a pivotal moment occurred—the Tet Offensive of January 1968. On the Vietnamese New Year, or "Tet," the Viet Cong and North Vietnamese guerillas staged a country-wide series of attacks. These included entering the U.S. Embassy grounds in Saigon and at least temporarily gaining control of several military bases and key strategic areas throughout South Vietnam. These attacks were widely seen on U.S. television news networks and reported in front-page headlines across the country. At the very least, the Tet offensive showed that after nearly twenty thousand American deaths over six years of U.S. military involvement, American forces were still bogged down in the Vietnam War, with no end in sight. It did not seem to matter that, after the dust had settled and the media hype focusing on the attacks (including dramatic shots of Viet Cong climbing over the walls of the U.S. Embassy in Saigon) had ended, in fact, the Tet offensive was a monumental military defeat for the Vietnamese communist forces. Every single one of their advances, while temporarily successful, were pushed back or retaken.

The Johnson Administration's credibility gap had now become an unbridgeable chasm. And while the military battle may have been won, the political war at home had been lost, at least as far as Lyndon Johnson was concerned, irrevocably. When General William Westmoreland, commander of U.S. forces in Vietnam, chose that particular moment to ask for an escalation of troop levels, all political Hell broke loose.

Let us not forget another issue. Opposition to the War grew much more rapidly as the military began to draft increasing numbers of middle-class and upper-middle-class college students. These children of suburban and ordinarily Republican parents had previously avoided the draft due to student deferments and special treatment by draft boards. Starting in late 1967 and 1968, those deferments were no longer available. The end of draft deferments certainly increased *my* interest in opposing the Vietnam War.

The Tet offensive and renewed challenges to Lyndon Johnson's credibility also spread to Johnson's authority to wage war without the declaration by the Congress required in the Constitution. In August 1964, the Johnson Administration obtained a nearly unanimous congressional resolution to authorize a military response to a questionable incident involving North Vietnamese gunboats attacking U.S. destroyers in the Gulf of Tonkin. Johnson then used that resolution as the legal basis for escalating the War to a commitment, at its peak, of over 500,000 ground forces and an ongoing bombing campaign.

Johnson chose this Gulf of Tonkin Resolution to authorize the War rather than seeking a formal congressional declaration of war. Americans never had the benefit of the debate, pro or con, regarding the War; and when the "light at the end of the tunnel" turned into a quagmire with no end in sight, Johnson had nowhere to go but down, politically speaking. The country was not yet ready to "cut and run"—Richard Nixon's election in 1968 showed that much—but clearly the American people on the right and left were frustrated by being caught in the crossfire of a civil war with no visible exit strategy (though as we now know in Iraq today, this would not be the last time the United States would find itself in this situation).

Finally, under a Republican president, Gerald Ford, America acknowledged the reality that "cutting and running" was better than "staying and dying" for no apparent reason. The left and the right came together in agreement on one slogan: "Win or get out." Since winning did not seem possible without destroying Vietnam, the only choice was to leave—some seven years and more than thirty-five thousand deaths after the Tet Offensive.

Make no mistake: the term "credibility gap" was a euphemism for the word "lie." President Johnson was accused of being a liar, and most people in both parties believed it. While accusing an American president of lying was not exactly historically unprecedented, never before had so many of the American people on a bipartisan basis believed the accusation. Looking back now, though we did not know it at the time, something fragile in the body politic had broken. What had started out as important dissent on policy had ended up as very personal and very ugly attacks on the character of the President of the United States.

But it was the Democratic Party and its liberal base that was most injured by Johnson's downfall. Not just because Johnson was a Democratic president responsible for the debacle in Vietnam, but also because his Vietnam War policy caused a fundamental split within the Democratic Party. That split, in turn, sent large segments of the historic New Deal coalition into the arms of the Republicans.

Mainstream liberal Democrats may have turned against the War and their own president in 1967–68, but they did not turn against the political process itself or fundamentally lose faith in American culture and values. Rather, they saw the ballot box as the best method for changing policies. However, these political process liberals were increasingly concerned about the more radical movements on the left. These were groups such as the "Students for a Democratic Society" or the even more radical "Weathermen," who suggested violence and revolution as the only answer. These self-styled "New Left" radical forces saw Lyndon Johnson and the War not just as wrong but as emblematic of an evil American society and culture. They chanted, "Hey, Hey, LBJ, How Many Children Did You Kill Today?" They marched and burned American flags. They also burned their Selective Service draft cards, which in and of itself was defined as a criminal act. They showed their condemnation for America as a whole by spelling it "Amerika."

They burned bras and smoked pot and did acid in public; and dared anyone to mind. And in some instances, they killed innocent people—for example, anti-war protestors at the University of Wisconsin, Madison, set off a car bomb at a campus building, which they thought was an Army-funded facility, killing a young researcher by accident.

So, almost without noticing, the legitimate anti–Vietnam War opposition within the mainstream liberal leadership of the Democratic Party had become tarred with the same brush as those who looked, acted, and talked in ways that threatened the broad American middle class and middle-American values. With only a few exceptions, Democratic liberals were not willing to challenge them or disown them. Indeed, many—perhaps it is accurate to say, most (including me)—facilitated, enabled, or even defended these nihilists of the left.

During the 1968 general election campaign, the far left so dominated and intimidated many Democratic Party liberals that they actually decided, at least until the late fall of the presidential campaign, that it was not worth trying to help Vice President Hubert Humphrey defeat Richard Nixon for the presidency. I remember attending a meeting of Connecticut liberals in Hartford, Connecticut, where someone actually said that it would be better to let Nixon defeat Humphrey and his "fellow pro-War Democrats," so we could "take the country back in 1972." I actually felt some sympathy for this stupid position after the 1968 Chicago Democratic Convention. I and many other young liberal activists were furious with Democratic presidential candidate Vice President Humphrey for not criticizing the police clubbing of anti-War demonstrators on the streets outside the hall of the Democratic National Convention in Chicago in August 1968. And I *almost* agreed that it would be better for Humphrey to lose. That is, until I thought about the poor people who would know the difference between the policies of a Democratic president versus a Republican president, while we upper-middle-class liberals sat safely in an upper-middle-class living room in Hartford, Connecticut.

The same phenomenon of sanctimony plus disingenuousness by liberals occurred in the 2000 election when Ralph Nader announced he was running as an independent against Democrat Al Gore and Republican George W. Bush. It was disingenuous enough that he claimed there would be no real difference to the country, to the poor and the middle class, whether George Bush or Al Gore was elected president. But the biggest lie of all was when Nader claimed that his candidacy would not help Bush and hurt Gore. He repeated that statement over and over again to liberal audiences he spoke to in 2000. This is a peculiarly Washington kind of lie: He knows he is lying, and he knows everyone knows he is lying, but he lies anyway as part of the game. We now know, indisputably, that the votes Nader won in Florida and New Hampshire, to name two examples, would have been the difference between a Gore presidency and a Bush presidency.

In sum, a pattern, or maybe more accurately, an infection, took hold. Liberals had been drawn into thinking that it was not enough to oppose the Vietnam War and Johnson. He and his friends had to be destroyed, and then we could be there to pick up the pieces, and, to use the favorite expression of those self-indulgent days, "reclaim America." To paraphrase Ross Perot some 20 years later, that sucking sound we did not hear at the time were the blue-collar and middle-American Democrats who loved their flag and their country as they slid down the drain into the basin of Republicans waiting to welcome them.

FROM CIVIL RIGHTS TO
FORCED BUSING AND RACIAL QUOTAS

The images on national TV and in newspapers in May 1963 of the fire hoses and vicious dogs of Bull Connor, the sheriff of Birmingham, Alabama, directed at courageous blacks peacefully marching to ask for basic civil and human rights repulsed a huge segment of America and drew wide sympathy and support for the Civil Rights movement. The peaceful August 1963 March on Washington, when Reverend Martin Luther King, Jr., delivered his historic "I Have A Dream" speech, was as positively viewed by the broad center of American politics as was the Bull Connor image viewed negatively. It was clear that the American middle class widely supported the Civil Rights movement that Dr. King and that march represented. It was the Democratic Party, however, that took the moral high ground and supported the Civil Rights movement of Dr. King. The conservative leadership of the Republican Party allowed themselves to be positioned in opposition (Senator Goldwater, for example, had voted against the 1964 Civil Rights Act and most Republicans in Congress had opposed the 1965 Voting Rights Act).

So the question is, how did liberal Democrats go from being on the right side of the American electorate in 1964 concerning Civil Rights to being on the wrong side just four short years later? In 1968, racial issues triggered a migration, first as a dribble and then as a hemorrhage, of massive numbers of traditionally blue-collar and suburban voters, to the national Republican Party. While it was not easy to understand back then and even to this day how this happened, it does appear to hinge on the Democrats' mishandling of two issues during the 1960s. These were forced busing to achieve racial balance in public schools and racial quotas to remedy past discrimination against minorities. In both instances, liberals jumped to support the position they thought was favorable to minorities because it seemed right and just. They failed to consider, however, whether it was right and just for all, including whites; and if it were not right and unjust for some, how could that be justified?

Forced Busing for Integration Purposes

For some reason, liberals chose to ignore the deep and personal threat that busing white schoolchildren out of their neighborhoods in order to achieve racial balance in heavily black neighborhoods (and vice versa) held for millions of parents. The reason was simple and was not about racism, at least as a general rule. You move into a neighborhood as a young couple primarily because of the school system that you want your kids to go to. As a result, it is not likely that you would take kindly to anyone telling you that your kids now have to get on a bus and go to another school that you perceive to be of inferior quality, security, educational standards, or whatever in order to achieve some larger social purpose. This is true regardless of how sympathetic you may be to that cause.

My friend Reverend Jesse Jackson used to oversimplify this issue by saying, "It's not the bus—it's us." For most people, certainly for most liberals like me opposed to forced school busing to achieve racial balance, that was only half-right. It was not the bus we were really objecting to; riding buses to school had been a long American tradition, especially in rural areas. But it was not about race either. Most Americans do not mind their kids riding a bus to the school they thought their kids would be attending when they moved into the neighborhood. They do mind, however, being told their kids have to go to another school, especially if it is one they perceive to be inferior. Changing the rules, at the expense of my kids, is not fair. It was as simple as that.

When Alabama Governor George Wallace first ran for president in 1964, it was just the beginning of what came to be called the "white backlash" to the busing issue. He attracted large crowds in traditionally Democratic blue-collar neighborhoods in the north over the issue. Even during Johnson's landslide victory in 1964, Wallace managed to draw a surprising number of votes on a national scale, securing nearly a third of the vote in the Democratic primaries of three states: Wisconsin, Indiana, and Maryland. When Wallace ran again in 1968, this time as a third-party candidate for the American Independent party, he seemed at times to base his entire campaign on this backlash. He was called racist by Democratic Party liberals and blacks. But the people who did not want their schoolchildren bused outside of their neighborhood schools were not all racist and they resented the implication. So, they became angry—and increasingly took it out on the Democratic Party, whose liberal leadership either supported forced busing or were complicit and silent in places where it had been ordered. They did so by voting for George Wallace and attending his rallies in increasing numbers.[9]

Between 1968 and 1972, President Richard Nixon effectively used the busing issue as a wedge to peel off traditional Democrats from the party to vote Republican. Democrats were in a quandary—but one of their own making. At the time, I recall virtually every liberal Democrat agreed that busing as a social tool to achieve better integration of public schools may be a worthy goal but not if it affected your own kids and your own schools. Yet very few national Democratic liberal leaders called for outright opposition to forced busing.

Why didn't we just have the courage to say no? Why didn't liberals say, "We're for civil rights, we're for de-segregated schools, and we're for integrated housing that will lead to integrated local schools. But we're not for forced school busing. It's not fair"? The main reason—and I can recall this vividly, as well—was fear and guilt or, perhaps more accurately, hypersensitivity to being seen by Blacks and minorities as not being sympathetic to the plight of inner-city black children going to segregated urban schools starved of funds and inferior to white suburban schools.

Whatever the reason, the result was that those people whose children were forcibly bused, or those who were incensed by the policy, became angry with Democrats. So, they started voting Republican, with this as the primary reason.

On the other side, the Republican right did not just disagree with Democrats who were trying to find a solution to the difficult problem of de facto segregation in inner-city schools. They accused Democrats of being anti-white, anti-neighborhood schools, and even anti-children! So, another chapter on the politics of demonizing the opposition was written, with the volatile issue of busing adding unneeded fuel to the fires.

Racial Quotas

Racial quotas did not create the same amount of visceral anger in the late 1960s or early 1970s the way forced busing did, but by 1972 the Republicans and President Nixon were already talking about the unfairness of racial "quotas" that caused "reverse discrimination."

How clever of the Republicans to figure out a way to justify years of racial and religious discrimination, as well as a way to make the word "quota" something liberals did to hurt Americans, rather than help rectify historic wrongs. They did, and liberal Democrats fell for it. As usual, rather than immediately and unambiguously condemning quotas as unfair and un-American, liberals equivocated. (This is true, even though, just as in the case of busing, very few liberals I knew could defend discriminating against a qualified white in favor of an unqualified minority in order to achieve a racial "quota.") One reason we equivocated is again due to the hypersensitivity described above—a fear of seeming anti-diversity and anti-black. Another is that we wrestled with a solution that would allow us to have it both ways—opposing numerical quotas but taking active steps to find qualified minorities to hire and admit to educational institutions in order to reverse years of racial discrimination. We called it "affirmative action."

While we believed in the concept of affirmative action and opposed "quotas" that would lead to favoring unqualified over qualified people based on race, in practice it did not always work that way. For example, Affirmative Action Programs or "AAPs" were required for all U.S. government contractors under an Executive Order established by President Johnson in 1965. But in practice, each contractor had to establish "numerical goals and timetables" based on the percentage of various categories of minorities in the surrounding population of the metropolitan area in which the federal contract had been awarded.

In the early 1970s, I was a young lawyer advising federal contractor clients on how to avoid violating this Executive Order at this time. As a result, I saw how contractors would go out and find enough categories of minorities (blacks, Hispanics, Asians, etc.) to "meet the numbers." Whatever it took to meet the numbers—that was what I heard again and again among employment officials and human resources specialists in federal contractor offices. Whites would be overlooked if it were necessary to meet the "numerical goals." In short, it walked, talked, and looked like a quota, and it was.

By trying to be fair, by trying to have it both ways, liberal Democrats ended up being branded as supporting "quotas." They supported injustice against qualified white applicants while trying to correct the injustice blacks and other minorities had suffered through years of racial discrimination. The result was that Republicans latched on to the accusation that Democrats supported policies that resulted in "reverse discrimination."[10] The bitterness between races and between left and right grew—and became more personal.

FROM CIVIL LIBERTIES
TO "CODDLING CRIMINALS"

From Thomas Jefferson to Andrew Jackson's founding of the Democratic Party, the conservative values of individual freedom, constitutionally protected civil liberties, and the right to due process as a protection against government oppression have been paramount. Yet, somehow, that concept of civil liberties and due process got turned on its head in the 1960s. By the end of the decade, Republicans had successfully made "civil liberties" synonymous with crime and civil disorder—and argued that liberal Democrats were sympathetic to both! It did not matter if it was factually true or not. It was an accusation made by conservative Republicans to win votes—and liberal Democrats played into their hands not only by failing to defend themselves but also by seeming to verify the Republicans' innuendo by speaking about the "roots" of crime in poverty and injustice (true!) as a reasonable justification for crime and violence (not true!).

By the late 1960s, crime, violence, and urban rioting were tragically intertwined with the race issue. This was mostly because the urban riots of the mid- to late 1960s occurred in inner-city black neighborhoods, where unemployment and social unrest were highest. The first major urban inner-city riot of the 1960s occurred in New York City in 1964, with more than a dozen flaring up over the next few years in cities across the country. Some of the most damaging included the riots in the Watts district of Los Angeles in 1966, where the cry of "burn, baby, burn" gained notoriety, followed by riots in Detroit, Cleveland, and Newark in 1967.

Then on the evening of April 4, 1968, when news of the assassination of Reverend Martin Luther King, Jr., in Memphis, Tennessee, was announced, cities across America went up in flames. From the Capitol in Washington, D.C., burning buildings and black smoke could be seen darkening the sky on April 5. Johnson called up over ten thousand federal troops to help bring the city under control. Marines even set up machine guns on the steps of the Capitol.

It is not possible to overstate the fears Americans had during this time that the social fabric and stability of the country was in real danger of unraveling. Even before the country had a chance to recover from the trauma of the King assassination and unchecked riots came the horror of Senator Robert F. Kennedy's assassination just two months later. Then, there was the violence on the streets of Chicago outside the 1968 Democratic National Convention, with police clubbing young protesters. Add to this the increasingly violent protests against the Vietnam War in 1969 and 1970, as protests organized by the ultra-left "New Mobilization" and other more radical groups supplanted the moderate "Vietnam Moratorium."

All in all, by the 1970 congressional elections, law and order was a major issue across the country and the political spectrum, and the Republicans had the upper hand. The Democrats somehow allowed the "gotcha" politics of the day to pin their party and its liberal ideology as a whole as one that "coddled criminals." If there was a pivotal moment when the Democrats did it right in addressing this law and order issue, it was the evening before the 1970 congressional elections, when Maine Senator Edmund S. Muskie responded to the charges by Republicans and President Nixon that Democrats were "soft on crime." The Republicans had run scary ads with rioting and sirens in the background. A strident Vice President Spiro Agnew campaigned using the rhetoric of fear and hate. He used racial code words about the need for "law and order" and defeating Democrats, whom he accused of being afraid to stand up to the rioters.

Muskie had impressed the country with his low key, "Lincolnesque" style and looks when he was the Democratic vice presidential nominee during the 1968 presidential campaign. As one of the leading choices for the Democratic presidential nomination in 1972, then chairman of the Democratic National Committee, Lawrence O'Brien, put Muskie on national TV to respond to this Republican charge. From his fireside seat in his small home in Kennebunkport, Maine, Muskie spoke sternly in words crafted by legendary John Kennedy speechwriter, Richard Goodwin:

> There are those who seek to turn our distress to partisan advantage—not by offering solutions—but with empty threat and malicious slander. They imply that Democratic candidates for high office . . . who have courageously pursued their convictions in the service of the republic in war and peace . . . actually favor violence and champion the wrongdoer. That is a lie. And the American people know it is a lie.

He continued, in words that might be worth a re-reading by today's Republican strategists as they try to exploit politically 9/11 and the War on Terror:

> There are only two kinds of politics. They are not radical and reactionary, or conservative and liberal. Or even Democrat and Republican. There are only the politics of fear and the politics of trust. One says: "You are encircled by monstrous dangers. Give us power over your freedom so we may protect you." The other says: "The world is a baffling and hazardous place, but it can be shaped to the will of men. . . . [C]ast your vote for trust . . . in the ancient traditions of this home for freedom. . . ."

This Muskie "election eve" speech as it came to be famously known had a dramatic effect. It was even more dramatic because it was preceded on the TV by Nixon waving his arms and sensationalizing the crime issue in a poorly recorded speech. The contrast could not be clearer. Almost instantaneously Muskie became the front-runner for the 1972 Democratic nomination, with broad appeal to moderate and even conservative Republicans as well as Democrats. And in the next day's congressional elections, the Democrats picked up a total of 12 seats in the House of Representatives though they lost three seats in the Senate.

Unfortunately, Republicans did not let the Democrats off the hook, and continued to declare Democrats as less than tough on crime, especially regarding minorities. As a result, Democratic resentment grew through the 1970s and 1980s, encouraging their search for the ever-desired payback.

FROM INDIVIDUAL LIBERTY TO THE "THREE AS"

As already noted, Democrats believe that they have historically held the political high ground on cultural tolerance and the protection of individuals from government intrusion going back to Thomas Jefferson. Yet, as if they did not have enough problems by being identified with anti-War flag burners, pro-busing and quotas, and lawlessness, Richard Nixon and the Republicans also masterfully promoted liberal Democrats and their 1972 presidential nominee, Senator George McGovern, as supporting the "Three As." This trio of issues—amnesty, acid, and abortion—seemed to prove that Democrats were out of touch with basic, middle-American, family and religious values. This was truly the beginning of the straight line from the 1960s to the Red State–Blue State division in the 2000 elections. Democrats were forced to write off huge swaths of the country because they never regained their footing after the emergence of these cultural wedge issues. They were firmly identified as supporting values and practices that offended the personal, religious, and family values of tens millions of Americans living in those areas.

Naturally, Democrats found a way to be depicted as sympathetic not only to draft dodgers who had fled to Canada but also with the long-haired protesters demanding amnesty. Senator McGovern tried to explain that he supported enforcing the law and was a patriotic American, but that perhaps when the War was over, there could be another look at amnesty. In fact, there was a historical tradition of granting amnesty to draft resisters, one that went back to the Civil War if not before, once a war was over. Given the polarization of the country over Vietnam, however, and the scenes of radicals and hippies burning the flag and denouncing the "fascist Amerika," the notion of ever granting amnesty to "draft dodgers" was unpopular, certainly while the Vietnam War was raging. But Nixon and the conservative right's demagoguery drowned out McGovern's nuanced position. He was pegged as sympathetic to protecting draft dodgers and people who had abandoned America. Period.

Democratic liberals sympathetic to the anti-War movement also carried the burden of the 1960s drug culture. Scenes of pot-smoking, LSD-dropping radicals and hippies actually had little, if anything, to do with the Democratic Party. But again, no Democratic liberal seemed willing to take the lead in denouncing the drug culture either. It was that sensitivity issue again—or maybe a question of civil liberties—or both. So, yet another stream joined the growing river of alienated Democratic voters shifting to the Republican side.

Finally, in 1972, abortion became a national issue in a presidential campaign for the first time in U.S. history. From the Civil War through the 1950s, every state banned abortion (except to save the life of the mother) except for Kentucky, whose courts judicially declared abortions to be illegal. But the effort to liberalize the exception to such bans gathered steam in the 1950s. It was then that the American Law Institute (ALI), a kind of super-think tank for U.S. lawyers, proposed a more limited "model" criminal abortion statute as part of its Model Penal Code that would allow abortions when childbirth posed grave danger to the physical or mental health of a woman, when there was a high likelihood of fetal abnormality, or when pregnancy resulted from rape or incest. The key change here is that it decriminalized abortions when the physical or mental health of a woman was at stake, rather than limited to saving a woman's life.[11]

The first U.S. Supreme Court decision that dealt with abortion was *United States v. Vuitch*, decided in 1971.[12] The Court upheld the Washington, D.C. abortion statute after being challenged on grounds of vagueness, in effect permitting an abortion where it was "necessary for the preservation of the mother's . . . health" (not just to save her life). A major legal and political Rubicon had been crossed. Anti-abortion forces—before they called themselves the "Right to Life" movement—realized (and they were right) that this exception opened the door essentially to abortion on demand—since a woman could almost always convince her doctor that an abortion was necessary to preserve her "health," which could include psychological and emotional as well as physical health.

During the 1972 campaign, everyone knew that there was a case, *Roe v. Wade*, pending before the Supreme Court that would determine whether an exception beyond saving the life of the mother was constitutionally protected. In any event, there were more and more liberalized abortion statutes that had been passed by some state legislatures. By 1972, four states allowed abortion on demand, one state allowed abortion for rape and incest only (Mississippi), and Alabama allowed abortions only to save a woman's "physical health." Thirty-one states allowed abortion only to save a woman's life.[13] Once again, the Democrats and Senator McGovern allowed the Republicans to paint the party as supporting the extremist position of "abortions on demand"—meaning all abortions, regardless of type, reason, or stage of pregnancy, were okay.

On January 22, 1973, shortly after Nixon's landslide victory, the U.S. Supreme Court ruled in *Roe v. Wade* that a woman had a limited constitutional right to an abortion because of the implied right to privacy and individual liberty under the Fourteenth Amendment.[14] The Court's key ruling was that at least in the first term, the right to an abortion was absolutely protected even if it was necessary just to protect a woman's "health"—i.e., her "psychological and physical well-being," not just to save her life.[15] The court went on to permit reasonable state regulation in the second trimester, and permitted state bans on abortion in the third trimester when the fetus was deemed viable, i.e., capable of surviving outside the womb.[16]

In fact, the irony is that Senator McGovern allowed himself to be associated with positions on all three "As" in which he did not himself believe. In an op-ed piece published in the *Washington Post* 16 years after his 1972 presidential campaign, McGovern insisted that he had been opposed to de-criminalizing possession of marijuana in 1972 even for a first-time offense (but favoring dropping that penalty from a felony to a misdemeanor). He also opposed amnesty for draft dodgers (at least as long as the Vietnam War continued and there were service men and women at risk in battle), and opposed abortion on demand without any regulation. He favored "regulation" of abortion by the states—though he did not explain what "regulation" meant. But Senator McGovern subsequently supported *Roe v. Wade*, decided after the 1972 presidential campaign was over.[17]

It is telling, however, that few of the American people, including McGovern's liberal supporters, much less conservative voters, knew that these were his true positions during the 1972 campaign. First, it is a fair question to ask Senator McGovern whether his own reticence to offend the unforgiving purist elements of his left-wing base worked to obscure his position as much as Republican distortion. Second, clearly Senator McGovern was not alone in the failing to "frame" issues before the Republicans were able to define him as being on the wrong side of the cultural divide. McGovern was the first of many Democratic presidential candidates, until Bill Clinton in 1992, who allowed the Republican Party and candidate to "frame" the issues in the worst possible way for the Democrats. The abortion issue is a clear and dramatic example—largely true to this day.

Senator McGovern and the Democrats failed on several points regarding the abortion issue in the 1972 campaign. First, they failed to explain that they did not believe the right to abortion was an absolute right under all circumstances. (For example, it is not an unrestricted right in the third trimester—consistent with the subsequent holding of *Roe*.) Next, and most importantly, they failed to immediately frame the issue as one about the "constitutional protection of individual liberty and privacy" from "government intrusion" in decisions that should stay between a physician and a woman. Nor did they immediately and repeatedly acknowledge the serious moral issues involved in any abortion and the painful and traumatic experience that any woman who has an abortion experiences.

Instead, the national Democratic Party allowed the Republicans to frame the abortion issue *first and repeatedly* as being about "baby killing" and "the right to life." It was only five months after the *Roe* decision, in May 1973, when the first mass publicity about the "right to life" occurred. This was when the National Right to Life Committee (NLRC) was incorporated, followed by a mass NRLC Convention that left the impression of a national movement that spanned the political spectrum. In January 1974 the first "March for Life" was held in Washington, D.C., on the west steps of the Capitol, as thousands of "pro-life" Americans, again apparently from all walks of life, received significant media coverage in most sections of the country.

It was not until years later that women's rights groups and the national Democrats recognized they had lost the initial round of defining the issue. They finally created the expression "pro-choice" rather than "pro-abortion" or "anti-Right to Life" (as the Republicans had already defined it). As we know, even the expression "pro-choice" did not resonate with those who had serious moral and religious problems with abortion.

In the final analysis, the abortion issue, perhaps more than any other issue, exemplified the personalized attack mode and demonization of the opposition that had entered the political process and metastasized quickly throughout the 1960s and early 1970s. From the "right to life" movement's perspective, people who supported allowing abortions under certain circumstances were not just wrong—they were morally evil. How could it be otherwise, since they regarded any abortion—even one in the first trimester to terminate a pregnancy that resulted from rape or incest—as the murder of a living being? So, anyone who supported *Roe* supported baby-killing. That is a pretty personal accusation, far beyond the norms of political debate and civil differences of opinion.

Those who supported the 1973 Supreme Court's 7–2 decision in *Roe v. Wade* naturally took the accusations of their being "baby killers" very personally. Both sides sharpened their knives. One side accused the other of baby-killing. The other side accused the other of favoring back-alley abortions and refusing to help victims of rape and incest. Things got personal, nasty, and hateful. And so, as the 1960s turned into the 1970s, another nasty seed in the gotcha cycle prepared to sprout.

PART II

WATERGATE
LEGACIES

CHAPTER THREE

THE
POST–WATERGATE MEDIA
REVOLUTION

"Where there is a will to condemn, there is evidence."

—*Jung Chang*[1]

I was raised in a liberal Democratic home, and I was taught to be tolerant of those who disagreed with me and not to hate. But there was one big exception—Richard Nixon. My father hated Nixon—and I learned to hate him, too. "Tricky Dick," the man, my father said, who had run against Helen Gahagan Douglas for California U.S. Senator by accusing her of being a communist, cutting out her picture and splicing it next to the American Communist Party chairman. I grew up thinking Nixon was evil. During the 1960 campaign, when I worked for Senator John F. Kennedy as a volunteer, I still thought he was evil—not just wrong, but evil. In the 1968 presidential campaign, I believed this even more so.

So when Watergate started to unfold and Woodward and Bernstein's articles began appearing in the Washington Post, I was ecstatic. "Finally," my father said to me, "we're going to get him." Every morning we Nixon-haters raced to our doorsteps to find the Post and look for another article by Woodward and Bernstein.

When Nixon's downfall finally occurred and he was forced to resign, leaving from the White House South Lawn with that final famous wave before boarding his helicopter on August 9, 1974, I felt no sadness or even empathy for the human and political tragedy unfolding. There was nothing but celebration among my liberal, Nixon-hating friends in Washington. I was filled with hatred for Nixon and joyous about his downfall (never once thinking about how tragic it was for him and his family). All I wanted to do was pack up my two little children, daughter Marlo, age 6, and son Seth, age 4, and drive them from suburban Maryland to 1600 Pennsylvania Avenue at 10 P.M. that night so they could look at the White House—Nixon-free—and share this historical, ecstatic moment with me.

When we arrived late at night in front of the White House, I expected to find many thousands of celebrants there for the same reason. Instead, what I found amazed and shocked me. There was literally no one there to share my excitement. We were alone, sitting in a car, my kids in the back seat, groggy and half asleep. I tried to talk to them, to share my sense of awe at this scene, suddenly realizing why it was so significant that we were the only ones there. Literally giddy with this visible proof of the strength of the American political system, I said: "Look kids, there is no one here—no troops, no tanks, no guns. This is the miracle of our democracy and the victory of the rule of law. The most powerful man on the face of the earth has been forced to resign his office and leave . . . and there's no one here. Remember this moment—this historic moment for all Americans that our system works." I was proud of my eloquence and hoped the kids would be, too. So I turned around to be sure that the kids, as young as they were, understood the significance of this occasion. They were fast asleep and hadn't heard a word.

Twenty-three years later, in the fall of 1997, I sat in my office in the Old Executive Office Building of the White House, now serving as Special Counsel to President Clinton with the responsibility of dealing with the media on "scandal" allegations and congressional investigations. And I was denouncing connect-the-dot journalists who were using anonymous sources to try to bring down Bill Clinton.

The breaking story: A writer for Insight Magazine, *an adjunct of the conservative* Washington Times *daily newspaper, had called to say he had evidence that a Clinton campaign donor had secured himself a burial site at Arlington Cemetery, even though he did not meet the criteria of service in the Armed Services. In other words, he had "bought" his burial plot through a campaign donation to President Clinton's campaign. Within minutes, before I had a chance to check the facts, the story circled the globe on the Internet, aired on the cable news stations, and major media outlets and newspapers were calling me on the phone for comment. "Wait a minute," I virtually shouted into the phone as several reporters prepared to publish these charges without confirming if the facts were correct. "You are relying on anonymous sources, and you haven't confirmed the facts—or given me a chance to confirm."*

A few days later the facts were clear and undisputed. This individual had papers that showed he served in the Merchant Marine; the decision to bury him at Arlington was made by the Secretary of the Army, without influence from the Clinton White House; and there was precedent for members of the Merchant Marine who served in wartime to be buried at Arlington Cemetery. The Secretary of Army, who cleared the burial, was at the time unaware that this individual had lied about his war record, a fact we subsequently learned after the story broke.

How could such Clinton-bashing hatred feed such a bogus story that circled the globe so quickly? I wondered. Why couldn't people just debate policy rather than let

their hate drive them to glee as they think of how they could bring down a presi-
dent? Where did that come from?

Of course, I conveniently forgot how just a few decades earlier my side of the
political spectrum had wallowed in hating Nixon and gloried in Watergate and his
downfall. Now the shoe was on the other foot. Suddenly, I wasn't such a great fan of
investigative journalists or the anonymous sources that fed them and allowed them
to thrive. Inspired by Watergate, too many journalists had learned to try to be first
before being sure they were right. And this strategy now worked to stoke the anger
of those people who "hated" Bill Clinton so much that they would believe anything
about him—even without first checking out the facts.

As theses two anecdotes illustrate, there is a clear danger inherent in the double standard practiced by the left and right in the years that followed Nixon's downfall—a hypocrisy that I now see I shared along with my counterparts on the right. That is not to say that Nixon's indisputably criminal conduct and abuse of presidential power that led to his resignation under pressure of a broad bipartisan consensus in both the House and Senate can really be compared to any of the post–Watergate scandals that followed. Certainly there can be no fair comparison between Nixon's abuse of presidential power and orchestration of a criminal conspiracy, on tape, from the Oval Office and the offenses that led to President Clinton's impeachment by the House for testifying falsely under oath in a civil case and his acquittal in the Senate.

Looking back, however, I see that the hatred of Richard Nixon and the Democrats' glorification of his downfall was the beginning of a dangerous pattern in American politics of demonizing the opposition and justifying whatever means necessary to destroy them.

Did it ever bother me or other liberals back then that Woodward and Bernstein sometimes relied on anonymous sources who had political or personal axes to grind against Nixon and the Nixon White House or that the reporters kept the grievances of those sources secret? No. Even my hero, Deep Throat, now known to be former FBI Deputy Director Mark Felt, had personal reasons—he had not been promoted to FBI director—that might, in part, have motivated him to help expose and bring down the Nixonites. For legitimate journalistic reasons, Bob Woodward and Carl Bernstein could not inform readers what they would liked to have known—that their key anonymous source had a political and personal axe to grind. For Democrats, though, the final result certainly seemed to justify relying on Felt's "deep background" revelations to Bob Woodward. Did it bother me that Mark Felt might have violated criminal laws for at least some of his disclosures to Woodward since he was, by definition, describing information that was the subject of an FBI investigation and that, in part at least, had been presented to a grand jury? No. If I had known that back then, I still would have celebrated what Felt did. After all, he brought down the hated Richard Nixon.

So while Watergate and Nixon's crimes may have been unique, the decision of partisans on the left such as myself to use that tragedy for political gain and to glorify Nixon's downfall without any empathy for him or his family, was not. Indeed, the Democratic response to Watergate helped build the foundation of the scandal culture and cycle of gotcha politics that followed.

The reporting techniques that Bob Woodward and Carl Bernstein used during the Watergate scandal of 1972–74, as well as the professional success they enjoyed, started a journalistic revolution whose impact on other journalists and the scandal culture that followed it cannot be overstated. Much has been written on this topic, but as one who 25 years later sat in the middle of a White House press corps in a scandal feeding frenzy, I can offer a personal perspective on the key legacies of Watergate and the *Post*'s role in bringing down Nixon that had the greatest impact on the scandal culture for years to come. Four come immediately to mind. First, there is the use of anonymous sources, which has become the lifeblood of investigative journalism; second, a growing habit of investigative journalists to draw conclusions, sometimes unconsciously, about what they want to say before finishing their reporting; third, very much related to the second, the temptation to "connect the dots" of circumstantial facts, suggesting a causal relationship between two events when, in truth, there is none; and finally, the lure among the next generation of journalists of the immense material and professional success on the scale of Woodward's and Bernstein's, which, I would argue, has contributed to the "talking head" industry where the lines between objective journalists, subjective editorialists, and celebrity personalities are often dangerously blurred.

ANONYMOUS SOURCES[2]

Long before the *Washington Post*'s Watergate success, investigative journalists have played an important role in our society, whether they were Muckrakers in the early twentieth century uncovering horrors of sweat shops and foul conditions in meat packing plants to the exposing of public health scandals like Thalidomide. But journalists digging for ugly facts where there is organized resistance and a cover-up must, of necessity, rely on unnamed sources who often would not speak to a reporter if their superiors knew their identities.

The problem with anonymity, however, is that sources can hide behind it in order to carry out an agenda rather than to report facts that help a reporter uncover the truth. Most good journalists, including Woodward, Bernstein, and their managing editor, Benjamin Bradlee, seek corroboration from other sources for information obtained from an anonymous source. But over the years that rule has been ignored or bent at times, especially under deadline pressures, such as when one anonymous source is asked to confirm the information obtained from another. One of the better known examples—thanks to the book and movie, *All the President's Men*, about Woodward and Bernstein's Watergate reporting—is when the two reporters obtained information from an anonymous source that Nixon's all-powerful chief of staff, H. R. Haldeman, controlled a secret cash slush fund that illicitly paid for Nixon's "dirty tricks" during the 1972 presidential campaign. Woodward and Bernstein thought that this information had been disclosed by the treasurer of the Nixon campaign committee, Hugh Sloan, when he testified before the Watergate grand jury. Bernstein thought he had a confirmation of this from another anonymous source based on a confusing system of counting to ten with a hang-up on the call as a means of confirming the fact, whereas the source thought the opposite. So the *Post* published the false information that Sloan had told the grand jury about Haldeman's involvement in the Watergate crimes. The truth was that Haldeman did have control of the cash slush fund—but Sloan had not told the grand jury, since the prosecutor had never asked him the question. So, the *Post* had to acknowledge it had made an error, and the admission set back the credibility of its Watergate coverage at a critical time.

Of course, it is arguable that when reporters are digging up wrong-doing in the government, reliance on anonymous sources and errors like this are inevitable, but the end result is worth it, regardless. In the years since Watergate, however, the reliance on anonymous sources has evolved from a necessary evil to protect sources who are disclosing wrongdoing involving their superiors in government to a shield for sources who have political agendas and want to attack the opposition from under a cloak of anonymity. That is a big change, and, unfortunately, too many government insiders resort to this tactic and too many reporters and editors are complicit in allowing them to do so.

The question of why both the sources and the reporters share the blame goes directly to the heart of the scandal culture that has evolved since Watergate. Instead of an appetite for journalism that uncovers government corruption and wrong-doing, editors, reporters and—let us not forget—readers have an increased appetite for "gotchas" of questionable legitimacy. These are the slashing attacks or innuendo that strike out at the opposition and are possible only if the reporters and editors are willing to grant the sources the anonymity they desire.

I certainly did my share of "on background" commenting (without attribution by name) on Republican Clinton critics in the Congress during my tenure in the Clinton White House. I would hide behind the negotiated anonymous designation of the day—such as "senior White House official," or "senior Administration official" (even better, since it hid my connection to the White House). Why did I want this anonymity? Simply, I did not want my name in the paper. If I were connected to an article attacking a member of Congress, it could lead to me becoming a personal target of that member. And why did White House reporters and their editors grant me that anonymity? Because they shared in the culture of attack, counter-attack, and counter–counter-attack that was the modus operandi of both sides of the aisle at the time; they enjoyed being in the middle of the fray, and they certainly believed that it sold newspapers.

So, this is the context in which Karl Rove and "Scooter" Libby talked to reporters "on deep background" (meaning no identifying attribution at all) in the summer of 2003 in the Valerie Plame matter. I am not referring to unproven charges that Libby allegedly lied to a grand jury. He remains to be tried on those charges. I am only talking about the technique of Rove, Libby, and certainly myself when I was at the White House, leaking information anonymously as a political weapon to defend the boss and attack the opposition.

In the case of Rove and Libby, it is interesting that there is very little controversy in the media as to why they insisted on anonymity, rather than being on the record, when they attempted to diminish the credibility of former Ambassador Joseph Wilson and his trip to Africa. Allegedly, because his wife, Valerie Plame, who worked at the CIA, had suggested that he was qualified to make the trip, this in some way made him unqualified or not credible. It seems that Rove and Libby believed that Ambassador Wilson was falsely encouraging the press to report that Vice President Richard Cheney had been behind his trip to Niger to investigate Saddam Hussein's purported attempts to purchase "yellow cake" uranium as part of an atomic weapons program. Their conversations with reporters—which we now know were explicitly encouraged by Vice President Cheney because he was angry at a critical op-ed by Wilson in the *New York Times*—were meant to refute this alleged assertion. But if it was wrong, why not refute it on the record? Perhaps the media was never interested in pursuing the question of why Libby, Rove—or Cheney—refused to criticize Wilson directly on the record because, after all, it is hard to criticize anonymous leaks at the same time you are benefiting from them.

What was truly unusual, but not totally unprecedented, was that the President of the United States himself—George W. Bush—chose to authorize the National Intelligence Estimate (NIE) to be declassified so that Scooter Libby could "leak" it (on "deep background"—without attribution).

As described in chapter one, President Kennedy, apparently unthinkingly, leaked classified information to then *Newsweek* Bureau Chief Ben Bradlee on the release by the Russians of U–2 pilot Frances Gary Powers. The big difference is that President Bush, apparently at the urging of Vice President Cheney, authorized the leak to attack former Ambassador Joe Wilson's op-ed piece in the *New York Times*, not for the purpose of informing the American people about a major news event that was coming out in hours anyway.

The other unusual aspect of President Bush's and Vice President Cheney's role in this leak episode is that they never took responsibility (at least up to the summer of 2006) for the outing of Valerie Plame's covert CIA status, even indirectly or unintentionally. Her life and her sources as a covert agent were clearly in danger. She was owed an apology. President Kennedy took responsibility for the Bay of Pigs disaster in 1961, even though it was not his, but his predecessor's (President Eisenhower's) plan. But somehow, in the post–Watergate culture of gotcha leaks—they leak to hurt us, we leak to hurt them, and back and forth again and again in the eighties, nineties, and now into the twenty-first century—such a public apology seemed politically unthinkable.

Clearly people doing Rove's job (or my job when I was at the Clinton White House) could not have succeeded if all the editors and reporters refused to play and we had no one to whisper our anonymous leaks to. But in the real world, since Watergate at least, that is not about to happen. Nor can you really blame White House reporters for accepting our "deep background" ground rules. It is a competitive business, and getting a scoop is huge for a journalist with any ambition to get ahead. It is no different for a lawyer who gets a big client away from a competitor or who wins a big case. Why should reporters be any less competitive than anyone else?

So, if everyone can be honest about the process, leakers and those who benefit from the leaks would acknowledge that all are complicit in this political, media-spin, gotcha game in Washington. That system of complicity between leaker and reporter, between political sources and journalists, became *the* modus operandi of the scandal machine and gotcha culture post–Watergate into the 1990s and the Clinton years, and now the Bush years, but it could not have reached the levels it did without the role it played in uncovering Watergate.

INVESTIGATIVE JOURNALISM AND THE ENDLESS SEARCH FOR SCANDAL

Post–Watergate, most news organizations dedicated greater resources, both in terms of people and money, to investigative journalism, shifting to proactive searches for wrongdoing, rather than simply reacting to and covering the news that broke each day. For example, in the closing days of the 1996 presidential campaign and in the immediate aftermath of the election, there was a team of reporters at the *Washington Post* and other major news organizations covering the Clinton White House who were dedicated to investigating instances of campaign finance "abuses" by the Clinton presidential campaign or the Clinton White House. I know this because I was at the White House at the time, responsible for dealing with the White House press corps on all "scandal" stories. There was intense competition not only between print and broadcast organizations to break the latest story on such "abuses" (a loosely defined term that covered any activity that seemed less than kosher, even if entirely legal), but also among reporters on the same team. The intensity of trying to find a new angle or a new story concerning the Clinton campaign's fundraising activities was intense. Sometimes I would get 40 to 50 calls a day from different reporters, some from the same organization, chasing different leads on different fundraising stories.

What was noteworthy was that almost all of these reporters started out their questions already assuming the worst—that someone had donated money in return for a "quid quo pro" from the Clinton Administration, or under suspicious circumstances, or possibly illegally—and it was up to me to overcome the presumption of wrongdoing. Sometimes I was able to do that by obtaining facts and documents, but proving a negative is very difficult. Often, when I was unable to offer facts disproving the presumed wrongdoing, the story still ran suggesting "abuse," but without proving it. In the cases where I did obtain facts that were inconsistent with or even contradictory to the assumptions that the reporter had when he or she started out, these would sometimes be diminished in the final editing or omitted entirely.

This predisposition toward a particular hypothesis is unconscious at times, but more often it is the engine driving the reporting. Great reporters and editors will constantly check and re-check themselves to be sure that their own opinions are not screening out facts and perspectives that run counter to them. But, as events have proven, even the best of them do not always realize that their personal assumptions result in a story that turns out to be wholly or partially unfair or untrue.

This danger of a predisposition that works to screen out inconsistent facts or to emphasize those that are in agreement sometimes infects the best of reporters. One of the journalists I admire most, Bob Woodward, arguably fell prey to this temptation on one memorable occasion when I was at the White House. I remember it well because late on the afternoon of February 12, 1997, Clinton Press Secretary Mike McCurry called and said, in effect, that if Woodward wrote the story he had just described to him, it could be the end of Bill Clinton. He said that Woodward was about to break a story showing that key contributors, including a Clinton and Democratic National Committee fundraiser, John Huang, had donated laundered Chinese government money to the Clinton presidential campaign, implying it was done with the President's, or at least his campaign's, knowledge. If true, and if President Clinton knew about it, the story could prove politically devastating to the President and, as we discussed, could lead to his impeachment and conviction.

Later that evening, however, McCurry called me back to say that the story was much softer than what he had originally understood and that Woodward was only reporting that there was a "plan" for such Chinese-government contributions to the Clinton campaign. Whether the "plan" had been implemented or not, or whether the Clinton campaign or White House officials even knew about such a "plan," was not clear, and we did not know how Woodward and the *Post* would report the story.

As it turned out, the story seemed a lot worse in its headline and lead paragraph than it turned out to be in substance. In fact, once you read the whole story, there did not seem to be a lot of facts there. On February 13, 1997, in a page-one lead story, Woodward (and *Post* reporter Brian Duffy) described a Chinese government "plan" to direct foreign contributions to the Democratic National Committee before the 1996 presidential campaign.[3]

The fact that it was a Woodward story and trumpeted by the *Post* as a page-one lead drove national newspaper and TV network news that evening and the next morning. But the dramatic headline, lengthy text, and all the hype in other media outlets belied the sparse evidence and lack of substance of the actual story. Indeed, it took a close reading of the Woodward-Duffy story to realize that there was *no evidence at all that such a plan had ever been implemented;* that is, the "plan," if it ever existed, never got past the discussion stage.[4] (Subsequently we learned that all this hype was spurred on by leaks and/or private congressional briefings by the FBI, headed by Republican Louis Freeh.)

The point is, despite the sparse hard facts underlying this story, the *Washington Post* and most other respected news organizations across the country played up the story because of a predisposition to believe that it had the element of truth and that sooner or later the facts would be uncovered and the truth revealed.

As we shall see, this unfortunate predisposition of reporters investigating and looking for scandals to assume the worst of those involved—often leading to misreporting or over-hyped reporting—is not limited to Bill Clinton's time in office or the Democrats, but has taken its toll among Republicans as well, both in the 1980s and today. As Joseph Alsop, the legendary national political columnist, once commented:

> I am horrified by what has happened to our business. . . . Independence, honest reporting, hard work, are the qualities that I value in newspapers. I do not value self-dramatization, self-righteousness, and self-appointment to be the moral censors of the nation. . . . All these rules seem to me to have been forgotten in the last years, and I am persuaded that our business will pay a heavy bill for this forgetfulness in the years to come.[5]

CONNECTING THE DOTS

A related journalistic by-product of Watergate is the movement from objective reporting toward what Edwin R. Bayley, in his definitive study of press coverage of Senator Joseph McCarthy, referred to as "interpretive" journalism—journalism that goes beyond reporting straight facts to convey inferences and to encourage subjective interpretations of those inferences by the reader.[6] Earlier, I have described this as "connect-the-dot" journalism.

Woodward and Bernstein used this technique to great effect during Watergate to expose the criminal conspiracy and cover-up involving the Nixon White House. Their methodology was to build a pattern of facts suggesting, but never proving, that President Nixon and his men were somehow involved and knowledgeable about the Watergate break-in and hush-money cover-up. Without their willingness to use "connect-the-dot" innuendo to suggest criminal conspiracy, it is entirely possible that the Senate Watergate Committee would never have been organized and all that put into motion the ultimate downfall of Nixon, from the discovery of the Nixon taping system to the forced resignation of Richard Nixon, would never have occurred.

So, no one is arguing that connect-the-dot journalism has no legitimate purpose. It certainly has been vindicated and at times is the only way to break stories involving government corruption and wrongdoing. But it also has its risks—great risks—because, more often than not, the "dots" do not actually connect or the apparently causal relationship between two events ends up being false. The Latin expression for seeing cause where none exists is "post hoc ergo propter hoc"—literally translated, "after this, therefore, because of this." A typical "post hoc" fallacy is to say that because the sun rises after a rooster crows, it is the rooster's crow that *causes* the sun to rise. And while believing roosters control the sun is merely foolish, post hoc thinking in journalism often ruins careers and works to fuel the scandal culture.

I have discussed this connect-the-dots technique with many reporters who were in the thick of the scandal machine, and I was surprised at how many agreed that this was a serious issue, although most would point to others as being guiltier than themselves. Tim Burger, a reporter who now writes for *Time*, provided me with a critical way of understanding the problem by noting the failure of reporters to differentiate between "correlation" and "causation." For example, assume a conservative businessman donates money to a conservative Republican congressman's campaign and the congressman later votes for a program that favors the business of the donor. There is obviously a relationship between the businessman contributing money and the congressman voting for a program that favors him, but merely by stating, "The congressman voted for a preferential program *after* receiving a campaign donation from a businessman," a quid pro quo is strongly inferred, i.e., causation—the campaign donation *caused* the congressman to vote the way he did. And if this were true, that would be bribery.

As Tim Burger explained, however, instead of causation, this relationship may be just a case of correlation. That is, the conservative contributor gave the donation because the congressman shared his political philosophy, and the congressman voted for the program not because of the donation but because he philosophically believed in it. That is the difference between correlation and causation, but journalists in the scandal machine chasing a story about "links" (a popular innuendo suggesting causation without proving it) between donations and votes almost never clearly make that distinction for their readers. In a public too prone to presume the worst about politicians, this distinction between causation and correlation is not likely to be appreciated.

A less subtle and more dangerous version of connect-the-dot journalism occurs when at least some of the claims are not publicly verifiable, but instead are based on anonymous and unreliable sources, which, as we discussed before, is a suspect journalistic practice in itself. Remember how even Woodward and Bernstein got tripped up on this in their Watergate coverage related to their charge that Haldeman controlled the slush fund, something they based on a mix-up they had with an anonymous source. As this shows, using information based on anonymous sources without first-hand knowledge only compounds the risks of getting things wrong when reporting an unconfirmed inference. An example is when the *Dallas Morning News* erroneously reported in January 1998 that Secret Service agents were prepared to testify that they had caught President Clinton and Ms. Lewinsky in a compromising situation. The story had been based on scraps of information, some from anonymous sources, that seemed to fit together but ultimately did not. Embarrassingly, the newspaper had to retract the story.[7]

More recently, the erroneous reporting by Judy Miller in the summer and fall of 2002 in the *New York Times* that claimed Saddam Hussein had developed weapons of mass destruction further emphasizes the dangers of connect-the-dot journalism, combined with reliance on biased anonymous sources not willing to be held accountable for the information they are transmitting to a reporter. Judy Miller relied on what she has subsequently described as erroneous information transmitted to her by anonymous sources to write these articles, many of whom had personal agendas to convince the American public that an invasion of Iraq was justified. That her sources were faulty, however, does not excuse the fact that the substance of the stories was wrong—and that being too quick to believe sources, perhaps because of an unconscious desire to believe them or to see the story in a particular way, can happen to the good journalists, as most people believe Judy Miller to be to this day. Indeed, most reporters prior to the Iraq War, and indeed, most of the national security apparatus of the Clinton White House (as well as the Bush White House) were predisposed to believing that Hussein indeed had weapons of mass destruction. So perhaps this is one reason why sources— whether questionable intelligence sources or questionable sources for journalists—were given more credence than they should have when they reported that Hussein had WMDs.

MATERIAL SUCCESS AND TALKING HEADS

It is difficult to understate the importance that the lure of material rewards— including fame, wealth, and ego gratification—a reporter earns for breaking a scandal story has had as a driving force in the scandal machine and the gotcha culture of the 1980s and 1990s. Many journalists aim to be the next Woodward or Bernstein.

Chasing after fame and fortune is human nature, so there is no reason to single out journalists over the members of any other profession, whether lawyers looking for the "big case" or businesspeople looking for the "big deal." But I have talked and worked with enough investigative reporters, whom I admire for their professionalism and integrity, to know that the prospect of becoming another Woodward or Bernstein is an important motivator and, at least in general, has fueled a good part of the scandal machine that started up after Watergate. The recognition that comes from covering scandals inevitably leads to invitations to appear on the evening cable talk shows, radio talk shows, Sunday morning network shows like *Meet the Press*, or maybe even a permanent slot as a commentator on one of the political panel shows. This, in turn, could lead to invitations for paid speaking engagements around the country, with speaking fees of $10,000 or more per engagement.

Often the same reporters who are supposed to be objective fact-finders during work hours appear on these panels and, while they attempt to be "balanced" and to show no political bias one way or the other, they know it will not be "good TV" if they are blandly neutral on the topic at hand. Almost invariably they will have an edgy tone or attitude toward a political topic, especially if they wish to be invited back on the show again. Yet these same reporters are back at their desks the next morning trying to report on the stories with factual objectivity and with no particular slant. It defies human nature to expect that achieving that objectivity will always be possible. Without challenging the integrity of journalists who choose to be talking heads on evening cable shows, it is certainly a fair question to ask whether they are able to seamlessly present themselves as credible fact reporters each morning after spending an evening of opinion-offering.

As we look back over the last 25 years or so, we cannot blame the scandal culture entirely on Watergate. But as the 1960s culture wars planted the seeds of venom and vitriol into the political process of the last 30–40 years, so Watergate followed from those culture wars and established the journalistic techniques and motivations that fueled the scandal machine and gotcha politics that followed.

What must be appreciated is that the new generation of journalists all looking to become the next Woodward and Bernstein—the journalistic legacy of Watergate and the foot soldiers of the scandal culture—is largely bipartisan. Post–Watergate, presidents, politicians, and the ideological partisans of both parties have genuinely believed, at one time or another, that the scandal press was biased and targeting them while favoring the other side. I am certain—absolutely certain—that the complaints I heard virtually every day in the Clinton White House about a biased, scandal-obsessed press aimed at destroying President Clinton through connect-the-dot journalism are the same complaints, perhaps word-for-word, heard in the Bush White House today—or in the Bush I, Reagan, Carter, and Nixon White Houses.

In fact, the bias in the press corps is largely not ideological, despite various surveys conservatives point to showing that journalists are more liberal than conservative. The real post–Watergate bias is the predisposition to see wrongdoing in politics, regardless of party, due to the professional and material incentives involved in bringing down public officials. Doing well by doing good has always been a win-win formula in life. And there is no reason why it should not apply to journalists as well as to everyone else.

So the new rules of investigative journalism, the legacy of Woodward, Bernstein, and Watergate, were now in place. Substantial material and professional incentives to follow those new rules were also in place. But these changes alone, though a key element of the scandal culture that we now find dominating American politics, were not enough to really get things started on the truly destructive path that followed in the late 1970s and 1980s, as we shall see. Two new changes were needed to fuel a new scandal machine—one, an excessive reaction to Watergate in which the subjective, sanctimonious values of hyper-ethicists came to dominate American political culture; and the other, the invention of what turned out to be an extra-constitutional monster called the "independent counsel."

CHAPTER FOUR

THE SCANDAL CAULDRON: THE 1980S

On May 23, 2005, the moderate "Gang of 14" Republican and Democratic senators announced a compromise on the issue of Democratic filibusters of President Bush's judicial nominees. The compromise headed off the so-called nuclear option that the Senate Republican majority had threatened. That option—first dubbed "nuclear" by former Republican Majority Leader Senator Trent Lott of Mississippi because of the radical change it would cause to a historic Senate rule—was to use a procedural "point of order" to shut down Democratic filibusters of Bush judicial nominees by a simple majority, rather than the 60 votes required for "cloture" (i.e., the rule allowing three-fifths of the entire Senate membership to limit debate and, thus, ultimately shut down the filibuster). Senator Lott called this a "nuclear" option (and most senators on both sides of the aisle agreed with him) because, in a body that honors tradition and custom more than almost anything else, the move to end-run Senate rules on a pure power play by the majority would offend traditionalists in both parties, something to be avoided if at all possible.

Both parties proved hypocritical in this debate. Republicans suddenly did not like filibusters that thwarted the principle of majority rule enshrined in the Constitution, including the Senate's power to confirm presidential judicial nominees by its "Advice and Consent."[1] But just a few years earlier when Bill Clinton was president, Senate Republicans were the ones trying to use the filibuster to prevent "up-or-down" majority votes of his judicial nominees. Indeed, when they won back majority control of the Senate in 1994, they often refused to allow nominees to be voted out of the Judiciary Committee or even to have a hearing, thus depriving them of the up or down votes they were now clamoring for on behalf of Bush nominees. The Democrats, however, were just as guilty of practicing a double standard. During the 1950s and 1960s, they characterized the filibuster as un-democratic when it was used to block majority votes on Civil Rights legislation. And of course they protested when Republicans blocked Clinton's judicial nominees from getting up-or-down votes.

The country outside the Beltway did not understand the procedural complexities of the argument nor the constitutional ones. But they understood the word "nuclear" and were disgusted over the hyper-partisanship and cynical double standards that once again seemed to paralyze the government from doing the people's business.

So when there was a dramatic announcement late in the afternoon of May 23 of a compromise, I was relieved. Fourteen Senators, dubbed the "Gang of 14"—seven Republicans and seven Democrats, with key roles played by Republican Senators John McCain of Arizona and Lindsey Graham of South Carolina and Democratic Senators Joe Lieberman of Connecticut and Ben Nelson of Nebraska—had forged a bipartisan compromise. The Democrats agreed not to support a filibuster of the President's judicial nominees except under "extraordinary circumstances." The Republicans agreed not to vote for the "nuclear option" and thwart the right to filibuster unless there were "extraordinary circumstances."

It all came down to the definition of that vague term, "extraordinary circumstances," which was left to each of the 14 senators to arrive at in good faith. Trust was the glue that made this compromise possible—as well as a mutual determination that the country could not afford continued bitterness over this issue—which is what made this all so unusual. These 14 senators came to an agreement based on faith and trust—two words that have not exactly exemplified the relationship between the two major political parties over the last 30 years.

Late in the afternoon of that day, I accepted an invitation to go on the Fox Cable News show Hannity and Colmes *to discuss the compromise and its political implications. The booker who called me assumed, knowing I was a liberal Democrat, that I would be critical of the compromise because it would likely make it more difficult for Democrats to thwart President Bush's conservative judicial nominees through the use of the filibuster. In fact, I had mixed feelings.*

On one hand, I was concerned about some of President Bush's more conservative judicial nominees, especially on the issue of whether they would support overturning Roe v. Wade *and allow the criminalization of abortion. I hoped that the threat of a Democratic filibuster would convince President Bush to reach out more to the middle in his judicial appointments. On the other hand, I was raised by FDR liberal Democratic parents and remember the days in the 1950s and early 1960s when my father denounced the filibuster, used by Southern Democrats to prevent up-and-down votes on Civil Rights legislation, as anti-democratic. When I saw Joe Lieberman and Lindsey Graham on TV explaining the compromise, I felt a rush of patriotism—that our democracy could work, that reconciliation could overcome partisanship, and that there were leaders of both parties willing to stand up to their base and cut through the threatened paralysis of government.*

So, when the conservative host Sean Hannity asked me on the air what I thought, I said: "You have fourteen Senators, Republican and Democratic, who compromised, who gave up on both sides. Neither side alone can declare victory, but both sides should declare victory for the moderate center, which is taking back the United States Senate, and I think can take back the country from people who are dividing the country apart through polarizing politics. I declare victory for the great center of this country."

Hannity and I had become friends over the years, confounding our colleagues on the left and right by at least being able to disagree agreeably. I regarded him as a sincere conservative—though way too far to the right for my philosophy. When I finished my opening comment about a victory for the "great center," I actually thought that on this one night Sean Hannity and I would agree on something. Boy, was I wrong. In a prior show on which I had been a guest, Hannity had called the compromise a "backroom deal" that would advantage the Democrats by allowing them to "characterize anybody as extreme right" and had criticized the Republican members of the Gang of 14 for not standing "on principle."

On this occasion, Hannity started out by saying to me, "This was the first time in 214 years the Democrats did this, where judicial nominees who would otherwise have been confirmed, they filibustered. First time that happened. . . ."

I quickly interrupted, "That's a false statement. That is a completely false statement."

I knew Hannity had inserted the phrase "where judicial nominees who would otherwise have been confirmed" as a way of distinguishing the Democratic filibuster from previous Republican ones. He meant that since the Republicans already were in the majority, it was worse for Democrats to filibuster because it thwarted the will of the majority.

But in prior shows we had already argued this point. I had reminded Hannity then that Democrats were in the Senate majority in 1968 when President Johnson had nominated Justice Abe Fortas to be Chief Justice of the Supreme Court, and Republicans filibustered that nomination until Fortas asked that his name be withdrawn. I also reminded him I thought this was a silly distinction: either an up-or-down vote is fair under all circumstances or it is not. When the Republicans took control of the Senate in 1994 they had denied more than 60 Clinton circuit court nominees of up-or-down votes, including denying some even a hearing before the Judiciary Committee.

So, after saying Hannity's comment was false, I went a step further. I added: "And you know it's false."

He responded, "I will bet you any amount of money on national TV. . . ."

I interrupted, "Sixty Clinton nominees never had an up-or-down vote. . . ."

Hannity tried to cut in, "Lanny—Lanny. . . ."

I continued, "That's a hypocritical statement."

Then he said, "Lanny, I'll make you a bet that my statement is true. And you name the amount of money. The first time in history that a judicial nominee would have otherwise been confirmed by the full Senate was filibustered. How much?"

There was that clever phrase again—"otherwise been confirmed by the full Senate"—but he was choosing to ignore the Fortas example, where the Democrats had a majority in the Senate and the Republicans filibustered.

I answered, "'That would have been confirmed. . . . First of all, Justice Fortas. . . .'"

He interrupted, "So is it a true statement or not? He wouldn't have been confirmed."

I said, "It's a false statement."

Hannity countered, "It's a true statement."

I raised my voice, pointing to several Clinton D.C. federal appellate judges who Republican Senators had tried to deny an up-or-down vote through a filibuster.

He interrupted once again, "You name—you name the amount of money and I'll make the bet."

Now I was nearly shouting. What about President Clinton's nomination of Judge Richard Paez to the Ninth Circuit in 1996, when some Senate Republicans had attempted to block an up-or-down vote by a filibuster? . . .

Hannity interrupted, "Lanny, you're going back to your old impeachment days, Lanny."

I added, " . . . and 60 Clinton nominees" (intending to finish, "were denied an up-or-down vote.")

He continued, "You're back to your screaming impeachment days. If you want to make a bet, you name the amount of money, and I'll win. So let me get back to the point."

I interrupted, "You can't accept the fact that centrists have won the battle for the center of America. . . . Don't be disappointed about the centrists winning, Sean."

And so it went. I left the studio feeling very depressed. For someone who hated the "food fight" TV shows and the political culture that encourages them, I sure had failed to resist jumping right in and participating in one.

On my way home, Hannity e-mailed me his strong objections to my having accused him of lying. I denied I had. But when I re-read the transcript several weeks later, I realized that I had added the sentence: "And you know it's false." And I realized that Hannity was right and I was wrong to add that, "you know it's false." That was the functional equivalent of accusing someone of lying. That was one of the lines I had been taught a long time ago not to cross during debates—taught by Senator John McCain, no less, who once scolded me in a CNN studio for attacking Independent Counsel Kenneth W. Starr's sincerity rather than his judgment. I knew I had crossed that line with Hannity—a similar line that President Clinton had warned us all not to cross during that memorable morning in the East Room during the portrait unveiling ceremony. I could have said Hannity was wrong without saying he was deliberately misstating the truth.

The next morning I heard from a number of Democratic friends who had seen me on Hannity. If Hannity was upset with the compromise, I assumed, at least my Democratic friends should be happy. But things do not seem to work that way anymore. My Democratic friends were angry, too. They argued that Democrats had now boxed themselves in from preventing a conservative Bush Supreme Court nominee from getting a floor vote. (As things turned out, they were probably right.) The bar of "extraordinary circumstances," they argued, was a clever trap. It would not likely ever be met, at least solely on philosophical grounds, as long as the nominee was unquestionably qualified. So, they argued, the compromise would do nothing to prevent Bush from stacking the Supreme Court with conservatives who would, among other things, overturn Roe v. Wade.

While I agreed that was worrisome, I reminded my friends that Bush did win the last two elections. We need to beat them at the polls—not through a filibuster thwarting an up-or-down majority vote. Haven't we Democrats always opposed the filibuster when it was used to block Civil Rights and progressive legislation? Well, that was different, was the answer; that was about getting Civil Rights legislation approved, not about preventing the right wing taking over the courts. I protested, wasn't the principle the same? Didn't we Democrats complain when the Republicans did the same thing to Bill Clinton's nominees in attempting to block Senate votes in the 1990s? They did it to us, my friends said. So now, it's payback time: We can do it to them.

So there it was, in clear, pristine terms: the double standard, the gotcha defense. The circle had been closed; the left and right were in agreement. They did it to us. We can do it to them.

What I experienced that night with Hannity and the next morning with my Democratic friends is, sadly, not an unusual phenomenon in American politics today. First, there is the double standard that both sides seemed to be willing to practice, shamelessly. Filibusters and personal attacks are okay if used by us for our causes, bad if used by them for their causes. It is depressing and, unfortunately, a reflection of the personal, venomous politics that now infects our culture.

The double standard in politics has been around for a very long time, but what is new is the personalization of political differences and the anger that has become an unfortunate hallmark of the political culture that had evolved since the 1960s and Watergate.

The gotcha cycle in which we are caught today, however, did not really start until after the election of President Jimmy Carter in 1976. Shortly thereafter, two new ingredients were added to the already heated cauldron of the mix started by the 1960s and the Watergate affair—one cultural and one legal—that led to primarily Democratic abuses of the scandal machinery in the 1980s.

The cultural development was the creation of a synergistic network of political leaders, ethics experts, reformers, and journalists, the most notable being President Jimmy Carter and those leading his 1976 presidential campaign, who promised a higher morality and ethics in government. It also included the good government organizations such as Common Cause and the Center for Responsive Politics that in their laudatory effort to remove the influence of money in politics were sometimes too quick to apply subjective judgments about what they considered to be "appearances" that were "inappropriate" or "unethical." The second development was the legal creation of the "Special Prosecutor" in 1978. (In 1984, the name was changed to "Independent Counsel." For simplicity's sake, this and subsequent chapters will refer to the "Independent Counsel," which is the name most people commonly use even when referring back in history.) This is an office and concept that had never existed before in U.S. history. By definition, the Independent Counsel is above politics and cannot be fired by the president or his attorney general once appointed, but rather, only by a three-member panel of judges "for cause." As things turned out, the Independent Counsel became a dangerous, unstoppable prosecutor with an unlimited budget and accountable to no one.

THE APPEARANCES CULTURE
AND ETHICS WARS

In the immediate aftermath of Nixon's resignation in August 1974, an intense focus on ethics and political reform emerged based on an almost reflexive assumption that "politics as usual" was dirty and that the system needed to be cleansed of money and political influence from top to bottom. This was not the first time in American history during which the pendulum swung mightily from an era of corruption to an era of reform. Recall the good government and anti-politics "Mugwumps" (mostly moderate Republicans) of the 1880s; Grover Cleveland's reputation as a reform mayor of Buffalo and governor of New York that got him elected president in 1884; the Civil Service reform movement that led to the passage of the Pendleton Act in the 1880s and Hatch Act in the 1930s, attempting to seal off federal employees from partisan political pressures; and the bipartisan Progressive movement at the turn of the twentieth century that included everyone from the trust-busting Republican President Teddy Roosevelt to the regulatory and financial system reforms of Democratic President Woodrow Wilson and the "Progressives" who backed both presidents.

So after Watergate, it was not surprising when a strong reform movement came forward, looking to raise ethical standards and end the system of "politics as usual." Jimmy Carter, reflecting this substantial focus on higher political ethics, ran on an anti-politics and anti-Washington platform and promised that members of his administration would be so ethical that they would be required to avoid even the "appearance of impropriety"—a favored phrase in the early days of Jimmy Carter's presidency. The problem with setting such high standards in such sanctimonious language is that old saw about being "hoisted on your own petard." Even a slight slip leads to exploitation by political critics on equally sanctimonious grounds charging hypocrisy, with little limits based on proportionality or perspective.

During Jimmy Carter's term a network of people who anointed themselves as ethics experts emerged and proved quick to pronounce this politician or that political practice as "inappropriate" or "appearing to be improper." Suzanne Garment, in her seminal 1991 book, also titled *Scandal*, called this network of political ethicists and self-described reformers the "Ethics Apparat."[2] The most famous and influential of these organizations was Common Cause, which criticized the influence of money in politics (rightfully so). However, they seemed too quick to attack the ethics of politicians on "impropriety," even honest ones, who, in order to get elected, accepted campaign contributions from those who had legislative interests before Congress, often during the same time period such legislation was being considered—as if they had any alternative so long as public financing of elections was politically unacceptable to most Americans.

In the almost hysterical atmosphere of this heightened ethical awareness, what was lost was how subjective these standards were and how this complicated the ability to determine guilt or innocence under the time-tested standards of due process of law.

This was a scary time to be accused of anything. Instead of the presumption of innocence guaranteed in the Constitution, as we shall see, the ugly combination of media willing to report on innuendo, partisan congressional investigations, leading to staffers leaking information to reporters, and ultimately the misuse and abuse of the unaccountable power of an independent counsel led to a culture dominated by a presumption of guilt based on subjective appearances rather than hard facts. As attorneys Peter Morgan and Glenn Reynolds wrote in their important 1997 book on the excesses of the appearances culture, *The Appearance of Impropriety: How the Ethics Wars Have Undermined American Government, Business and Society:*

We live, in short, in an Age of Appearances. . . . [I]t is, ultimately . . . a story of the substitution of appearances for substance, of technicalities for judgment, of opportunism for self-discipline. . . . [A]lthough the post-Watergate explosion of ethics rules has produced enormous benefits for parts of society . . . [i]t has deterred good people from seeking to serve in public office, where it is so possible to be condemned and even destroyed based on subjective standards and the absence of due process. In fact, faith in government and corporate America has probably never been lower as a direct result of this presumption of guilt, subjective culture of the ethics apparat.[3]

THE FIRST VICTIM: BERT LANCE

The first tragic victim of these subjective ethical standards where "appearances" were deemed to be more important than substance—and probably the first example of post–Watergate payback by Republicans—was T. Bertram Lance, President Carter's budget director. There is little doubt that Bert Lance's painful downfall was a Watergate gotcha. William Safire, Nixon's former speechwriter who left the Nixon White House to become a columnist for the influential *New York Times*, made this very clear when he dubbed the affair "Lancegate," apparently the first use of "-gate" as a suffix for scandal after Watergate.

Context here is hugely important. As noted, Jimmy Carter had run for president on the post–Watergate theme of raising the ethical standards to unprecedented levels for anyone who served in his administration. As he proclaimed when he accepted the Democratic nomination for president: "We can have an American government that has turned away from scandal and corruption and official cynicism and is once again as decent and competent as our people." For his top appointees, President Carter established what Suzanne Garment described as the toughest conflict-of-interest guidelines ever seen in the federal government—with the effect of barring even an attenuated, far-removed *appearance* of "possible" conflicts of interest.[4]

Bert Lance was an old friend of Carter's from Georgia. Author and journalist Bob Woodward described him as "the closest person to a Bobby Kennedy that Carter had in his administration, almost a brother."[5] When Carter was elected president he appointed the 45-year-old banker as White House budget director. Lance owned a controlling interest in a small bank in Calhoun, Georgia, and was a major stockholder in the National Bank of Georgia. Because Lance's position as Carter's budget director was a staff position—that is, he only made recommendations to the president and had no independent legal authority of his own—the notion that he had any power to benefit himself or his Georgia bank interests through his appointment as budget director should have been absurd on its face. For the ethics mavens and media thirsting for scandal, however, this signaled prey ready for their first post–Watergate pack attack.

We need to recall that Carter imposed on all his senior staff and cabinet secretaries requirements to sell off investments and financial disclosures that went well beyond the law or any standards then applicable. Under this atmosphere, where appearances were more important than reality, Lance rashly promised senators during his otherwise noncontroversial confirmation hearings in January 1977 that he would sell all the stock he owned in the National Bank of Georgia by the end of the Carter Administration's first year, December 1977, even though this was *not* required by law but only by Jimmy Carter's own ethical requirements.

No one at the hearings ever asked him why owning stock in a bank constituted any conceivable conflict of interest with his service advising the President on the overall federal budget. It is conceivable that by making a budget recommendation that helped the banking system that the President accepts, Lance could have indirectly sustained the value of his bank stock, but this could be called a conflict of interest only in its most attenuated sense, which demonstrates just how absurd this fervent atmosphere of hyperethics was at the time.

Six months later, however, the market value of the National Bank of Georgia stock had substantially dropped for reasons having nothing to do with Lance's activities. Realizing that dumping all of his stock at once would have a devastating effect on an already depressed stock price, Lance asked the Senate Committee for an extension—even though he was under no legal requirement to sell his stock, much less to ask a congressional committee's permission for delay.

Lance's real problem was that he had borrowed $3.4 million from a Chicago bank to purchase the bank stock, similar to buying stock from a broker on margin. So with the stock price down, he faced the functional equivalent of a margin call. Selling his stock holding all at once would just drive the price down further, increasing the economic hole in which he already found himself, and hurting other shareholders.

In any case, the committee had no problem with granting the extension. Senator John Glenn, the former astronaut, known on both sides of the aisle for his honesty and integrity, made a comment that, unfortunately, was neither appreciated nor understood for its prescience at a time of such dangerous ethical sanctimony. Senator Glenn said that Washington had gone "ethics happy."[6]

The tragic ending that followed for Bert Lance has become the classic pattern of the post–Watergate scandal culture ever since: vague allegations of wrongdoing leading to leaks and news stories and an accelerating feeding frenzy of reporters smelling scandal. The public headlines, in turn, led to re-newed congressional interest, more hearings, more stories, and more contro-versy. It is amazing that at the time and in the years since so few people saw how ugly this was—how frightening it should have been to anyone who cares about due process, civil liberties, and principles of fundamental fairness.

William Safire played a key role in maintaining focus on Lance through his *New York Times* columns. The very fact that the columns appeared in the *Times*, seen then (as now) as a liberal Democratic editorial page, made the impact even greater. Safire's guilt-by-association language hurt as well. He began his attack on July 21, 1977, with a column headlined, "Carter's Broken Lance." He referred to the $3.4M loan from the Chicago bank to purchase the National Bank of Georgia bank stock and loans from the Teamsters' pen-sion fund in vaguely pejorative terms (the latter ironic given Richard Nixon's closeness to the Teamsters, who endorsed him for president in 1972). He lamented that President Carter's budget director—the man "in charge of the nation's books," in his exaggerated words—was "dangerously in hock."[7]

In subsequent columns, Safire grew even less subtle about evoking analo-gies to Watergate—repeatedly referring to the scandal as "Lancegate" and using the expressions "cover-up," "smoking gun," "stonewalling," and the need for a "special prosecutor" repeatedly in his columns over the course of several months.[8] The editorial page editors of the *New York Times*, for some unknown reason, let Safire proceed with this barrage of charges based largely on innuendo concerning Lance's conduct.

By way of explaining Safire's focus on this case, Bob Woodward wrote, "Safire believed that Democratic presidents should be held to the same stan-dards of scrutiny that Nixon had faced. . . . *Safire was framing the language of scandal for the post-Watergate era.*"[9] What Safire never explained is how any issue or allegation raised concerning Lance's personal financial problems and mistakes bore any resemblance whatsoever to the criminal conspiracy, ob-struction of justice, and abuse of power by President Nixon that were the sin-gular and undisputed reasons why he was forced to resign by Republicans as well as Democrats.

Even when the Comptroller of the Currency, the chief bank regulator in the federal government, issued a 394-page report that found no illegal conduct, the innuendo and suggestions of wrongdoing continued.[10] The fact that Lance and his family had depended on overdrafts on accounts in his own bank was played up as further evidence of "impropriety" or at least the "appearance of impropriety." More leaks and headlines created a sense within the Washington scandal corps that Lance was in deeper and deeper trouble.

In the end, the controversy itself, as opposed to any actual evidence of illegal behavior, became enough to "prove" wrongdoing. The inevitable calls for Senate investigations followed from ethics groups like Common Cause. (I hate to seem like I am picking on Common Cause, since it was one of the great political reform organizations that emerged after Watergate, and it serves as an important public interest counterweight to the special interest lobbyists in Washington. It is just that their raison d'être was pronouncing ethical judgments on politicians and lobbyists—the stuff of reality in Washington politics. Too often these subjective judgments had the aroma of the presumption of guilt that was too easily misused by partisan politicians looking for scandals to bring down their opponents.) Then came calls for Lance's resignation including those from Democratic and Republican senators on the oversight committee, Senator Abe Ribicoff and Senator Charles Percy.[11] Their calls omitted any explanation as to exactly what laws he had actually or even potentially violated to justify such a damaging forced resignation. According to Suzanne Garment's book on scandals: "[People] talked and wrote this way because they were afraid that if they did not, they would not seem moral enough for the post–Watergate times. Their fear was a sign of the definite shift toward a type of modern Puritanism, a movement that had taken place in the political culture and its notions of morality."[12]

Finally, President Carter's top White House aide, Hamilton Jordan, yielded to the excesses of this appearances culture by advising President Carter in an "eyes-only" memo: "You pledged that you would not tolerate wrongdoing or *even the appearance of wrongdoing*. We cannot allow this or any other incident [to] erode the moral authority of your presidency."[13]

As Bert Lance commented years later, "Sooner or later the cumulative weight becomes too much to handle. The pressure builds. People say, 'You're harming the president,' or 'you're harming the party.'"[14] Brave, Lance refused to go down without a fight. On September 15, 1977, facing calls for his resignation, Lance voluntarily testified before the congressional committee again. His testimony should have been a clarion call to decent Americans of the dangers of the new hyperethics McCarthyism dawning in the post–Watergate era. As part of his statement, he asked: "Is it part of our American system that a man can be drummed out of government by a series of false charges, half-truths and misrepresentations, innuendoes and the like?"[15] The answer should have been a resounding no. Had it been from Democrats and Republicans alike, the history of the scandal machine and its politics of personal destruction that followed might well have been different. Instead, there was silence. One wonders today whether there is anyone from that committee—or any other then Democratic or Republican leader—who is now ashamed of their silence in the face of this gross violation of Civil Liberties and the presumption of innocence.

Five days later, Bert Lance was summoned to the White House by his old and close friend, President Jimmy Carter, who started out by praising him for his testimony and for "proving that the system does work."[16] Then Carter asked Lance to resign, despite the danger that doing so could injure Lance's reputation in the future. Lance submitted his resignation letter two days later. So much for the system working.

Lance's wife, LaBelle, a longtime friend of President Carter as well, said the few words that actually captured the authentic outrage at what Carter and his fellow sanctimonious members of the ethics culture had committed at the expense of Bert Lance and his family. "You have stabbed my husband in the back after all he's done for you," she said furiously. "I want to tell you one thing—you can go with the rest of the jackals, and I hope you're happy."[17]

After his resignation and departure from Washington in disgrace, Bert Lance and his family spent the next decade in litigation with the government. In the end, Lance was indicted for bank fraud, giving him the chance to face his accusers, respond with the facts under rules of due process, and allow a jury of his peers to determine guilt or innocence. At trial, the jury acquitted him on nine counts of the government's indictment and deadlocked on three. The government chose not to retry him.[18] Not once, I believe, was an apology ever offered to Lance or his family. And so ended the first chapter of post–Watergate gotcha politics.

A CONSTITUTIONAL NIGHTMARE: THE INDEPENDENT COUNSEL

The distrust of politics and the political process as an adequate check on abuse of power was the underlying assumption after Watergate that led to the creation of the legal monster called the "Special Prosecutor," five years later changed to the more frequently used name, "Independent Counsel."[19] Whatever complaint Democrats might have had about Judge Kenneth W. Starr, the Independent Counsel who investigated President Clinton, it was actually their party—liberal, post–Watergate Democrats caught up in the rush to impose subjective "ethics" on politics—that was primarily responsible for the creation of this monster. Over the 21 years of its existence, Democrats also bear the most responsibility for the increased limits on the attorney general's discretion to refuse appointing an independent counsel, even when partisan politics, media leaks, and innuendo were the driving force behind the call for one.

Two issues related to the legislation governing the appointment of an independent counsel proved to be crucial in making that position the bane of those opposed to the cycle of gotcha politics and scandal mongering in American politics. The first issue was the question whether the president and the Executive Branch should control the hiring and firing of a "special counsel" or whether that power should be given to the Judicial Branch, thus insulating it from political pressures. Despite arguments from Republican conservatives against allowing any prosecutor to operate outside of the Executive Branch, Democrats, led by Watergate Committee Chairman Senator Sam Ervin and his Chief of Staff Sam Dash, pressed for an independent counsel appointed by a judicial panel, which would not be subject to removal by the president or the attorney general. This was, of course, a reaction to Nixon's firing of the Special Prosecutor Archibald Cox in October 1973, called the "Saturday Night Massacre."[20] In retrospect, their concerns seemed misplaced, since Nixon was brought down by the successor to Cox, Leon Jaworski, who Nixon appointed due to pressure from the political process. In fact, the people who knew best—all four Watergate special prosecutors: Cox, Jaworski, Henry A. Ruth, Jr., and Charles Ruff—opposed the concept advocated by Ervin and Dash of an independent counsel supervised only by the judiciary.[21]

In 1976, President Ford agreed to offer a proposal for the establishment of a "special prosecutor" appointed by the attorney general with high standards that must be met before the prosecutor could be removed. The proposal passed the Senate by an overwhelming margin but stalled in the House, and Congress actually ended up debating more than 35 different proposals over the next two years. Finally, in 1978, those who did not want the Executive Branch to give up prosecutorial power—which, they argued with strong justification, was where it resided according to Article II of the Constitution—and those who wished to prevent a president or other executive official opposed to an investigation from firing the special prosecutor reached a compromise.[22]

The compromise in the resulting Ethics in Government Act of 1978 vested in the attorney general the discretion to begin a "preliminary investigation" as well as to determine whether a "Special Prosecutor" was necessary. But it vested the power of appointment and, more importantly, of removal in the judiciary. A "special division" of the prestigious D.C. Circuit Court of Appeals composed of three judges would make those crucial appointment–removal decisions, with the chief judge appointed by the chief justice of the Supreme Court. It is unlikely that those who drafted this compromise realized at the time exactly what havoc this hybrid monster would create or how little supervision the judicial panel would have over the independent counsel, let alone firing one.

The second issue, however, is what ultimately led to the worst partisan abuses of the independent counsel. This concerned the evidentiary threshold necessary to require the attorney general to initiate the "preliminary investigation" and the standard required for asking the three-judge panel to appoint an independent counsel. This occupied the majority of the debates between Democrats and Republicans each time the statute came up over the years for re-enactment (every 5 years). When the Republicans controlled the White House and the Democrats the Congress in the 1980s, the Republicans wanted to narrow the attorney general's discretion to seek appointment of an independent counsel and Democrats wanted to expand it. Then when things switched around in 1995, with President Clinton in the White House and the Republicans controlling the Congress, both parties flip-flopped and shamelessly reversed their positions. The Republicans now supported a lower threshold of evidence to require the attorney general to seek the appointment of the independent counsel, and the Democrats wanted to raise the standard to enable the attorney general to resist pressures to do so.

The final outcome, however, that evolved over the years was that the threshold remained so low that it was virtually politically impossible for the attorney general, whether a Republican or a Democrat, to resist the pressures to seek an independent counsel. In the final version of the statute, the standard to initiate a "preliminary investigation" by the Justice Department was an accusation of a crime against a senior administration or party official supported by "credible" and "specific" evidence—even if there was no significant corroboration. Once that standard was met, the attorney general had to ask the judicial panel to appoint an independent counsel if there was a "reasonable basis" for doing so.[23] As we shall see, from the first year after its creation, this low standard resulted in the attorney general appointing an independent counsel virtually every time the "preliminary investigation" was completed. As Attorney General Civiletti put it at the time, he had to recommend a special prosecutor any time a serious crime was alleged against a senior administration official unless the allegation was "so unsubstantiated that it warrants no further investigation."[24] Even where the source was not credible or involved a first-time offense that would not ordinarily lead to a federal prosecution, such as the case investigating Carter's Chief of Staff, Hamilton Jordan, for an alleged use of cocaine at a night club, Civiletti felt compelled to seek appointment of an independent counsel.

When the act came up for renewal in 1983 and the Republicans were now in control of the Senate with Ronald Reagan in the White House, Republicans led the charge to expand the attorney general's discretion to decline to appoint an independent counsel. Under the Republican-sponsored amendments, the attorney general could now take the credibility of the source of the information into account. Also, the scope of those covered under the act was narrowed and any official investigated but not indicted could be reimbursed for attorney's fees.

When the Democrats re-took the Senate in 1987 and the act was once again up for renewal, they attempted to *restrict* once again the discretion of the attorney general to decline to appoint an independent counsel in order to put maximum pressure on him or her to appoint independent counsels to investigate Reagan and then Bush Administration officials. They did so by lowering the threshold of the standard of evidence that would require the appointment of an independent counsel after the conclusion of a "preliminary investigation." And they succeeded, with innocent people serving as victims of their success. It was only in retrospect, after seeing the roles reversed in the 1990s when President Clinton became president, that some of these same Democrats had any regrets.[25]

THE WORST OF THE INDEPENDENT COUNSELS INVESTIGATIONS FROM THE 1980S

As noted, those abusing and misusing this modern-day political golem alternated between Democrats and Republicans, depending on which party was in control of Congress and not in control of the White House at the same time. In the 1980s, the Democrats clearly carry most of the shame—and the burden—of triggering the gotchas of independent counsel abuses by the Republicans against the Clinton Administration in the 1990s. The victims of the independent counsels appointed by Democratic prompting against Reagan and Bush I officials are many, but it is worth looking at the worst cases that make up a kind of Hall of Shame to understand the payback the Democrats eventually received from the Republicans in the 1990s.

The Dubious Investigation of Hamilton Jordan

Counterintuitively, the first person with the dubious honor of being prosecuted (and, as it turned out, unjustly so) by the first independent counsel called for by Democrats was one of Jimmy Carter's senior aides, Hamilton Jordan. This is the same Hamilton Jordan who was so concerned about ethical standards that he was ready to push Bert Lance out of office and out of town because of a concern about appearances. Certainly, once he suffered the unjust investigation he was forced to go through, he must have regretted what he had done so facilely to Bert Lance.

The individual most culpable for launching this entirely unnecessary use of an independent counsel was Carter's highly intelligent and impressive attorney general, Benjamin Civiletti. The charge, made by people who turned out to be of questionable reliability, was that Jordan had used cocaine in a famous New York City nightclub, Studio 54. Civiletti conducted the preliminary investigation called for by the independent counsel statute and found no corroborative evidence. Yet, for reasons that are still not clear even in hindsight, purely out of fear of political appearances, he decided to unleash an independent counsel. (This lack of political backbone by an attorney general is exactly what Justice Scalia referred to in his dissent to the Supreme Court case upholding the independent counsel in 1988.)

The one individual who clearly recognized Civiletti's poor judgment and political hypersensitivity was the man asked to serve as the independent counsel to investigate Jordan—Arthur Christy, a former U.S. attorney who had made his reputation prosecuting organized crime. Christy was unhappy about the assignment, could not understand why Civiletti was insisting on appointing an independent counsel, and actually tried to turn it down when the chief judge of the special panel asked him to take the post. He regarded the charge of a one-time use of cocaine as not worthy of federal prosecution, much less by a special prosecutor, but the chief judge pressured him into accepting.[26]

After conducting a four-month investigation that cost Jordan over $100,000 in legal fees, Christy found no credible evidence against Jordan and refused to prosecute. On May 21, 1980, the grand jury accepted Christy's recommendation unanimously and voted "No True Bill"—not to indict Jordan. This was the result of 19 grand jury sessions and 33 witnesses over 2 months.[27] Jordan has described the experience as a personal nightmare. The fact that it was avoidable should have forewarned everyone of the dangers of this monstrous new creature, but it did not.

The Unnecessary Investigation of Theodore Olson

The next on the list is the investigation of Theodore Olson, former head of the Justice Department's Office of Legal Counsel under Reagan (and later solicitor general under President George W. Bush), prompted by Democratic congressional leaders. On March 10, 1983, Olson testified before a House Judiciary subcommittee chaired by Representative Peter W. Rodino, famous for chairing the Nixon impeachment committee hearings. The controversy between the committee and the Reagan Administration was whether the Environmental Protection Agency had turned over all documents requested (but not subpoenaed) by the congressional committee concerning violations of the Superfund statute. (Superfund was a program for cleaning up hazardous waste dump sites financed through a combination of congressional appropriations and industry contributions.) The Justice Department, with Ted Olson spearheading the effort, had taken the position that some of these documents were subject to confidentiality restrictions and "executive privilege" because they reflected the deliberations of Executive Branch officers advising the president. Thus, under the Constitution's separation of powers doctrine, they could be withheld from Congress under most circumstances. Incidentally, Olson and his colleagues were clearly correct in this position.

Olson testified, not under oath by the way, that the Justice Department had turned over all relevant documents, with the exception of those that were withheld on grounds of executive privilege. When asked about his own personal notes he answered, "I didn't include handwritten notes of my own" and "I'm not sure that we've included everything." Unhappy with this, the Democratic House committee leaders insisted on a full-scale investigation of whether the administration had turned over all documents. Two years later, in December 1985, they produced a four-volume, 3,129-page report on what had now become a media controversy, though no one could quite put a finger on what the charge of wrongdoing was all about or why the Democrats had wasted so much time, effort, money, and paper on this issue.[28]

At this point, Chairman Rodino, otherwise a fair and highly respected member on both sides of the aisle, demanded an independent counsel to investigate whether Ted Olson, who had now been out of government for two years, had lied to the subcommittee when he answered the questions about the Justice Department's production of documents. For some reason not clear even to this day, Attorney General Meese decided that the murky testimony of Olson could be the basis of "credible evidence" of a possible crime and, thus, he was required to seek appointment of an independent counsel by the judicial panel—because, as he explained, the "threshold is so low."[29] The first choice, James C. McKay, had to withdraw because of a conflict of interest (his law partner, Charles Ruff, future White House Counsel during President Clinton's impeachment and former Watergate prosecutor, had advised the House committee on its investigation of Olson).[30] In the end, the judicial panel appointed McKay's deputy, Alexia Morrison, as the independent counsel.

Morrison began her work in April 1986. She went into high-energy mode, seemingly without boundaries and without a sense of proportion, the virus that seems to infect virtually every subsequent independent counsel once they realize there is no supervision and no budget limitations. Morrison called Olson to testify under oath before her, half a dozen of her lawyers, and FBI agents on her staff for an entire day. All Olson's friends to whom he may have made comments about the case were also hauled before the grand jury. Then Morrison asked Olson to waive his right to make a constitutional argument against the independent counsel law, but he refused.[31]

Within six months, Morrison concluded that Olson's testimony three years before was "literally true" and probably did not constitute a prosecutable offense. Even after reaching that conclusion, however, Morrison demanded that Olson waive his rights to be protected under the "statute of limitations" (because the alleged false statements had occurred more than three years before). If he refused to do so, she said, she would seek to indict him—even though she had already concluded he was probably not guilty! Under the then existing independent counsel statute, Olson would lose his right to be reimbursed for legal fees if indicted, even if he were acquitted afterward. So under these circumstances, Morrison's threat to indict has been characterized by some critics as abusive prosecutorial conduct. Olson had no choice but to waive his statute of limitations rights.[32]

Despite all this, Morrison did not complete her investigation for more than two additional years after she had concluded Olson's congressional testimony was "literally true," ultimately spending a total of $2.1 million. She issued her final report filing no charges in March 1989—to her credit. One reason for the delay is that she sought to expand her investigation to include an EPA official as well as two former Justice Department officials. Meese, however, refused her request to expand her investigation (to his credit), and, in one of the few instances that the panel turned down an independent counsel on anything in its entire history, the judges backed Meese and rejected Morrison's request.[33]

In fairness, another reason for the delay in Morrison's bringing the Olson investigation to a close was Olson's decision, backed by Republican conservative groups, to challenge the constitutionality of the Independent Counsel Act. Olson believed strongly that the Constitution clearly invested prosecutorial power only in the Executive Branch of government in Article II and that, as currently structured, the independent counsel was effectively independent of the Executive Branch and, thus, unconstitutional.

Olson took the challenge to the D.C. Circuit Court of Appeals, and in January 1988, by a 2–1 vote, the court ruled against the independent counsel in an 84-page decision written by conservative Circuit Court Judge Laurence H. Silberman. In retrospect, Silberman's prescience on the abuses inherent in the creation of a prosecutor outside the supervision of the executive branch of government is nothing short of brilliant.[34] The Supreme Court, however, in June 1988, with conservative Justice William H. Rehnquist writing a majority 7–1 opinion, upheld the act, ignoring Silberman's separation of powers constitutional concern by pointing to the discretion vested in the attorney general to decide whether or not to appoint the independent counsel as a sufficient role for the Executive Branch. The Rehnquist majority also gave credence to the supervisory power of the three-judge panel, ignoring the political reality that the "for cause" power to remove would be, in practical terms, rarely if ever exercised.[35]

The only dissenter in the *Morrison* case, Justice Antonin Scalia, castigated the majority for this naïveté in ignoring political realities. With equally amazing foresight as that shown by Judge Silberman on the appellate court, Scalia predicted that the attorney general's initial discretion on whether or not to recommend an appointment of an independent counsel (which was the key basis for the court's upholding the constitutionality of the office) would be virtually meaningless. "As a practical matter," given the political pressures from the opposing party that the attorney general would face if he refused to do so, "it would be surprising if the attorney general had any choice." He predicted that if the president refused to back such an appointment, Congress had the power to retaliate. "The context of this statute," he wrote, "is acrid with the smell of threatened impeachment."[36] In a famous phrase, Scalia predicted that suggesting that an independent counsel could be moved by the supervising judicial panel was like referring to "shackles as an effective means of locomotion."[37]

Finally, Scalia captured the dangers of allowing political and policy goals, however laudable—in this case, the desire to prevent another "Saturday Night Massacre," with a president firing a prosecutor to cover up his crimes—to influence a law that went beyond the limits of the Constitution. He predicted that once enacted, the Independent Counsel Act would be difficult to repeal—and difficult not to misuse, because politicians simply could not resist the temptation to misuse it:

> *The notion that every violation of law should be prosecuted, including—indeed, especially—every violation by those in high places, is an attractive one, and it would be risky to argue in an election campaign that that is not an absolutely overriding value. . . . Let justice be done, though the heavens may fall. . . .* [But for politicians elected to Congress], it is difficult to vote not to enact, and even more difficult to repeal, a statute called, appropriately enough, the Ethics in Government Act. If Congress is controlled by the party other than the one to which the president belongs, it has little incentive to repeal it; if it is controlled by the same party, it dare not. By its shortsighted action today, *I fear the Court has permanently encumbered the Republic with an institution that will do it great harm.*[38]

As can be seen by the italicized words, Justice Scalia clairvoyantly predicted the partisan misuse of the low threshold for triggering an independent counsel and the consequences of unaccountable prosecutorial zeal likely to result once the independent counsel got appointed:

> Unless it can honestly be said that there are "no reasonable grounds to believe" that further investigation is warranted, further investigation must ensue; and the conduct of the investigation, and determination of whether to prosecute, will be given to a person neither selected by nor subject to the control of the President—who will in turn assemble a staff by finding out, presumably, who is willing to put aside whatever else they are doing, for an indeterminate period of time, in order to investigate and prosecute the President or a particular named individual in his administration. The prospect is frightening. . . . [39]

These words of Justice Scalia must be read by every victim of independent counsels from the first to the last—from Republicans Ted Olson, Casper Weinberger, and Ed Meese to Democrats Mike Espy, Henry Cisneros, and Bill Clinton—with a chilling appreciation of their truth. Scalia's entire dissent should be required reading for anyone considering re-enacting an independent counsel statute.

Olson was an innocent man. He never should have been investigated. Democrats who called for him to be investigated by an independent counsel for his testimony should have apologized to him. Morrison compounded the injustice by offering her opinion in the final report she issued on March 14, 1989, stating that while Mr. Olson's 1983 testimony was "literally true," it was also "less than forthcoming" (without defining that phrase or explaining why it was appropriate for her to offer such an opinion).[40] This was not, unfortunately, the last independent counsel to decide that his or her public opinions mattered, were needed, or were somehow fair and just outside of due process.

The Abusive Investigation of Ed Meese

Another strong candidate for one of the democrats' most abusive uses of the independent counsel statute is the hounding of Reagan's Attorney General Ed Meese, which ultimately caused him to resign in disgrace. To this day, he still has never been convicted of any crime, much less indicted—a classic victim of the appearances culture and the scandal machine that lives on innuendo as a surrogate for facts.

First, in typical fashion, various unsubstantiated allegations surfaced concerning the sale of Meese's home in San Diego and various bank loans during his confirmation hearings to become attorney general in early 1984. Then, according to the unfortunate classic pattern, Democrats, who feared the conservative Meese might be Reagan's future choice for a Supreme Court slot, started leaking other allegations to the media, including some involving his wife and an accusation that Meese had accepted jade cuff links from a South Korean government official that were worth $375 when regulations limited such gifts to under $140. The media firestorm grew. Finally, Meese himself called for an independent counsel investigation to clear his name, which the Attorney General, William French Smith, could not ignore in the politicized environment. Smith agreed to appoint an independent counsel, even though the threshold of any credible evidence of a crime had surely not been met.

Jacob Stein, a distinguished attorney, was appointed independent counsel in April 1984 as leaks from Democratic senators and staff in Congress about Meese continued to flow, including unsubstantiated allegations about trips Meese had taken paid for by private groups. These were eagerly published by the scandal press corps without verifying the facts or determining whether or not these alleged actions actually constituted wrongdoing. In September 1984, Mr. Stein published a report in which he stated—in words that constituted a direct challenge to the ethics culture and its influence on triggering independent counsel investigations—"Nowhere in the statute or the order [appointing me] is there a directive to investigate and report on the propriety or the ethics of the respondent's conduct." In other words, Mr. Stein concluded that there was no evidence to warrant criminal prosecution, but he also did not declare Mr. Meese innocent.[41]

Thus, Meese was not out of the crosshairs of the scandal machine yet, where facts and evidence are not as important as innuendo. Meese ended up being confirmed as attorney general, but a legal cloud continued to hang over him—and, as he discovered, the scandal machine energized by partisan Democrats would not let it ever go away. As a result of their pressures, another independent counsel, James C. McKay, was appointed in February 1987 to investigate Reagan political aide Lyn Nofziger for alleged lobbying violations of the Ethics in Government Act involving a Bronx, N.Y., defense contractor called Wedtech.[42] McKay, however, broadened his investigation to include a senior adviser and old friend of Attorney General Meese, E. Robert Wallach, and then Meese himself.[43] McKay ended up issuing a public "report," in the summer of 1988 as he was permitted—*but not required*—to do at the end of his investigation. McKay chose to editorialize on the various allegations of financial improprieties against Attorney General Meese as well—though he, McKay, had never brought charges against Meese. These opinions of Meese's alleged prior conduct involving ownership of a small amount of telephone stock and a minor non-disclosure on one year's tax return led McKay to opine that Meese should not be prosecuted—but that he had "probably violated the law."[44]

McKay's decision to offer his opinion on the subject of his investigation, without having to prove it in court, was an abuse of discretion and principles of fairness also perpetrated by many of the independent counsels in subsequent years. It was in contrast to the statement made by Meese's actual independent counsel, Jacob Stein, who specifically stated he did not have a right to offer such opinions.[45]

In any event, just to show the malicious mischief such voluntary opinion-offering can create for an innocent person, here are the two contrasting headlines that resulted from McKay's gratuitous public report on Ed Meese—one published in the *New York Times* and the other, on the same day, in the *Washington Post:*

MEESE FOUND FREE OF SERIOUS BLAME IN MAJOR
SCANDALS
—*New York Times*, July 19, 1988

MCKAY REPORTS 4 "PROBABLE" MEESE OFFENSES
—*Washington Post*, July 19, 1988[46]

What could be better proof of the entirely ephemeral and subjective standards of the scandal media culture and the independent counsel, working together? Both headlines are right, but clearly, in the world of appearances, everything is in the eye of the beholder.

Democratic Shame: The Persecution of Raymond Donovan

The case of Raymond Donovan represents perhaps the very worst Democratic misuse of an independent counsel to hound and ruin an innocent man. Here, without any doubt, the Democratic congressional leadership, not a particular independent counsel, led the charge against Donovan and would not leave him alone until he was a ruined man. In retrospect, all Democrats who participated in this repulsive campaign of innuendo should, in retrospect, be ashamed.

Donovan's nightmare began after he, a big fundraiser in New Jersey for Ronald Reagan, was nominated to be Reagan's Secretary of Labor, and he appeared for his Senate committee hearings in January 1981. Donovan and his New Jersey construction company firm, Schiavone Construction Company of Secaucus, New Jersey, had already been the subject of whispers in the Washington media (of course appearing in print without attribution) as having connections to organized crime. (One does not have to be an over-sensitive Italian American to wonder whether such whispers of mob connec-tions would have ever been published if the firm had been called the Smith Construction Company rather than the Schiavone Construction Company.) There is little doubt that some of these leaks came from Democratic staffers preparing for the congressional hearings, but the hearings established no such links, and the FBI testified it had found no evidence of wrongdoing, saying: "If it were a criminal investigation, we would have ended it a long time ago."[47]

Surprisingly, or perhaps not, the FBI's assessment did not end the matter. More and more stories suggested wrongdoing by Donovan, and Democrats continued to pressure Attorney General William French Smith to appoint an independent counsel. Things got so bad for Donovan that he took the initia-tive and himself requested that the attorney general appoint an independent counsel to clear his name. Smith granted Donovan his wish at the end of 1981, and the judicial panel appointed Leon Silverman, a lawyer with a na-tional reputation, as independent counsel. Between 1982 and 1987, Silver-man opened and closed three separate investigations. The first two, in 1981 and 1982, ended with the curious phrase that there was "insufficient credible evidence" to warrant prosecution. For the last one, Silverman offered his opinion, again not required under the statute, that there was "some evidence to support an indictment" regarding alleged kickbacks at the Schiavone firm but not much chance of getting a conviction. Each time, Donovan was left to try to continue his professional and personal life with a cloud hanging over his head—neither guilty nor innocent, but suffering from the presumptive guilt imposed by the scandal culture and the world of appearances still em-braced by much of Washington.[48]

After the first two investigations ended with no indictments, President Reagan allowed Raymond Donovan to remain as Secretary of Labor. But in October 1984, shortly before the presidential election, a politically ambitious Democratic Bronx district attorney, Mario Merola, called "one of the best DA's in the state" of New York, brought a multi-count indictment against Donovan. At first, Donovan voluntarily took a leave of absence from his post as Labor Secretary to fight the charges. Six months later, however, when it appeared that it would still be a significant amount of time before he would be tried, he was forced to resign.[49]

Merola and his assistant, Stephen Bookin, had no compunctions about trying their case in the media and keeping the pressure on Donovan. They were known to regularly brief reporters about their case against Donovan, leading to a barrage of stories and headlines. Their media campaign certainly did not offend the New York media, and, surprisingly, it did not seem to offend the presiding judge either.

The core charges against Donovan were that he and Mr. Schiavone misused a minority firm in order to qualify for a federally subsidized contract worth $12.4 million; in short, they had used fraudulent methods of meeting federal affirmative action requirements. Merola publicly accused Donovan of committing a "fraud upon the minorities of the people of New York."

It took two years for the case to come to trial for reasons Merola and his deputy Bookin never explained, beginning in September 1986. The prosecution's case was so weak that the defense chose to present no witnesses and simply let the jury decide on the basis of the one-sided presentation of the prosecution. The jury deliberated for less than ten hours. When they returned to the courtroom, surprising everyone with their speed of decision, the judge asked the usual question, whether they had reached a verdict. The response proved quite unusual. The jury foreman rose and asked the judge whether they were required to state that a defendant was "not guilty" or allowed to declare him to be "innocent." The judge said they could describe their verdict any way that they wanted. So, each juror stood up and said, "Innocent." After the jury announced its verdict, Donovan turned to the deputy prosecutor Bookin, who had been so singularly responsible for bringing this outrageous case, and asked him the now famous question that has resonated ever since: "Which office do I go to to get my reputation back?"[50] It appears that Mr. Bookin offered no answer—and no apology.

Mr. Donovan certainly was not the last innocent victim of the independent prosecutor statute created in the ethics-obsessed culture following Watergate, but he serves as a powerful example of just how egregious things can get in politics when partisanship and "holier than thou" attitudes of the hyper, post-Watergate ethics culture join together. From Bert Lance forward, Democrats and Republicans have both been hurt, as well as have tried to inflict hurt, by the power of the independent counsel. However, like the Golem from Jewish mythology, the independent counsel is a monster that had escaped the control of its makers. It became an integral part of the scandal culture that helped keep the cycle of gotcha politics in motion, as the 1990s clearly demonstrate. But before moving on to that, there was another event in the 1980s that has played a key role in creating politics as we now know it.

CHAPTER FIVE

TO BE "BORKED" AND "GINGRICHED"

President Ronald Reagan nominated Robert Bork, then a member of the prestigious D.C. Circuit Court of Appeals, to the Supreme Court on July 1, 1987. He was nominated to replace retiring Justice Lewis F. Powell, Jr., who had established a moderate record as a Supreme Court justice. There will never be agreement, even among political moderates, on whether Robert Bork was, or was not, treated fairly prior to and during his confirmation hearings by Democrats on the Senate Judiciary Committee and the extensive network of liberal organizations and interest groups that organized a broad, grassroots campaign against him.[1] It is true that Bork's liberal opponents sometimes used exaggerations and outright distortions, including those made in print and TV ads, to inflame public opinion against him. It is also clear that some of them (even if just a few) were indefensibly inaccurate or at the very least misleading. The fact, however, that he was defeated by a 58–42 margin, the largest negative vote on a Supreme Court nominee in history, including negative votes from six moderate Republicans and all but three conservative Democrats, belies the notion that he was defeated just because of a liberal campaign of distortion. Despite this, the Republican right never forgave and they never forgot, and to "Bork" or "to be Borked" became an accepted synonym, even among many in the mainstream media, for smear tactics, as well as a conservative battle cry. So, how exactly did these events lead to such an outcome?

At the time of Bork's nomination in 1987, Democrats controlled the U.S. Senate by a 54–46 margin, and the chairman of the Senate Judiciary Committee, Joseph Biden, was a liberal Democrat with great skepticism about the unabashed conservative ideology and jurisprudence of Judge Bork. He and the top staff of the Judiciary Committee worked closely and unapologetically with a network of liberal organizations to develop a media campaign publicizing the negative aspects of Bork's judicial record and philosophy. Fair enough. These organizations represented a "who's who" of

American liberalism of the last 25 years or more. There were the leading civil rights groups, such as the National Association for the Advancement of Colored People (NAACP) and the Leadership Conference on Civil Rights; women's groups, such as National Organization for Women (NOW) and the National Abortion Rights Action League (NARAL); the American Civil Liberties Union (ACLU); Common Cause; Public Citizen; leading labor organizations, such as the AFL-CIO; the People for the American Way; and the Alliance for Justice, just to name a few.

Members of this coalition started with an impressive, meticulously researched book analyzing all of Bork's writings and judicial decisions over a career spanning two decades, from Yale Law School to service in the Nixon Justice Department to his many written decisions while he served on the prestigious D.C. U.S. Court of Appeals. It was ultimately referred to as the *Book of Bork* and was completed during the early summer weeks of 1987. Journalists and critics alike used it as a reference text. But while the *Book of Bork* focused on substance, the anti-Bork strategists recognized that reliance on judicial philosophy and decisions alone might not be sufficient to defeat a nominee for the Supreme Court if he was viewed as highly qualified and of sound judicial temperament to serve on the highest court in the land. As the authors of *People Rising* put it, "As of July 1, 1987 [with the Bork Senate hearings just two months away], it was not at all certain that the Senate would even open the pages of the 'Book of Bork.' And even if it did so, and found the constitutional views therein abhorrent, it seemed unlikely that a majority of the Senate would consider it appropriate to reject Bork on that basis."[2]

As a result, the anti-Bork liberal coalition made a critical strategic decision to organize what was tantamount to a political "campaign" against the Bork nomination, i.e., to put together paid print and TV ads, leaks to newspapers, and constant media strategies.[3] Calling themselves the "Block Bork Coalition," they went to work at the grassroots level of all of their organizations, raising money to pay for their ads and deploying their leaders and members to knock on doors of U.S. senators in a massive lobbying effort. The campaign proceeded the nationally televised Senate Judiciary Committee hearings, chaired by Biden, beginning on Tuesday, September 15, 1987, and continued for all five days of the hearings. Bork's nomination was rejected by a decisive 58–42 margin one month later, including votes in opposition by Republican Senators John Chafee of Rhode Island, Arlen Specter of Pennsylvania, Bob Packwood of Oregon, Robert Stafford of Vermont, John Warner of Virginia, and Lowell Weicker of Connecticut.

Republican conservatives have insisted (including in *The Tempting of America*, a book written by Bork himself) that the only reason Bork was rejected by the Senate was because of the liberal coalition's campaign based on distortions and smears having little or nothing to do with the facts or Bork's actual judicial philosophy and temperament. Charles Krauthammer, a conservative *Washington Post* columnist, making a comment typical at the time, described the coalition's campaign against Bork as "one of the most mendacious media campaigns ever launched against a public official" and the "meanest national campaign of this decade."[4]

The accusation that distortions and smears were primarily responsible for defeating Robert Bork, however, simply does not hold water. The sheer number of votes against Judge Bork, including the six moderate Republicans just mentioned as well as many conservative and moderate Southern Democrats, including Alabama Senator Howell Heflin, Louisiana Senator Bennett Johnston, North Carolina Senator Terry Sanford, and Arkansas Senator David Pryor, Jr.—as stated, producing the biggest negative margin for defeat of a Supreme Court nominee in history—is proof of this. Surely, a margin that great, including many Republican moderates, could not be entirely attributed merely to smears and distortions.

In fact, there were two more valid reasons for Bork's defeat, even if one disagrees with them as justifiable reasons for opposition: his judicial philosophy and his personal temperament. Regarding his judicial philosophy, one needs to go no further than his speeches in 1987, the year he was nominated by President Reagan, and his own articulation of his views in his 1990 book, which was intended to articulate his judicial philosophy in detail. A few key examples suffice to show there were valid reasons for viewing Judge Bork as too far out of the mainstream, even beyond conservative judicial philosophy.

First, there was Judge Bork's unapologetic opposition to the result in *Griswold v. Connecticut*, arguing in his book as well as earlier during the Senate hearings that the 14th Amendment of the Constitution and its specific guarantee of individual liberty free from intrusion by states does not prevent a state from imprisoning a married couple simply because they had chosen, in the privacy of their bedroom, to use contraception.[5] To many people, not just liberals, that position alone was enough to disqualify a Supreme Court nominee. Judge Bork did not even give solace to those troubled by that position by giving deference to the doctrine of stare decisis—meaning respect for the Supreme Court's past precedents that have become "settled law" over time. In fact, he told the Federalist Society in January 1987, just months before he was nominated to the Supreme Court: "I would think an originalist judge would have no problem whatever in overruling a non-originalist precedent, because that precedent by the very basis of his judicial philosophy has no legitimacy."[6]

By contrast, years later, both Justices John Roberts and Sam Alito, clearly judicial conservatives, during their confirmation hearings in late 2005 and 2006 not only supported the holding of *Griswold* and its finding of a right to privacy implicit in the 14th Amendment in that case, but also confirmed their overall belief in the doctrine of stare decisis. These were code words, of course, on both sides that they would be at least reluctant to overturn *Roe v. Wade* outright.

Bork also challenged the use of the Equal Protection clause to ensure that each citizen's vote would have the same weight, regardless of whether he or she lived in a rural area or an urban area. The concept of "one man, one vote" has been the law of the land as protected by the 14th Amendment's Equal Protection clause since 1962 when the Supreme Court decided the case of *Baker v. Carr.*[7] Yet in 1987, Bork disagreed that there was such a protection for the right to equal voting, regardless of where a citizen lived within a state. The Supreme Court, he said, "stepped beyond its allowable boundaries when it imposed one man, one vote under the Equal Protection Clause. That is not consistent with American political theory, with anything in the history or the structure or the language of the Constitution."[8] And Bork can hardly claim to have been "Borked" by his own words.

That does not mean that there are no legitimate constitutional arguments to support his positions or legitimate reasons to have supported his nomination to the Supreme Court. His book, *The Tempting of America*, is brilliantly written and on many points, especially those arguing deference to democratic principles and deference to state legislatures, he is, to me at least, affirming core liberal, not just conservative, values. But it *does* mean that there were legitimate reasons to oppose him that had nothing to do with some distortions or half-truths in ads run by the Block Bork coalition.

Besides judicial philosophy, a second legitimate cause for concern regarding Judge Bork was the question of whether he had the appropriate judicial temperament, especially for the Supreme Court, which rules over the third branch of government for the whole country. This is not just a question of how he came across during the televised hearings, which, candidly speaking, given aspects of his appearance and voice, was not very positive. In fact, he often came across as arrogant, condescending, and patronizing. More solid proof of Judge Bork's arrogance and close-mindedness, however, is readily found in his own book. Check out the title of Chapter Twelve concerning his justification for relying on the "original intent" of the Framers of the Constitution as a guiding constitutional principle. Bork calls this chapter "The *Impossibility* of All Theories that Depart from Original Understanding."[9] For Judge Bork to suggest that it is "impossible" for anyone to disagree with him is the best evidence that his temperament may have made him unsuitable to serve on the Supreme Court.

Judge Bork's level of arrogance and inflexibility about his own views was a fatal flaw in the eyes of many students of the Supreme Court. This characteristic is not only bad in a Supreme Court justice; it is, at least for many Supreme Court experts on both the left and right, disqualifying. Because there are only nine justices on the highest court in the land, it is essential that they have the personal temperament to be collegial with their fellow justices, willing to listen to opposing views, and to keep an open mind after reviewing the facts and listening to colleagues argue the law.

That could be the strongest reason why Justice Roberts and, to a lesser extent, Justice Alito were confirmed in 2005 and 2006 but Judge Bork was not. Even liberals who disagreed with the judicial decisions Judges Roberts and Alito had taken in past decisions found them to be affable, open-minded, and likely to be collegial with colleagues. Given Bork's documented close-mindedness, then, one could reach the conclusion in good faith that he was not fit for the Supreme Court without needing to use half-truths or innuendo in order to defeat the nomination.

Given the legitimate and accurate reasons for opposing Judge Bork, it seems even more unnecessary and unfortunate that the Block Bork liberal groups chose to use political campaign techniques, including TV ads and oversimplified sound bites, that sometimes distorted complicated judicial decisions. We can debate how many times these distortions occurred, how material they were, and what their real impact was, but there can be no debate that they occurred.

The respected legal affairs journalist Stuart Taylor Jr., found that many of the ads "painted a frightening portrait, based upon exaggerations of and highly creative extrapolations from his past statements [and decisions.]"[10] Even the authors of *People Rising* admit that "there were rhetorical excesses and oversimplifications."[11] Rather than go through some examples used by conservatives to show the "Borking of Bork," however, I have chosen one case that is a clear, horrific example of the liberal groups' distortion of Bork's record—one that has escaped the attention of most liberal chroniclers of the Bork treatment. This neglect alone offers great insight into the blindness of these liberal groups to how blatant some of their distortions were—and thus, their lack of understanding as to why the right was so outraged by some of the tactics they used against Bork. The example I have chosen is the accusation that Bork favored forced sterilization of women.

There is no doubt that the Block Bork Coalition made that charge—repeatedly. For example, People for the American Way, one of the leading groups organizing opposition to Bork, published a full-page ad on the day the hearings began, with the headline: "Robert Bork vs. the People." And one of the sub-heads blared: "Sterilizing Workers." Ohio Senator Howard Metzenbaum repeatedly made that charge during the televised hearings. And it was repeated over and over again in the media.

The charge was false. It was based on a 1984 case decided by Judge Bork titled *Oil, Chemical and Atomic Workers (OCAW) International Union vs. American Cyanamid Company.*[12] Judge Bork wrote the decision for a unanimous 3–0 decision. The two other judges who joined him in the decision were then Circuit Court Judge (and later Supreme Court Justice) Antonin Scalia and a visiting senior judge from the Central District of California, David W. Williams. Judge Williams had been the third African American municipal court judge in the history of California before President Nixon appointed him as a U.S. District Court Judge in 1969.

The facts of *OCAW v. American Cyanamid Company* were that American Cyanamid had determined that one of its divisions had ambient air that contained levels of lead that would put the fetuses of pregnant women at risk. The Administrative Law Judge for the Department of Labor who heard the case found that there was no feasible way for the company to reduce that ambient air to levels that would be safe for pregnant women. So the American Cyanamid company announced to the women of child-bearing age that they had two options: transfer to lower-paid, safer areas of the facility, if they were available; or, if they chose, demonstrate proof that they had been sterilized and keep their positions in the area with levels of lead that could endanger fetuses.

The only legal issue the court was asked by the lawyers to decide was whether the company's announcement of those two options was a workplace "hazard" as defined by the Occupational Health and Safety Act (OSHA). The Labor Department's Administrative Law Judge decided the case first after the union representing the women challenged the company's policy concerning those two options as an "occupational hazard" in violation of OSHA. But the Administrative Law Judge said no—that Congress had defined an "occupational hazard" covered by OSHA to be "processes and materials which cause injury or disease" in the workplace, and that the policy itself could not therefore be defined as an occupational hazard under OSHA, even with a stretched interpretation of legislative intent.

The independent Occupational Safety and Health Review Commission heard the union's appeal of the Administrative Law Judge's finding and unanimously affirmed. The Secretary of Labor had the right to appeal from the Commission decision, and chose not to do so. The union then appealed the Commission's decision to the three-judge panel of the D.C. Circuit Court of

Appeals. Judge Bork, writing for a unanimous 3–0 panel, affirmed the decision of the ALJ and the Commission:

> It is clear that American Cyanamid had to prevent exposure to lead of women of childbearing age, and furthermore, that the company could not have been charged under the Act if it had accomplished that by discharging the women or by simply closing the Department, thus putting all employees who worked there, including women of child-bearing age, out of work. The company was charged only because it offered the women a choice. . . . The women involved in this matter were put to a most unhappy choice. But no statute redresses all grievances, and we must decide cases according to law.[13]

In fact, as Judge Bork pointed out in his book discussing this case and as the second to the last sentence indicates, he was not personally happy with the company's policy.[14] In addition, in a footnote at the very end of his decision, he offered another possible remedy for the women workers who were offered the option of working or sterilization. He suggested that they could have filed a grievance of an "unfair labor practice" under the National Labor Relations Act or a "forbidden sex discrimination under Title VII of the Civil Rights Act of 1963." He went on to note that the court had been informed by counsel to the union that the affected women had, in fact, made such a filing under Title VII and that American Cyanamid had settled the suit.[15] The OCAW union chose not to appeal the Bork unanimous decision to a full "en banc" rehearing by the full D.C. Circuit Court of Appeals. Nor did it seek an appeal to the Supreme Court.

The point is, all the Block Bork Coalition did was to permit the impression that Bork either favored forced sterilization or, in some more careful formulations, that he simply supported a company that offered women "the gruesome choice of getting sterilized or getting fired."[16] Of course, none of the Block Bork Coalition ads or leaders pointed out that the holding was limited to interpreting the scope of OSHA as an appropriate statutory remedy and had nothing to do with supporting the company's policy on the merits. Nor did any of the ads or leaders mention that the Bork decision was a 3–0 decision; that the decision by the OSHA Commission was unanimous and came down the same way; that the Administrative Law Judge did so as well; or that the union did not even choose to appeal to the full D.C. Circuit Court of Appeals or the U.S. Supreme Court.

It is interesting how the book on the liberal groups' Bork battle, *People Rising*, handled this example of a gross distortion of the truth. It describes how on the fourth day of the Bork hearings, Senator Metzenbaum of Ohio asked Bork about the *American Cyanamid* case and quotes Bork's response as, "They

[American Cyanamid] offered a choice to women; some of them I guess did not want to have children." Then the book quotes a telegram composed by two women who had sued American Cyanamid and was read by Metzenbaum to the committee: "'I cannot believe Judge Bork thinks we were glad to have the choice of getting sterilized or getting fired. . . . It is incredible that a judge who is supposed to be fair can support a company that does not follow OSHA rules.'" Of course, as anyone who read the decision knew at the time, this telegram was a gross distortion of the truth. Judge Bork had not said the word "glad" in his response—he was just describing factually that some women had chosen to be sterilized. Yet this telegram was read openly and was used to provide, according to one leader in the anti-Bork effort, a "vehicle for showing just how outside the mainstream [Bork] was. . . . We showed a candidate for the Court who was capable of little or no sympathy, let alone empathy. This was the 'Book of Bork' and this example breathed life into it."[17]

Is there any wonder, from this one example of the use of the *American Cyanamid* case alone, why the political right who supported Bork was so outraged by these tactics—and never forgave and never forgot? Is it any excuse to say, well, this is just one example, or there were only a few other examples, and while the use of the *American Cyanamid* decision was not entirely accurate, it symbolized the larger truth that Bork was "not empathetic" and did not deserve to be on the Supreme Court? As history has shown, you cannot use a little bit of poison in distorted political attack ads and not expect the poison to be returned in kind, if not in significantly bigger amounts when the other side gets its chance. You cannot be almost accurate, or sometimes accurate, or justify distortion with the larger goals at issue. Truth and facts are not relative words. They are absolutes. Intentional or even careless distortions are not defensible sometimes, even if they can be used to symbolize what might be seen as a larger truth.

By using distortions like the *American Cyanamid* case against Bork during the "campaign" to defeat him, even if there were just a few instances, liberals gave the conservative movement their red meat anthem for the 1990s and beyond—"Borking"—and a pressing need for payback they would never forget. And, as we shall see, Bill Clinton and many members of his administration paid the price again . . . and again . . . and again.

CLOSING THE 1980S: THE GINGRICH CAMPAIGN TO DESTROY SPEAKER JIM WRIGHT

Just around and after the time of the Bork hearings, between 1987 and 1989, a brilliant, charismatic, young Georgia Republican back-bencher in the

House of Representatives named Newt Gingrich began a campaign to attack and bring down then Democratic House Speaker Jim Wright on ethical and other charges. The attack techniques he used had been historically common in political campaigns but, with few exceptions before Gingrich (Senator Joe McCarthy being a notable one), they had rarely been used by members of Congress against one another. These included public criticism as well as the use of rhetoric, personal attacks, and innuendo apparently aimed not just at defeating the opponent but also destroying him or her personally.

Because there were few rules or restraints on the public rhetoric Gingrich could use about Speaker Wright, at least off the House floor, it appears he decided it was worth keeping the public pressure on Wright, raising doubts, and, thus, hurting Congressional Democrats who tried to defend him, even if he used excessive and reckless charges and rhetoric. Even back then, Newt Gingrich had his eye on the objective that most people at the time described as impossible—winning back the House of Representatives for Republicans for the first time since 1954.

Gingrich found two main issues on which Wright had at least the appearance of impropriety. One was a minor charge that Wright had lobbied a regulator in the Federal Deposit Insurance Corporation on behalf of a savings & loan bank (S&L) constituent in his district (not exactly a new story in Washington, nor a particularly shocking one, so long as he did not ask the regulator for special treatment for the S&L, which he said he had not).[18] The second one got more traction: that Speaker Wright had used a book contract with a local publisher to generate both unusually high royalties and outside income to get around House rules. Wright had published a memoir, *Reflections of a Public Man*, under a publishing contract with a Texas friend and publisher, Carlos Moore, whose companies had received more than $600,000 worth of printing business from Wright's reelection committees in the previous 10 years (though no one questioned the legitimacy of that work nor the price paid).

Gingrich pointed out that Wright had earned $55,000 in royalties from the book on the sale of only 20,000 copies—an unusually high royalty rate of 55 percent per book, as opposed to the traditional author's top rate of 10 percent–15 percent. Moreover, Wright was accused of "influencing" lobbyists who had legislative interests he could affect to make bulk purchases of the books. The suggestion—without hard evidence—was that the unusually high royalty rate was a return favor by his friend Moore for all the business Wright's campaign had given his printing and election service companies over the years and that the bulk purchases were a way of muscling lobbyists to supplement Wright's income via the inflated royalty rate by buying lots of books.

The charges were investigated by the Democratic-controlled House Ethics Committee, but only after nearly a year of Gingrich's pounding, and were never finally adjudicated because Wright chose to resign.

Speaker Wright did not help his cause much by attacking Gingrich politically rather than being transparent and immediately getting all the facts out as early and as quickly as possible. For example, during a national TV interview in June 1988, Wright justified the high 55 percent royalty rate by pointing out that he received no advance up front, as many authors do. He attacked Gingrich as "one little Republican congressman" engaged in a "flimsy" partisan effort designed to embarrass him.[19]

The purpose here is not to adjudicate whether or not Gingrich was right or wrong on the merits. He certainly had an ethical argument. Speaker Wright's defense seemed, at best, to suggest that he had found a loophole to get around the limits on outside income and had taken advantage of it. And his communications with the FDIC in the middle of regulatory investigations of S&L banks in his congressional district arguably showed a political tin ear, at least with the wisdom of hindsight. But clearly, the language Gingrich used in attacking Wright was over-the-top, personal, exaggerated, and violated the unwritten rules of political partisanship that congressional members on both sides of the aisle largely respected. For example, Gingrich called Wright "the most corrupt speaker in the 20th century." In speeches, Gingrich repeatedly attacked Wright personally—at one point publicly comparing him to Benito Mussolini, Italy's Fascist dictator, by accusing Wright of "betrayal of America's friends and allies. In World War II, I guess 'collaborator' or 'quisling' would have come the closest terms to describe Wright's role." (Gingrich had accused Wright of revealing government secrets about U.S. provocations against the Nicaraguan government then led by left-wing (some said communist) Daniel Ortega, charges he repeatedly made but that were never shown to be true.) As Gingrich admitted to an author who wrote about his campaign to bring down Wright, his tactics of repeatedly attacking Wright personally was for the purpose of undermining the House Democratic majority's power structure. "Wright's a useful keystone to a much bigger structure," Gingrich reportedly said.[20] He used the words any political campaign manager would use about a negative attack strategy on a political opponent in a campaign: "I'll just keep pounding and pounding on his ethics. There comes a point where it comes together and the media takes up on it or it dies."[21]

Wright was finally forced to resign on May 31, 1989. In his resignation speech, in words that would come back to haunt Gingrich, Tom DeLay, and future Republican partisan leaders once the Republicans took over the House in 1995, Speaker Wright called on his colleagues, Republicans and Democrats alike, "to bring this period of *mindless cannibalism* to an end."[22]

This phrase "mindless cannibalism" perfectly summed up the personal destructiveness that had come to infect the body politic. This phrase ironically reappears, as we shall see, at the close of the 1990s, used by—of all people—Republican Tom DeLay when, as hard as it was to believe on the occasion of Wright's being driven from office, things actually would get a lot worse.

Four weeks before Wright's resignation, on May 1, 1989, Dan Balz, a leading political reporter for the *Washington Post*, assessed the consequences of the changed atmosphere of incivility and personal vilification reflected in the Gingrich campaign against Wright, as well as other indicators of heightened partisanship in the Congress. The piece perfectly summarized the cumulative legacies of the post–Watergate scandal machine, foretelling the impact of TV and new communications technologies in the coming decade that would magnify the negative effects of that gotcha culture where opponents were not just defeated but demonized. Balz opined: "The characteristics of campaign-style politics are now familiar: sharp, negative attacks; the use of trivial issues for tactical gain; greater attention to questions of character; the emphasis on style over substance; the power of television; and the hothouse of news media attention that forms around issues or individuals."

As a Democratic member of Congress, David R. Nagle of Iowa commented on the dangers of converting disagreements between members on issues into political campaigns of attack and counter-attack: "The negative campaign has moved from the campaign to the House," he told Balz, which, in retrospect, is clearly an understatement.[23]

POST-SCRIPT ON THE
CONGRESSIONAL CAMPAIGN CULTURE:
CONFIRMATION HEARINGS OF JUDGE ALITO

In mid-January 2006, the weekend after the Supreme Court confirmation hearings for Judge Sam Alito had concluded, the newspaper analyses were filled with stories about Democrats having failed to establish a convincing political or substantive case for rejecting Alito. What was striking about those stories was the total obliviousness of both Democrats and Republicans to how the Bork experience 15 years before had dominated the thinking of both sides during the confirmation process.

The Democrats paid for the conscious or unconscious memories of "Borking," through their hypersensitivity to any appearance of personal disrespect toward Alito. This drove partisan liberals and bloggers crazy, believing Democratic senators had been too soft in cross-examining Judge Alito (which really meant, not engaging in partisan attack questions that might have succeeded in getting Judge Alito to "make a mistake"). The Bork effect had been even more apparent in the hearings two months before concerning Judge John Roberts as the nominee for chief justice to replace the late Chief Justice William H. Rehnquist. Despite clear conservative views and judicial philosophy, Judge Roberts' qualifications were so impressive and answers on the controversial social issues so diplomatic that he ended up being supported by liberal Senator Patrick Leahy, the ranking Democrat on the Judiciary Committee, and sailing through the Senate with more than 70 votes.

The Republicans, by the same token, with memories of Judge Bork firmly in mind, focused on protecting Judge Alito from answering any questions on his constitutional views on the most important substantive issues, such as abortion and the right to privacy, deference to Congress, and the powers of the Executive during wartime. Conservative groups ran TV ads not focusing on praising Judge Alito's ample conservative writings and judicial record, but rather—again with the Bork legacy clearly in mind—arguing that Alito should be confirmed based solely on his indisputably impressive resume.

But it was more than the ghost of "Borking"—pro or con—that haunted both the Democrats and the Republicans. It was also the legacy of the gotcha culture reflected in the "campaign" of Newt Gingrich against Speaker Jim Wright and the negative attack campaign culture that had become staples of the post–Watergate scandal machine in the late 1970s and 1980s. This was certainly reflected in media coverage of the Alito hearings. It seemed to be a given in virtually every news story and analysis, on the blogs and on the Sunday morning talk shows, that there would be no real substantive debate on constitutional issues coming out of the Alito (or Roberts) hearings. Rather, it was a waiting game of whether someone would get a "gotcha"—leading to a headline, a gaffe, a "stumble" that might cause controversy, extended hearings, attacks and counter-attacks—in short, the running media question was: Would this become another round of gotcha politics and divisive partisanship or not?[24]

The campaign type of atmosphere of the Bork confirmation hearing seemed to be present in the Alito hearings, but the anti-Alito liberal groups appeared discouraged by how effective Judge Alito was (as was Judge Roberts in his hearings). Judge Alito did not necessarily avoid showing his true conservative views, but he was very good at avoiding mistakes. Much as if it were a presidential campaign debate, things seemed to come down to the "gaffe" watch. The only serious question, so consistent with 20 years of the gotcha political culture, was whether or not Judge Alito would "f**k up," as one liberal opponent of Alito put it to me during the hearings. As we now know, he did not.

The one Democrat who seemed to get to the core of the post–Bork legacy of a political campaign applied to the Alito hearings was Senator Ted Kennedy. Kennedy, the most respected and influential voice of liberalism in the Democratic Party, clearly understood and was frustrated over the fact that he and his fellow Judiciary Committee Democrats had failed to draw Judge Alito out to discuss serious substantive issues about his constitutional approach and philosophy. He seemed to understand that it was not enough to play gotcha in the campaign style of the Bork hearings when he said: "These issues are so sophisticated—half the Senate didn't know what the 'unitary presidency' was, let alone the people of Boston," referring to the doctrine that some conservatives have endorsed favoring a strong presidency. "I'm sure we could have done better." He added: "But what has happened is that *this has turned into a political campaign.* The whole process has become so politicized that I think the American people walk away more confused about the way these people stand."[25]

Senator Kennedy was, of course, right. What he and other Democrats didn't seem to recognize is that the way they had treated Judge Bork 19 years or so earlier was one reason why this campaign atmosphere surrounding judicial nominees continued. And Republicans are equally in denial that some day the tables will turn and it will be they who face Democratic TV ads demanding that senators not ask judicial nominees of a Democratic president substantive questions but instead vote solely based on an impressive curriculum vitae.

It is ironic how quickly both sides in a gotcha culture forget the inevitable truth to the ancient biblical phrase, "As ye reap, so shall ye sow."

PART III

THE 1990S SCANDAL MACHINE IMPLOSION

INTRODUCTION

The last decade of the twentieth century marked the pinnacle of the destructive power of the scandal machine. Two successive presidents from different parties, different generations, and with far differing political philosophies—George H. W. Bush and William Jefferson Clinton—shared the common pain and injustice of a scandal culture and gotcha politics gone completely out of control. Both suffered, most of all, from the consequences of men who used the unaccountable prosecutorial powers of the independent counsel with an apparent complete loss of good judgment and proportionality.

In the closing days of the 1992 presidential campaign, President George H. W. Bush suffered from one of the worst examples of poor, even reckless, judgment by an independent counsel. In this case, it was Lawrence Walsh, the independent counsel then in his sixth year investigating Iran-Contra and approaching $40 million in expenditures.

By the time President Bill Clinton had taken office, the Independent Counsel Statute had been allowed to expire, thanks in no large part to the excesses of Lawrence Walsh that Republicans and President Bush had witnessed. President Clinton, however, ignored President Bush's wise advice not to support renewal of the statute. As a result, it was resurrected in mid-1994—just at the time that three new ingredients to the scandal machine were mixing together. As discussed earlier, these were the telecommunications revolution, a political revolution, and the end to the "gentlemen's agreement" regarding media coverage of public officials' sexual activities. Together, these three combined with the newly enacted Independent Counsel Statute to become weapons of mass political destruction faced by no other president in U.S. history, with the result of nearly destroying Bill Clinton's presidency.

A careful study of the scandal headlines that plagued the Clinton presidency shows that there was little behind all the noise and commotion. Certainly, there were some unseemly fundraising practices in the 1996 presidential campaign, mostly on the Democratic side, as well as other media and congressional-driven "controversies." However, in the final analysis, there was no finding of criminal wrongdoing involving a Clinton Administration official other than a misdemeanor plea following one of the most abusive independent counsel investigations ever. At the time, few people in the public and media made the distinction between political controversies based on questionable "appearances" versus those based on actual wrongdoing substantiated under objective rules of due process. At the same time, a series of independent counsels who abused their discretion against Clinton Administration officials and friends seemed to arouse little, if any, media or public outrage. This may have been because the Democrats had done the same thing against Reagan and Bush Administration officials.

The scandal culture came full circle at the peak of the scandal machine of the 1990s. First, the boomerang caught two of the Republican leaders of the House impeachment drive—House Speaker Newt Gingrich and Speaker-to-be Bob Livingston in December 1998—prompting their downfall. Second, it resulted in the impeachment of President Clinton by the House of Representatives and his acquittal by the Senate.

There were hopes that with the dawn of the twenty-first century the scandal machine's destructive energy had dissipated. Not only did the independent counsel statute expire in 1999, but also, general "scandal fatigue" seemed to set in across the political spectrum immediately after the final vote was cast acquitting President Clinton. Unfortunately, as we shall see, reports of the demise of the scandal culture and gotcha politics are premature.

CHAPTER SIX

PRESIDENTS GEORGE H. W. BUSH AND BILL CLINTON: BOOKENDS TO THE SCANDAL CULTURE

On the Friday before the 1992 presidential elections, independent counsel Lawrence Walsh announced that he was re-indicting former Reagan Defense Secretary Caspar Weinberger for obstruction of justice. The indictment also mentioned that Secretary Weinberger's notes claimed that President Bush had "favored" the arms-for-hostages deal.

I was working as a volunteer in the Clinton presidential campaign in Maryland. We knew the election was close, and we knew this announcement changed everything. As soon as the news broke about the Weinberger indictment, my phone started ringing with gleeful Democrats writing President Bush's political epitaph. "It's over," was the general reaction; and they turned out to be right.

We knew that if the situations were reversed, the Republicans would have jumped all over this with spin messages and innuendo about the Democratic candidate having "lied" about Iran-Contra. The fact that our side could not—and did not—resist the same opportunity did not surprise anyone. Indeed, it would have shocked everyone if we had.

During my door-to-door work that weekend I referred to the Walsh indictment as a "smoking gun." Did I point out to the voter that, in fact, an indictment is not evidence of anything? No. Did I remind the voter that a prosecutor presents entirely one-sided evidence to a grand jury, without opportunities for cross-examination and balance? No. Did I explain that there is some truth to the line that a prosecutor could indict a ham sandwich if he wanted to? No.

I will be the first to admit, now, that this was not fair nor just. While we may not have wanted to rely on a prosecutor to hand down an indictment the Friday before an election, we certainly didn't mind if it helped us get back the White House.

"How could that be bad?" we asked ourselves with some comfort. "It was happening to the other guy."

As we celebrated Walsh's decision and Bush's political pain that weekend, none of us saw the double-standard—the politically expedient hypocrisy—we Democrats were exhibiting. Nor did we dwell on the possibility that it could come back to bite us if the Independent Counsel Statute were revived and the Republicans took over both the Senate and the House. Little did we know how Bill Clinton would pay some very serious consequences in the next gotcha cycle of the scandal culture.

GEORGE H. W. BUSH AND THE POOR
JUDGMENT OF LAWRENCE WALSH

L awrence E. Walsh was one of the most outstanding lawyers in the United States when he was appointed independent counsel in 1986 to investigate the Iran-Contra matter. His investigation would not formally conclude until seven years later. In summary, the Iran-Contra investigation focused on the question of whether top Reagan Administration officials had surreptitiously violated, or at least evaded the restrictions of, a law called the Boland Amendment. This law banned any form of U.S. government financial aid to support the "Contras"—the pro-U.S. (and CIA-supported) guerilla forces opposing the then leftist forces of the "Sandinistas" who controlled the government of Nicaragua.

In 1979, the Sandinistas overthrew the Somoza dictatorship that had ruled Nicaragua since the 1930s, and their leftist approach and rhetoric sounded and looked very much like the hated Fidel Castro and his communist regime in Cuba. The Carter Administration opposed the Sandinistas, and the Reagan Administration's anti-Sandinista attitude was even more hostile. Beginning in the first year of the Reagan Administration, Reagan's National Security Adviser, Admiral John Poindexter, and his CIA director, William Casey, devised various ways of sending money, arms, and ultimately American personnel to help the rightist Nicaraguan "Contras" wage guerilla warfare against the Sandinista government.

But between 1982–84, with the legacy of Vietnam and Watergate very much in their minds, congressional Democrats opposing Reagan's interference in Nicaragua (even though they may not have had much love for the Sandinista government) enacted two restrictive amendments.[1] Both were aimed at using congressional powers to restrict the Executive Branch from executing foreign policy—raising serious constitutional questions. The second amendment (the Boland Amendment) stated that any executive agency, including the Defense Department and the CIA as well as any other government "agency or entity," could not spend money "directly or indirectly" on "military or paramilitary operations in Nicaragua."[2] But in subsequent amendments and actions (in fact, five different Contra funding policy amendments in four years), Congress sent mixed signals as to how it wanted to direct and control U.S. foreign policy regarding Nicaragua.[3] It allowed money to be spent on "humanitarian aid" and then on "communications" aid. And in 1986, Congress actually resumed funding the Contras to the tune of $100 million.

The ambiguities abounded. What constituted "humanitarian" or "communications" aid? What was a government "entity"? Was a department of the White House reporting directly to the president and deemed part of the president's staff, like the National Security Adviser, such an "entity"? Putting aside the unseemly actions of Executive Branch officials violating congressional mandates and then covering it up, it is important to understand that what followed was a constitutional struggle between two branches of government on a foreign policy issue. Congress placed severe limits on the Executive Branch's right to set foreign policy, which prompted a political and constitutional showdown. Rather than vetoing or trying publicly to amend or oppose these Boland amendments, the Reaganites chose to find ways to thread the legal needle using ambiguities and loopholes to continue helping the Contras.

Finally, key officials in the Reagan White House were also forced to admit that they had indirectly sold arms to Iran. The hope was that such sales would result in the release of U.S. hostages held in Lebanon by groups generally believed to be under Iranian control, if not directly then at least indirectly. When it came out that a junior National Security Council aide, Colonel Oliver North, had conceived and implemented the idea of secretly diverting the profits from the arms sales to aid the Contras, this added a huge burst of energy to the scandal machine.

By the end of his seven-year, $47-million investigation, eleven persons were convicted, Walsh managed to extract five guilty pleas, but his two highest profile convictions—of National Security Adviser Aide Colonel Oliver North and National Security Adviser Admiral John M. Poindexter—were reversed on appeal. This was because the independent counsel could not establish that the convictions were not at least partially based on immunized testimony given before the congressional committees, and thus out of bounds.

THE INDICTMENT(S) OF CASPAR W. WEINBERGER[4]

The Walsh prosecutor team first indicted former Secretary of Defense Caspar W. Weinberger in June 1992. However, the judge dismissed the key conspiracy to obstruct justice count of the indictment on September 29, 1992, on technical grounds. That is to say, the indictment did not allege specifically enough that Weinberger had worked with others in the Reagan Administration to obstruct the investigation. The judge had indicated his expectation that the flaws in the indictment would be fixed and re-filed within a month. With Iran-Contra going into its sixth year, this must have frustrated Walsh and his team, since they still had not landed a serious blow against President Reagan, Vice President Bush, or senior members of the Cabinet. As is so often the case, when prosecutors are unable to prosecute on the underlying crime, they look for "false statements," "perjury," or "obstruction of justice" crimes as surrogates. That appears to have been the case in the decision to re-indict Weinberger not only on the obstruction count but also on making a "false" statement (not under oath) to federal investigators.

It seems that Weinberger initially told Walsh's senior FBI agent that he had not really taken any notes since 1981 and had no relevant notes to turn over concerning Iran-Contra. He said that if there were notes they might be scribbled on the back of classified briefings, which he made available to the prosecutors. In the fall of 1991, however, a young associate of Walsh's accidentally discovered boxes of handwritten notes among the unclassified section of Weinberger's files at the Library of Congress. Some of them contained references to sensitive military and intelligence secrets, including about 1,700 pages of notes from meetings Weinberger attended from the Iran-Contra period.

The substance of the notes was not harmful to Weinberger. Quite the contrary, they showed that Weinberger had vehemently opposed the concept of arms-for-hostages and did not indicate any knowledge on his part about the North plan of secretly diverting Iranian arms profits to the Contras. They also showed that Weinberger considered the arms sales to Iran to be illegal due to U.S. law preventing sales to Iran, even though they were funneled through Israel at the time.[5]

Weinberger's attorney unsuccessfully tried to convince Walsh that Weinberger had forgotten about the notes because taking them was second nature to him. He even produced a report from a memory expert to substantiate the theory. Walsh did not buy it, though. On June 16, 1992, with the Democratic National Convention and Republican Convention weeks away, Walsh convinced the grand jury to indict Weinberger on five felonies, including obstruction of justice, making false statements to federal investigators, and perjury.[6] So why did the indictment have such a huge potential to hurt President Bush if it was just about Secretary Weinberger allegedly withholding relevant documents?

The answer goes back to an interview Vice President George H. W. Bush had given the influential political journalist David Broder of the *Washington Post* on Iran-Contra. This was the first truly definitive on-the-record interview by the Vice President regarding his involvement or knowledge concerning the controversial arms-for-hostages deal. Bush had largely escaped the crosshairs of both Walsh's prosecutor team and the media up to then over Iran-Contra because he and his aides had insisted that he was neither involved nor knowledgeable. In August 1987, he was more explicit with Broder. He said *both* that he had not been told that the Reagan White House was trading arms with Iran in order to free the hostages held in Lebanon and that he was not aware that Secretary of State George Shultz and Secretary of Defense Caspar Weinberger had objected to that deal. "If I'd have sat there and heard [Secretary of State] George Shultz and Cap [Secretary of Defense Caspar W. Weinberger] express it [opposition] strongly, maybe I would have had a stronger view. But when you don't know something, it's hard to react. . . . *We were not in the loop.*"[7]

Throughout Bush's 1988 presidential campaign, there was an undercurrent of questions and stories about the level of Bush's involvement or knowledge of Iran-Contra, but the phrase "out of the loop" achieved a life of its own. Even though there were many indicators that Bush had attended many meetings on the Iran arms sales, and even though the leaks coming from the Walsh prosecutors and from Secretary of State George Shultz indicated Bush played at least a minor role, the conventional wisdom remained that he stood apart from Iran-Contra. And there was certainly never any indication that he had favored the arms-for-hostages deal; indeed, quite the contrary.

WALSH'S RE-INDICTMENT DECISION: TIMING *AND* CONTENT

That was how things remained after Bush was elected President and as the Iran-Contra investigation and scandal surrounding it seemed to wind down. Even after Walsh got an indictment of Weinberger in June and then again in September, it did not appear that this would have much impact on Bush's re-election campaign. Partisan Democrats could not resist making some attenuated "guilt by association" arguments, but they had little effect.[8]

What made the timing of the re-indictment so politically devastating to Bush and what reflected so badly on the judgment of Walsh and his team, however, was the decision to include a specific reference in the indictment. It referred to the contents of one of the notes Weinberger took during a January 7, 1986 meeting, at which President Reagan allegedly approved the

Iran-for-hostages deal. This note, which Weinberger had taken (he was apparently a prolific note-taker at all meetings), consisted of two unexplained words: "VP favored."

There are three reasons that make Walsh's decision to include these words very difficult to understand. First, including these words in the indictment would automatically prompt the public into believing that Bush had lied in the past. They could be persuaded that he had lied about not being involved or "in the loop" about the arms-for-hostages issue—as well as the fact that he had opposed the concept. The reality is that, for most people, an indictment is seen as a presumption of guilt or as guilt itself and the accusations in the indictment as at least presumptively true.

Second, there was no certainty as to what Weinberger meant by those words. It was at least ambiguous whether Bush had attended the entire meeting on January 7. It was also not clear whether Weinberger knew with certainty that the "VP favored" arms-for-hostages because that is what Bush said at the meeting or whether he was just repeating an erroneous impression.

Finally, and most importantly, the two words were—according to members of the Walsh prosecutor team—*not* a piece of evidence necessary to convict Weinberger.[9] So, if inclusion of those words was not necessary and could have a potential impact on the presidential election, then why did Walsh's prosecutors choose to go forward on October 30? Why was the re-indictment handed down on October 30 rather than a week later, and why were the words "VP favored" included? The reasons appear, in retrospect, nothing short of bizarre.

The person most responsible for the decision was a distinguished and experienced trial attorney with a national reputation, James Brosnahan, who was slated to conduct the Weinberger trial for the prosecution. Brosnahan had asked the prosecutor who had helped prepare the re-indictment, John Barrett, to check out the Justice Department guidelines on the issue of the timing of prosecutorial decisions. He also had Barrett look into the specific question of whether to include the words "VP favored" in the indictment. Barrett reported back that the department guidelines said that such decisions were not supposed to take political considerations into account.

According to one of the young prosecutors who opposed the inclusion of the phrase because of its political ramifications, there was a staff meeting with Brosnahan to discuss the timing and content issue. (According to Woodward in his book *Shadow*, Brosnahan claims not to remember this meeting.) Brosnahan was said to read the Justice Department guidelines to mean that they should proceed with the indictment immediately, including the "VP favored" language, because to do otherwise would violate the guidelines by taking "political" considerations into account and would not be acting "in the ordinary course of business." Then, he reportedly went on to say that if they did not include the "VP favored" language in the indictment, "people might be furious" if Bush won narrowly and they had been deprived of this information.[10]

This view raises serious questions, however. By including the language "VP favored" to avoid a political reaction seems merely to take different political considerations into account. To state the obvious, Justice Department "guidelines" are "guidelines" rather than "mandates," precisely because they allow for discretion and good judgment.

What makes the decision to hand down the indictment on October 30 and to include these words even more baffling is that Walsh himself was never completely engaged in the debate, despite the serious consequences of the decision. One of the younger prosecutors, Ken Parsigian, went to Walsh's deputy, Craig Gillen, to appeal Brosnahan's decision and to ask him to take the matter directly to Walsh. Gillen reportedly agreed that including the two Bush words was a "nuclear bomb."[11] Yet, incomprehensibly, he decided not to take the matter to Walsh because he did not want to second-guess or undercut Brosnahan. Parsigian also decided it was not his role to go directly to Walsh one-on-one, so he dropped the argument.

NOT A "BIG DEAL"

So, what did Lawrence Walsh think when he read a draft of the indictment, saw the words "VP favored," and still had a chance to strike those words? No political innocent, Walsh had served as a prosecutor in the Eisenhower Administration and a District Court judge. Yet, he reportedly told the prosecutor who drafted the indictment, John Barrett, that he did not consider the words "VP favored" a "big deal."[12]

It did not take long to prove how wrong and politically naïve Walsh and Brosnahan's decision proved to be. Front-page headlines and stories in every major newspaper in the country virtually ignored the substance of Weinberger's indictment and focused instead on those two words, "VP favored." The *New York Times* headlined the indictment on its front page as follows: "'86 Weinberger Notes Contradict Bush Account on Iran Arms Deal." The lead paragraph of the story was consistent with the focus on President Bush's credibility: "Newly disclosed notes on a White House meeting in January 1986 contradict President Bush's assertion that he was unaware at the time that arms sold to Iran were part of an arms-for-hostages deal."[13]

The Washington Post headline writers also focused on Bush's credibility: "Bush Stance, Iran-Contra Note at Odds, Weinberger Memo Says President 'Favored' Arms-Hostage Plan." And the *Post*'s lead paragraph similarly emphasized the hit to President Bush's credibility: "A 1986 note written by then-Defense Secretary Caspar W. Weinberger, released yesterday by a federal grand jury, contradicts statements by President Bush that he had not known U.S. arms sales to Iran in 1986 were intended to free U.S. hostages and was unaware of strong opposition to the plan from two Cabinet members."[14] So much for Lawrence Walsh and his assistant prosecutor's judgments regarding what was, or was not, "newsworthy."

BUSH TAKES A POLITICAL HIT

Meanwhile, the formidable Clinton campaign war room led by George Stephanopoulos and James Carville was quick to jump on the indictment and the conclusion that it "proved" that Bush had lied. "It's never pretty to see a defense secretary question a commander in chief, but this is conclusive evidence [sic] once and for all that George Bush was as deep in the loop as you can get on the Iran-Contra," said Stephanopoulos. Vice presidential candidate Al Gore, also unable to resist overplaying the issue, agreed that it was a "true smoking gun."[15]

Lest there be any doubt about the political impact of Walsh's decision, particularly the unnecessary inclusion of the phrase "VP favored," on Bush's presidential campaign, the proof was in the polls. On Friday morning, October 30, before the re-indictment containing the two words was announced, the Bush campaign's internal tracking poll showed the race was 39 percent Bush, 39 percent Clinton, 12 percent Perot (the independent billionaire candidate from Bush's home state of Texas), with an unusually large 10 percent still undecided even on the last weekend before the election. Gallup had published a similar poll a day or so earlier—Clinton 41, Bush 40, too close to call.[16]

On Saturday, October 31, after the overnight media and headlines similar to the *Times* and the *Post* were published all over the country, Bush's tracking polls revealed the severity of the hit Bush had taken. It had gone from a dead heat on Friday to a substantial seven point drop for Bush, with all the defectors apparently going to Perot: Clinton 39 percent, Bush 32 percent, and Perot up to 19 percent, with 10 percent still undecided. Obviously, the story had hurt Bush, but it did not particularly help Bill Clinton at first. The drop-off in the polling from the day before seemed to benefit only Ross Perot—with 10 percent still undecided on this last weekend. The final results on Election Day show that Bush recovered some of those undecideds, but not enough, with Clinton 43 percent, Bush 38 percent, and Perot staying at 19 percent.

Of course, it is impossible to prove that this result would have been different had Walsh waited a week to hand down the indictment or had chosen to delete the phrase "VP favored"—one that his own prosecutors deemed to be legally unnecessary to include in the indictment. But the decision to include that phrase shows poor, and arguably reckless, judgment by Walsh and his team, weighing their own perception that it was not really necessary against its obvious potential to have a significant adverse effect on President Bush in an extremely tight election. For that reason, Walsh's decision—or non-decision—is an appropriate, if tragic, emblem of how the convergence of the media scandal machine and an out-of-control independent counsel who had no accountability for misjudgments has affected the course of American history.[17]

Did anyone in the media hesitate before publishing this story on the Friday before the election? We do not know for sure but judging by the saturated negative coverage President Bush received on this last critical weekend, it does not seem likely. While most news organizations have long-standing policies against breaking any news in the final weekend before a presidential election, some argued that the grand jury re-indictment could not be ignored. Whatever one's view on that debate, it is clear that the media did not put the information regarding the re-indictment in its proper context. That is to say, the phrase "VP favored" was evidence of nothing and that Weinberger may not have had certain knowledge of the Vice President's position when he wrote the notes.

On the other hand, it appears the Bush campaign was not well prepared with a rapid-response crisis management team. Rather than getting all the facts out, the President was so furious at the media and at Walsh that he spent most of the weekend and run-up to Election Day bashing the media. He even told Frank Sesno of CNN that weekend when he was asked for his reaction to the story: "I don't think people believe this. This is the same old charge that's been refuted . . . but it does seem a little weird on a Friday before an election that something like this is elevated." Instead of dealing with the substance of the issue, Bush chose to denounce the press: "I think the press has been the worst it's ever been, ever."[18]

So, President Bush was the latest victim of the scandal machinery gone awry—and we Democrats were overjoyed to watch it happen. In fact, we did whatever we could to exploit it, feed the frenzy, and of course celebrated on election night when Bill Clinton became the nation's forty-second President of the United States. We also did it with no regrets or questions asked about the fairness of Lawrence Walsh's decision (but certainly with some gratitude felt).

Little did we know how soon after our night of celebration that the shoe would be on the other foot when it was our ox being gored by the same scandal machinery and out-of-control independent counsel system. Bill Clinton was certainly the beneficiary of poor judgment by an independent counsel, excessive prosecutorial zeal by his invested deputies, and a media machine ready to go into high gear even in the closing days of an election. Little did he know the price he would pay when that pendulum inevitably swung back in his direction.

BILL CLINTON AND THE
SCANDAL MACHINE IMPLOSION

President Clinton must have recognized the immense political benefit he received from Lawrence Walsh's indictment of Caspar Weinberger during the closing days of the campaign. He also must have been aware of the rise of a more polarized political culture where hate and hyper-partisanship too often replaced civil discourse and disagreement between the parties since the 1960s and especially since Watergate. In addition, he must have seen the indiscriminate, unjust, and unaccountable effects of the independent counsel on the reputations of mostly Republican administration officials during the 1980s. But he could not have anticipated the unparalleled destructive power of the combination of the independent counsel, the telecommunications revolution, the political revolution (and there is no other word to describe the upheaval reflected by the 1994 congressional elections), and, lastly, the ending of the "gentlemen's agreement" already discussed.

The result of these four developments all joining together during the first several years of the Clinton presidency was, for Bill Clinton, the functional equivalent of a political nuclear detonation. It was an implosion of the weapons of mass political destruction that had accumulated over the last quarter of the twentieth century. The rules had changed—drastically. As one noted professor of sociology put it, "the rules of engagement among politicians have broken down."[19]

The Re-Birth of the Independent Counsel

The hypocrisy of both Democrats and Republicans concerning the independent counsel is dramatically displayed by what leaders of both parties said, or left unsaid, when the statute was up for renewal in 1994. As one writer put it, reflecting in hindsight on the wisdom of Justice Scalia's 1988 dissent to upholding the Independent Counsel Act, "It is indeed hard, as Scalia cautioned, to know who deserves the most blame for an investigation that continues to hurtle toward an ever more elusive destination. Is it the Republicans, who now embrace the statute they recently attacked, or the Democrats, who now attack the statute they recently embraced?"[20]

President Bush I strongly resisted the renewal of the Independent Act in 1992, which is one of the key reasons why the act was allowed to expire while he was in office. Ironically, Bush reportedly warned then President-elect Clinton not to support renewal of the act or it would be a decision that would come back to haunt him. Talk about foresight!

When members of Congress began debates in 1993 and 1994 concerning the act's renewal, the Clinton Justice Department actually requested *broader authority and less discretion* for the attorney general over initiating an investigation under the Independent Counsel Act. It is almost as if Democrats remained stuck in their post–Watergate mentality—forgetting that now that *they* controlled the presidency and the Executive Branch, it was Democrats who could be the targets of independent counsels pressured to be appointed by partisan Republicans. On the other hand, because they controlled both houses of Congress after President Clinton's election with seemingly unbeatable margins in the House of Representatives, perhaps they felt no need to worry that the Republicans would win control of either chamber in the foreseeable future.

To their credit, congressional Republicans at first showed some intellectual honesty and consistency on this issue and opposed the two measures reducing the attorney general's discretion to resist pressures to appoint an independent counsel. Many still opposed revival of the law in its entirety, believing in the constitutional problems this unaccountable prosecutorial power raised. No doubt they also remembered the abuses of the independent counsels throughout the 1980s, especially Lawrence Walsh.

When legislation was introduced in 1994 primarily by Senate Democrats to re-enact the Independent Counsel Act, there were two important issues debated. Both would have substantially lowered the standard for triggering an appointment of an independent counsel, that is, would have reduced the discretion of the attorney general to resist political pressures and *not* appoint an independent counsel. The Clinton Justice Department supported extending the trigger for the attorney general's preliminary investigation any time the "subject matter" raised—not just a charge against an individual person—presented a political "conflict" of interest for the Justice Department to investigate.[21] If enacted, it would have required an independent counsel to be appointed every time something like a charge of "campaign finance abuses" was made against the Democratic National Committee and was supported by a modicum of credible evidence. This is due to the fact that, by definition,

"subject matter" involving the Democrats would arguably create at least a political "conflict of interest" for a Democratic attorney general to investigate.

The second issue concerned whether an "actual" conflict of interest had
to be present to proceed or if only an "appearance" of conflict was enough to
appoint an independent counsel. In other words, if a Republican congressman made an accusation of wrongdoing against any member of the administration, based on someone's "specific" and "credible" allegation of
wrongdoing, even if there was no corroboration, this would be enough to initiate the appointment of an independent counsel *based on appearances alone*.

Fortunately for Bill Clinton and the Democrats (and really, in the long
run, for both parties), the Republicans and some wise Democrats joined together to reject these two proposed changes. So, the Independent Counsel
Act was renewed in June 1994 without them—when the Democrats were still
in control of both the White House and the Congress.[22]

The intellectual honesty Republicans showed in opposing these two
provisions disappeared after the November 1994 elections, however, when
the Republicans dramatically took control of *both* the Senate and the
House. Suddenly, the Republicans were new converts to the notion that it
should be *easier* to require an attorney general to appoint an independent
counsel. After all, it was just a year before that they had been complaining
about Lawrence Walsh's abuses, and two years is such a long time. Meanwhile, the Democrats, suffering from similar short-term memory loss and
the intellectual double standard, suddenly saw danger in reducing the attorney general's discretion *not* to appoint an independent counsel. As
Thomas Mann, a political scientist at The Brookings Institution, stated:
"When a Republican was in the White House, Democrats were champions
of the independent counsel law and quick to demand its use at the slightest
provocation."[23] House Republican Bob Barr stated in early 1998: "Most
targets of independent counsels prior to the Clinton Administration were
Republicans. . . . Now it's the Democrats' turn." Congressman Henry
Hyde, who chaired the Republican-controlled Judiciary Committee that
voted to impeach President Clinton, also conceded: "When the Reagan
Administration and the Bush Administration were in the White House,
why, there was great Democratic support for independent counsels. Now
that the shoe is on the other foot, the Republicans are looking more kindly
at this institution."[24] Curiously, given that the media loves to point out the
hypocrisies of politicians on both sides of the aisle, there was little written
at the time noting the ironic, even delicious, flip-flop between the Democrats and Republicans on the independent counsel issue now that the other
guy's ox was being gored.

The Telecommunications Revolution

Bill Clinton can certainly blame himself for priming the Clinton-era scandal machine with his decision to help bring the dead independent counsel law back to life, ignoring the advice of President Bush I. Undoubtedly, he would agree this was a mistake with the wisdom of hindsight. He cannot be blamed, however, for the second development: the telecommunications revolution in cable TV and the Internet.

There is no underestimating the powerful magnifying effect that the *combination* of the 24/7 cable news programs on CNN, CNBC, MSNBC, and, by the end of the 1990s, Fox News, as well as the newly emerging power of the Internet and the bloggers' geometric networking power had on the scandal machine. President Clinton was the first president in U.S. history to face this lethal combination in a political atmosphere already focused on scandal and energized by the misuse of the independent counsel. He faced a continual and unending news cycle where rumors of scandal could break, be hyped up, circle the globe, and be seen as fact even before the information could be proven false.

By the mid- to latter part of the 1990s, Internet search engines began to show their destructive power within the context of scandals. Once misinformation got on the Internet, cyberspace served as an echo chamber where it could live on forever. Quick searches on prior stories would repeat the misreporting, and through this repetition alone they took on the appearance of fact. The story was now "out there," so reporting on it without verification seemed justified. Add to this the increasing power of the conservative radio talk shows and cable news shows, with talking heads engaging in political food fights every night. With so much time to fill, producers turned to the newest Clinton "scandals" to increase ratings or keep viewers turned on and tuned in.

The 1994 Elections: The Political Revolution

President Clinton was the first president in 40 years to see his own party lose control of *both* houses of Congress, switching from that of the president's party to that of the opposition party, during mid-term congressional elections. The last time that happened is when President Dwight Eisenhower, elected in 1952, enjoyed a Republican-controlled Senate and House of Representatives in 1953–54 but saw both chambers dramatically switch back to the Democrats after the November 1954 elections.[25] But the consequences for President

Eisenhower were much different. There was yet no Watergate and its impact on the scandal-searching media; no independent counsel; and no 24/7 cable news cycle or Internet. Most importantly, in the days of Eisenhower, Democrats and Republicans would fight it out on the floor of the Senate and House and then go off to play golf or dine together in the evenings.

Clearly the collapse of the Democratic congressional party in the 1994 elections had much more serious consequences for Bill Clinton because of the new scandal machine phenomena that were slowly converging. Also, in sheer numbers, the change in control was remarkable. The U.S. Senate switched from 57 Democrats and 43 Republicans in 1992 when Bill Clinton was elected to 52 Republicans and 48 Democrats in 1994. The House switched from 267–176–1 controlled by Democrats in 1992 to 230–204–1 controlled by Republicans in 1994—an incredible swing of 117 seats for the Republicans in one congressional election. While the Gingrich-sponsored "Contract with America" received a lot of post-election credit for "nationalizing" the election, polling data and other anecdotal evidence suggest that there was wide disillusionment with the Clinton presidency and the Congressional Democrats. Most likely, the 1994 election would have been a debacle for the Democrats even without Gingrich.

More significant than the "Contract with America," however, was Gingrich's ideological call for a "revolution" to erase the liberal consensus government in place since FDR. His goal was to replace it with a radical anti-government, anti-tax, and religious-right-dominated government, which energized the ideological base of conservative voters drawn to this platform.

Thus, the political upheaval Bill Clinton faced was not just a change in party control of Congress, as faced by President Eisenhower, but a radical change in the political culture in Washington. Everyone on and off the Hill quickly noticed the difference. The days of the Democratic Speaker Tip O'Neill and Republican Minority Leader Bob Michel fighting it out on the floor of the House followed by playing a round of golf together later in the day were clearly over. Mean-spiritedness, talk of revenge by Republican congressional staffers, acts of pettiness, and partisanship now seemed to be the order of the day, especially in the halls of the House.

It is not an exaggeration to say that "hate" was now more the rule rather than the exception in private and public political rhetoric. This was true not just on the right-wing radio talk shows and the nightly cable TV shouting fests, but also in the House office buildings and on the debating floor. Hate was a word frequently uttered—on the record, "on background," and off the record—about Bill and Hillary Clinton. It came from members themselves, their staffers, and by ideologues back home. It became clear to some, and very clear now with the clarity of hindsight, that the agenda had changed radically from defeating a political opponent over ideas to destroying a political opponent because he or she was seen as evil.

One is hard pressed to recall any President of the United States who faced a Congress controlled by the opposition that not only hated him personally and wanted to destroy him politically but that also was willing to use congressional subpoena power and public hearings to engage in a full-scale war against the president. In 1988, then a back bencher, Newt Gingrich himself said that "an aggressive investigator with subpoena powers might find something" if he kept at it long enough. Six years later, just before the 1994 congressional elections, Gingrich said, "Washington just can't imagine a world in which Republicans have subpoena power."[26]

Another major factor in the hyper-partisan Republican-dominated House of Representatives was the evolution over the years of essentially one-party, non-competitive Congressional districts, effectuated by manipulative gerrymandering by *both* Democratic and Republican controlled state legislatures. This meant incumbent House members who had no real general election political worries, but rather, only worried about avoiding primaries from their purist ideologically bases. (This is one reason why House Republicans, despite their net losses in November 1998, persisted in proceeding with impeachment. Their own right-wing party bases strongly favored doing so—and they cared little about overall voter sentiments in their districts.[27]) It was in this context that shortly after the 1994 elections Speaker Newt Gingrich and his ideological, self-styled "revolutionary" leadership team, especially Majority Whip Tom DeLay of Texas, set out to use all the committee investigatory powers of the House to bring down Bill Clinton. For most of the next three years, up to the Lewinsky matter, Republican chairs issued subpoenas to obtain White House and Executive Branch documents, sometimes by unilateral signature by the committee chair without even going through the motions of consulting the Democratic minority.

Democratic Congressman Henry Waxman of California estimated that between the end of 1996 and early 1998 "thousands" of subpoenas were issued in the area of the campaign finance investigations by Republican House committees alone. Federal agencies received hundreds of requests for documents, which, according to Government Accounting Office estimates, cost them over $9 million to comply with. Waxman and his staff also estimated that the total amount spent in 1997 and 1998 by House Republican congressional committees looking for Clinton and DNC campaign finance abuses exceeded $14 million, reaching a total of $23 million of taxpayers' money on this one issue.[28] Arguably, it was the worst partisan abuse of congressional investigatory powers since Senator Joseph McCarthy and the House Un-American Activities Committee during the Red Scare years of the late 1940s and 1950s.

At the time, few Republicans, much less conservative members of the Federalist Society, seemed very concerned about the challenge the Gingrich-led attack on the White House made to the Constitution's separation of powers. (If they were, they at least did not issue many press releases about it.) The Gingrich-led House committees ignored, even ridiculed, claims of executive privilege and attorney-client privilege involving legal advice provided by the White House counsel to the President. When the White House resisted and asserted the constitutional grounds of separation of powers and executive privilege, the subpoenas came to the floor of the House, and specific White House officials, including the White House counsel, were threatened with being held in contempt of Congress.

The Clinton White House tried to resist the abusive subpoenas and partisan demands of the House Republican committees, as they did with the D'Amato Special Whitewater Committee organized in the early months of 1995. (Today's Secretary of Homeland Security, Michael Chertoff, was counsel to Senator Al D'Amato, the Whitewater Committee chairman, and Chertoff's tactics and guilty-until-proven-innocent attitude set the bitter, partisan tone for the televised hearings. This ultimately hurt Senator D'Amato, costing him his Senate seat when he ran for reelection in 1998.) At the end of the day, despite public battling, media frenzy, and questions about their reluctance to hand over documents if there was nothing to hide, the White House surrendered and gave them up.

Today's Bush White House learned some lessons from those days for sure. When Dick Cheney refused to disclose what energy company officials his Energy Task Force met with, he was following in a long tradition of White Houses resisting disclosure of their internal deliberative processes. The Bush White House also successfully resisted turning over e-mails and other documents concerning the days leading up to the Katrina disaster in New Orleans. The double hypocrisy was the number of congressional Republican leaders who defended Cheney's assertions of executive privilege—and the number of Democrats who suddenly forgot the days of defending the Clinton White House claims of Executive Privilege. These were the same Republicans who clamored for documents from the Bill Clinton White House travel office or Hillary Clinton's Health Care task force files. This time the Bush White House actually litigated the issue of whether they had to turn over the energy task force records to the GAO, and won.

The End of the Gentlemen's Agreement

The last change to the political atmosphere that helped take the scandal machine to a new level in the Clinton era was the end of the "gentlemen's agreement." The understanding was that the press would not report on the sexual or private life of a public figure unless there was a clear and direct connection to public performance or public policy. The one incident that most people see as the turning point on this is the Gary Hart–Donna Rice incident that scuttled his campaign to be the Democratic presidential nominee in 1988. In fact, there were two other key moments: the Clarence Thomas Supreme Court confirmation hearings in 1991 and *Newsweek*'s decision to publish an article in the summer of 1997 about an alleged sexual advance made by President Clinton.

The Gary Hart Dare.   Since his first run in 1984, the press had repeated rumors that then-Colorado Senator Gary Hart had a reputation as being a womanizer, despite being married. These rumors, however, remained buried deep inside stories or stayed within the inside-the-Beltway "buzz." After Senator Hart lost the Democratic nomination to Vice President Mondale in 1984, the issue seemed to die down. But it still lurked not too far under the surface.

When Senator Hart emerged as a probable front-runner for the 1988 nomination, the rumors of his dalliances again gained currency, and this time started to leak into the inside pages of the mainstream press and national news magazines. Still, this was not all that different from past instances in U.S. history described in chapter one. The rumors about Maria Reynolds and Hamilton, Sally Hemmings and Jefferson, and Nan Britton and Warren Harding were actually pretty widespread, known by people both in the know and slightly outside the know. Then, after declaring his candidacy for president in April 1987, something very basic changed in media culture, and, as a result, America's political culture would never be the same.

For reasons known only to himself, when asked a question about rumors among the press corps concerning his extracurricular sexual life in an interview with the *New York Times*, Senator Hart responded: "Follow me around. I don't care. I'm serious. If anybody wants to put a tail on me, go ahead, they'll be very bored."[29] One newspaper, the *Miami Herald*, decided to take Hart's dare, and the rest is history. After an anonymous tip, two reporters from the *Herald* observed a young woman named Donna Rice coming out of Hart's Washington, D.C., townhouse late on the evening of May 2, 1987. The *Herald* published the story on May 3.

Hart at first tried to deny the story, and then tried to deny the details of the story. The result was a classic media frenzy that made him unable to address any serious issues. For example, during a 51-minute press conference at Dartmouth College in the critical primary state of New Hampshire, Hart was confronted with what was said to be the most hostile questioning of his career, including whether he had ever committed adultery. He responded: "I don't have to answer that." *Time Magazine* wrote: "There on network TV, *a taboo of sorts was broken*, and the questioning of presidential candidates is likely to grow blunter and more personal."[30] Shortly thereafter, the Hart campaign reportedly heard that the *Washington Post* was working on another story involving another Hart affair. That was it for Hart. On May 7, less than a week after the Donna Rice incident, he decided to withdraw his candidacy.

With the breaking of this story and with Hart's withdrawal, very few people in politics realized that a fundamental paradigm shift had occurred. The *Herald*'s decision to publish this story did represent a significant break with the past. Clearly something fundamental had changed in the long-accepted rules between the media and politicians regarding sex and private behavior. No longer could a politician assume that extramarital activity or sexual affairs would be off-limits.

The paradigm shift occurred even though polls suggested that the American people were not much concerned with the sexual infidelity of politicians. A Gallup poll taken shortly after Hart was forced to withdraw his candidacy showed that nearly two-thirds (64 percent) of those surveyed thought the media treatment of Hart was "unfair." A little over half (53 percent) responded that marital infidelity had little to do with a president's ability to govern.[31] However, the point was not that the American people cared. It was that the media had changed the rules, regardless of whether the American people cared.

It was interesting and significant that the *Herald* changed its rationale for publishing the story as time went on. In the beginning, the reporters and editors involved insisted that the rules had not changed. Gary Hart had issued a public dare, and the arrogance and ultimate hypocrisy of the dare made it fair game in a political campaign. Even if that explanation is not entirely persuasive, it is true that Hart egged on reporters to do exactly what they did. Then, some at the *Herald* felt a need to justify their journalistic decision on a moral level, and this is where the gentlemen's agreement really suffered a fatal blow. In response to the Hart campaign's accusation that the *Herald* had engaged in character assassination and tabloid journalism, the *Herald*'s executive editor, Heath Meriwether, replied that they were justified because Hart's personal activities raised "*questions concerning the candidate's judgment and integrity.*"

These words could have been written by the feminist left or the Christian right—the private lives of politicians had become fair game.[32]

Any of a number of presidents and high public officials would not have survived that standard if applied to sexual indiscretions—such as Alexander Hamilton, Thomas Jefferson, Grover Cleveland, Warren Harding, Franklin Roosevelt, Dwight Eisenhower, Lyndon Johnson, John Kennedy, to name a few. If the *Herald*'s new rationale that extramarital affairs reflected on character and character was a valid media issue in a presidential campaign was correct, then, rightly or wrongly, this radically changed the rules of the game. In any event, most politicians did not focus much on the reasoning offered by the *Herald* editor at the time. Most still saw the Hart incident as an exception to the understanding, and that Hart's dare was just a stupid mistake not to be repeated.

The Clarence Thomas Hearings.   Much as been written about the controversy surrounding Justice Clarence Thomas's confirmation hearings in October 1991, but little of it explores how they represented a further erosion of the gentlemen's agreement.

When President Bush I nominated Clarence Thomas to the U.S. Supreme Court in the summer of 1991, most observers on both sides of the aisle believed that the nomination might prove controversial because of likely opposition by Civil Rights organizations and liberal groups. There were concerns that it would lead to another "Borking" experience with divisive televised confirmation hearings in which personal and character attacks would occur. There were more than enough substantive reasons for liberals to oppose Mr. Thomas on philosophical grounds. During his televised hearings, he seemed reticent to support the right to privacy on which *Roe v. Wade* was based, and he was also ambiguous, at best, on the role of Congress and the federal government to set national social and economic policies despite opposition at the state level of government. No one could have imagined, however, that the Thomas confirmation hearings would deteriorate into an awful nationally televised spectacle of a "he said, she said" exchange of personal charges about Mr. Thomas's alleged sexual harassment in the workplace, habits, preferences, and vocabulary.

A 35-year-old woman named Anita Hill, who had worked for Mr. Thomas at the Education Department and accompanied him as a staffer when he went to serve as the chairman of the Equal Employment Opportunity Commission (EEOC), came forward and made various accusations against Mr. Thomas. They concerned what she said constituted abusive behavior, sexual harassment in the workplace, and worse. Ms. Hill stated in the nationally televised hearings that during work meetings Mr. Thomas would turn to the topic of sex, with "vivid" accounts of pornographic films involving such material as "women having sex with animals" and a pornographic star famous for his endowment, known as "Long Dong Silver." She quoted him as referring to his own endowment as "larger than normal" and then described an incident in which he allegedly questioned her about a pubic hair on a Coke can. Many were horrified that this level of sexual detail would be discussed in a confirmation hearing, much less on national television, and it all became fodder for late-night comedians. What was done under the guise of "fact finding" looked much more like a partisan sneak attack.

When Mr. Thomas was finally allowed to offer his version of events, it was late in the evening. Most of the viewing audience had dropped off by then. His outrage, whether genuine or a cloak for deceit, was justified purely on grounds of fairness. "Enough is enough," he said, virtually shaking with anger. "I am not going to allow myself to be further humiliated in order to be confirmed." Thomas categorically denied all of Hill's accusations and then, rightly or wrongly, played the race card (despite the fact that Anita Hill was African American and that his critics on the Senate Judiciary Committee were mostly pro–Civil Rights liberal Democrats). Thomas denounced the confirmation process as a "high tech lynching . . . for uppity blacks."

This is not an attempt to litigate who was telling the truth—much has been written on the subject.[33] There were only two witnesses to these conversations, Ms. Hill and Mr. Thomas, and as Senator Herbert H. Kohl said at one point, "Clearly, one is lying and one is telling the truth." What is most significant about the Thomas hearings in the context of this book was the decision by the Democrats on the Democratic-controlled Judiciary Committee, chaired by Senator Joseph Biden, to allow Hill's charges of sexual harassment and misconduct to go out over national television before Thomas or his attorneys had a sufficient and complete opportunity to cross-examine Ms. Hill, rebut her charges, or question her credibility.

Many people at the time and to this day wonder whether Senator Biden and the Judiciary Committee Democrats did the right thing in allowing Anita Hill's accusations to be put out on national television before they could be fully investigated. Many conservatives and some liberals concerned about due process and fairness were troubled by their decision to do so. Of course, Senator Biden and the Democrats had an obligation to air publicly serious questions about a Supreme Court nominee who might have been guilty of serious sexual harassment. Senator Biden, however, perhaps with the wisdom of hindsight, might concede that he had a better alternative: He could have required an executive session. He could have had Ms. Hill subpoenaed and subjected to cross-examination under oath by Thomas's attorneys before allowing any of these charges to be made public. Some would have criticized the delay such a process would cause, but it would have been fair. It also would have given Judge Thomas the privacy rights protections that so many liberal Democrats hold as an important value. It would have given Judge Thomas a fair chance to rebut the charges or present evidence concerning some inconsistencies in Ms. Hill's story—*before* it was permitted to go out on national television.

This did not happen, and, at the time, most liberal Democrats cheered Joe Biden's decision. Liberals loved seeing Judge Thomas squirm in embarrassment and instinctively accepted Ms. Hill's version of events. It was a gift that kept on giving, and if it led to Clarence Thomas's rejection by the Senate, which up until then had been seen as hopeless, then all the better. Liberals could get over the fact that Thomas had been treated shabbily, because the larger purpose of saving the Supreme Court from the conservatives made embarrassing Thomas worth it.

In retrospect, what was done to Clarence Thomas during the nationally televised Senate Judiciary Committee hearings—putting aside the question of whether he or Ms. Hill was telling the entire truth (if that's possible)—should have made many civil liberties Democrats cringe. When the same type of public humiliation and fundamental unfairness occurred at the hands of Senator Joseph McCarthy in the 1950s, there was no hesitancy on the part of liberals to speak up, even if the person being accused turned out to be a real communist. Yet the silence was obvious about decisions to broadcast unproven and personally damaging charges on national TV without thorough investigation and due process for the accused.

And, like a time bomb ticking away, this erosion of the gentlemen's agreement further changed the rules governing how and when private sexual conduct becomes a public issue.

Newsweek's *Decision to Publish the Kathleen Willey Story*. On August 11, 1997, *Newsweek* decided to publish a story by Michael Isikoff that related the story of a woman named Kathleen Willey and an alleged incident involving President Clinton. Whatever else might be said about this story and the alleged incident, two facts remain indisputable. First, from the beginning to this day it is a "he said, she said" story and second, whatever happened had nothing to do with national security.

Newsweek and Isikoff considered the story reportable not because of the alleged sexual advance alone. Isikoff later wrote in his best selling book about the Clinton–Lewinsky scandal, *Uncovering Clinton*, that the "rules of this game—a decade after Gary Hart—were still something of a blur."[34] But, according to Isikoff in his book as well as a recent interview by the author, *Newsweek* and Isikoff saw the story in a broader context than just about an alleged sexual advance, welcome or unwelcome. Notably, they saw it as relevant to the merits of the sexual harassment case filed by Paula Jones against President Clinton the year before. And Willey was seen as a newsworthy figure. The United States Supreme Court had recently decided in a unanimous decision to allow Jones' attorneys to compel a sitting president to testify under oath based on the filing of the complaint alone.[35] Willey was the first recipient of a subpoena by the Jones legal team after the Court's decision. The attorney in the Jones case, Joseph Cammarata, believed that if Willey's story checked out, it could be evidence of a "pattern and practice" relevant to Jones' sexual harassment charges and, thus, would be valuable to use during the deposition of the president—and as a way to exert further pressure on him to settle for a high price.

Also, according to Isikoff, *Newsweek* legitimately had to consider the historical context of the renewed attention to sexual harassment in the workplace ever since the Clarence Thomas confirmation hearings. After all, Willey was a volunteer in the White House social office and, if the incident were true, might be able to make her own case of sexual harassment, just as Anita Hill did.

Newsweek, however, still had to wrestle with the fact that the Willey story concerned the private conduct of a president and had no apparent relevance to public policy or national security. Nor was there a Gary Hart–type of dare to justify publication. Even more problematic, Ms. Willey and her lawyer not only refused to confirm the story but also praised the President. Ms. Willey's attorney was quoted by Isikoff in the story as saying that Willey "had and continues to have a good relationship" with President Clinton, although as Isikoff noted in the story, the attorney "declined to comment" on whether the incident had in fact occurred. The President's lawyer also denied that an advance had occurred.

So *Newsweek* was forced to rely on one on-record witness who had only indirect evidence that some advance had occurred. She was a White House secretary named Linda Tripp—someone known to love to gossip and who later decided to betray a young confidante and tape the confidences of a young woman named Monica Lewinsky without telling her. While Tripp seemed to confirm that Willey had had an intimate exchange with the President, by describing her smudged lipstick and other aspects of her appearance, she went on to tell Isikoff that far from the advances being unwelcome, Willey was "flustered, happy, and joyful" after the alleged incident. Thus, *Newsweek* made the decision—and Isikoff describes it in retrospect, during the same interview with the author, as a "difficult" decision and a "close call"—to publish the unsubstantiated allegation of an intimate encounter between the President of the United States and Ms. Willey based entirely on indirect, circumstantial second-hand hearsay (i.e., what Linda Tripp inferred from her contact and observations of Ms. Willey).

In retrospect, it is fair to second-guess *Newsweek*'s sourcing and rationale for publishing this story. Certainly there was a broader context, as Isikoff argues, for the story given its possible relevance to the *Jones* sexual harassment allegations that made it a close call for the magazine and the increased public interest in that issue since the Thomas hearings. But here is the problem with that rationale: The *Newsweek* story itself contradicts the possibility of sexual harassment since, according to its only on-record witness, Linda Tripp, the advance, if it occurred at all, was not unwelcome and therefore there could not be, by definition, a legal case for sexual harassment.

One is left to surmise that a similar shift in rationale that had occurred at the *Herald* after publication of the Gary Hart story was going on then at *Newsweek*. In both cases, the original rationale was superceded by the idea that it was worth publishing the story because it concerned "character and integrity." Isikoff has written and said on various television interviews that the character issue raised by President Clinton's sexual indiscretions did disturb him and might have made the Willey incident newsworthy in and of itself.

In short, the rules of the game had clearly changed (or at least, to use Isikoff's words, had become "something of a blur") from the days of John Kennedy, much less Thomas Jefferson. The Willey story should have signaled to most politicians at the time, especially President Clinton, that if the gentlemen's agreement had not completely been turned upside down, it was at least in the process of being turned sideways.[36]

The interesting question is why, at the time, so few journalists and politicians noticed and appreciated the significant paradigm shift represented by Isikoff's Willey story and took lessons from it to avoid future dangers. Indeed, as we shall see, even after the break-out of the Lewinsky matter, there were still many politicians in Washington—including leaders of the Republican congressional opposition morally condemning President Clinton's conduct with Lewinsky—who still believed that the old rules still applied, and if there were new rules, that they only applied to Bill Clinton.

So, the four elements were in place, and the stage had been set for the truly devastating power of the Clinton scandal implosion.

CHAPTER SEVEN

THE CLINTON "SCANDALS": MUCH SMOKE, LITTLE FIRE

The Republicans must have figured that if they created the appearance of scandal and corruption in the Clinton White House by making enough charges about the "culture of corruption" surrounding Clinton and if they generated enough public hearings that spurred enough headlines, then people would start believing them. As the old slogan goes, "where's there's smoke, there's fire." It turns out they were right—not about the fire but about creating the impression of fire. "Scandal," "corruption," and Clinton were used so often together in the media that they became virtually synonymous.

In 1998 Speaker Newt Gingrich vowed that he would never give another speech without talking about corruption in the Clinton Administration.[1] In 1995, even before Whitewater and other independent counsel investigations of the Clinton Administration heated up, the *Philadelphia Inquirer* described "a Clinton Administration ethics meltdown that is beginning to match that of the Reagan era."[2] In the summer of 1996, California Representative Robert K. Dornan called President Clinton one of "the most corrupt persons to sit in the Oval Office in 209 years."[3]

Living through those times as a Clinton supporter and hearing those words repeated over and over again, not just by Clinton-haters but also from national newspapers with reputations of being more sympathetic to Democrats, like the *New York Times*, the *Los Angeles Times*, and the *Washington Post* was very painful. Reading the words "scandal" so many times in the paper and hearing it repeated so many times on TV would make anyone wonder whether there may be some truth under the bluster.

Just how often were Clinton's name and the word "scandal" linked together? Looking at the *New York Times*, the *Los Angeles Times*, and the *Washington Post* in their coverage of the Clinton "scandals" during the five years

between the first day of the Clinton Administration and the breaking of the
Monica Lewinsky story (i.e., between January 20, 1993, and January 20,
1998—the Lewinsky story broke on January 21, 1998), this is the breakdown
of articles:

New York Times: 1,503
Los Angeles Times: 1,358
Washington Post: 1,699

That means in each year that Clinton was in office until the Lewinsky story,
each paper, on average, mentioned Clinton in association with the word
"scandal" about *six out of seven days of the week, every week, 52 weeks a year.*

When looking at these numbers, though, it is important to remember
two facts. First, *no matter how big a number is, whether ten or ten million, if you
multiply it by zero, you always get zero.* Second, despite eight separate independent counsels who collectively spent over $116 million investigating nine
people in the Clinton Administration—President Clinton, Mrs. Clinton, five
cabinet secretaries, and two senior officials—*there was not a single conviction of
any administration official for conduct that occurred during President Clinton's eight
years in office.*[4]

Given all the publicity about "scandal" in the Clinton years, this second
fact seems so counterintuitive and at odds with overall public and historic impressions that some further explanation and clarification is necessary. First,
this excludes the guilty pleas of two Clinton Administration officials—former
Associate Attorney General Webster Hubbell and former HUD Secretary
Henry Cisneros—because *neither of their pleas involved conduct having anything
to do with their service in the Clinton Administration.* (Hubbell's guilty pleas in
1994 and 1999 were for conduct that had occurred at or relating to his Little
Rock law firm *before* he came to Washington. Cisneros's plea to a misdemeanor in 1999 was for a false statement he had made to an FBI agent during
the vetting of his candidacy *before* he was confirmed as HUD Secretary.) Also
note that the Lewinsky matter is *not* an exception to the statement because *at
no time did President Clinton ever acknowledge a criminal violation*—despite all the
innuendo and various charges made to the contrary by impeachment managers and Republican critics. Independent Counsel Robert W. Ray accepted
an agreement in which President Clinton acknowledged he testified mislead-
ingly and falsely in a civil deposition, paid a civil fine of $25,000 to cover the
legal costs of the Arkansas Bar Association's investigation, and had his law li-
cense suspended for five years.[5] So what about all the other widely publicized
"scandals" of the Clinton Administration? With nearly daily controversies in

the newspapers and over the airwaves, surely there must be more than nothing. What about Whitewater, Travelgate, Filegate, Fostergate, and the rest?

The answer remains, despite what a wide swath of the American people have been led to believe, that there has not been a single finding of criminal conduct by any member of the Clinton Administration for actions during the eight years of the administration. Of course, critics can still insist that any of these "scandals" involved "improper," "inappropriate," or "unethical" conduct. That is a perfectly legitimate opinion, as long as everyone is clear that there is a difference between subjective judgments and objective violations of law as determined under standards of due process.

The most insidious problem with subjective claims is that through repetition, especially repetition in the mainstream media and on editorial pages, they become confused with objective violations. For example, surveys at the time of the 2004 presidential elections showed that two-thirds of the American people mistakenly believed that Saddam Hussein had something to do with the attacks of 9/11. This is a misunderstanding that was encouraged by White House officials who spoke of Hussein and 9/11 together repeatedly during the build-up to the war and its mismanaged aftermath.

To assess the specific damage this avalanche of innuendo wrought during the Clinton years, I will examine the major "scandals" of the 1990s to try and put them into accurate and balanced historical perspective, if that is at all possible. After reading this litany and having a glimpse of what it was like to be in the Clinton White House trying to do the people's business in the midst of this scandal machine frenzy, the reader can judge for himself or herself whether the widely accepted accusations of the so-called scandalridden Clinton Administration are almost entirely, as Shakespeare put it long ago, "full of sound and fury, signifying nothing."

Before proceeding to read the list of so-called Clinton scandals—such as Whitewater, Travel Office, FBI Files, or White House Coffees—ask yourself how much can you really remember about these scandals? The answer—despite countless front-page headlines, thousands of column inches of stories across the nation, breathless TV broadcast network evening news reports, shouting matches and food fights virtually every night on cable TV, hour after hour—is: not much.

WHITEWATER: A BAD INVESTMENT—
NOTHING MORE THAN THAT

The most famous "scandal" of all involving both Clintons is Whitewater. This is what led to the appointment of former D.C. Circuit Court Judge

Kenneth W. Starr as independent counsel and ultimately led to the impeachment of President Clinton on a partisan vote by the House and his acquittal by the Senate four years after Judge Starr's appointment. It is also a notable example of the din and hype of the scandal machine at its worst. Whitewater created so much controversy, cost so much, and split the country so deeply, but, in the final analysis, it was based on so few facts.

Whitewater concerned the Clintons' modest investment in 1978, along with business partners James B. and Susan McDougal, in 220 acres of land along the Whitewater River in Arkansas' Ozark Mountains. James McDougal, a longtime political friend of Bill Clinton's, owned several banks, including the Madison Guaranty Savings & Loan, and had some experience in real estate financings and development. In total, the Clintons invested $203,000 borrowed from a bank. They hoped to repay the loan over the years with money received selling parcels of the land. They formed the Whitewater Development Corporation to do this. From the very beginning, both the Clintons and the McDougals understood that James McDougal would fully control and manage the deal—and at no time was this disputed by the prosecutors. The Clintons were never to be more than passive investors. When McDougal approached the Clintons to make the investment, he promised them he would take care of everything responsibly, and that they would have no role in managing or operating the company. At the time, they had no reason to doubt him.

Ultimately, the Clintons lost about $40,000 on this land deal. McDougal appeared to have misused funds from his bank, Madison Guaranty Savings & Loan, to subsidize part of the debt service of the Whitewater Corporation. Most people forget, however, that McDougal was indicted and acquitted in 1990 of bank fraud charges related to his management of Madison. The Clintons denied any knowledge of misconduct or indirect use of Madison's funds to subsidize Whitewater or any other wrongdoing associated with the venture. No person ever presented credible evidence at any time contradicting that denial. There was a highly suspect claim made by a former local judge and, ultimately, convicted felon (on a charge regarding misuse of Small Business Administration loan funds) named David Hale. Also, shortly before his death, James McDougal, under pressure and threat from Starr's prosecutors, suddenly had a revived memory that Bill Clinton had been more involved in incidents relating to the David Hale/small business/Madison case, but no one but a few reporters (and the Starr prosecutors) who had heavily invested in his credibility took him seriously. And that was really about it as far as the Whitewater story and the Clintons' involvement is concerned. All the rest is smoke.

Mrs. Clinton's Legal Work for Madison: Myths and Facts

There was a sideline controversy involving Mrs. Clinton that further fueled the story. Mrs. Clinton supposedly used her position as the wife of the governor to influence the state regulator to help Madison Guaranty. Jeffrey Gerth of the *New York Times* broke the Whitewater story on March 8, 1992—three weeks after the February 18, 1992, New Hampshire presidential primary as the race for the Democratic nomination was still running hot. The story was published in prominent headlines on page one of the *Times*, which inevitably influences national and TV news coverage. A review of the crucial first two paragraphs shows how little actual wrongdoing was reported in this story, but the innuendo was there for readers to draw negative, false inferences of wrongdoing by the Clintons: "Bill Clinton and his wife were business partners with the owner of a failing savings and loan association that was subject to state regulation early in his tenure as Governor of Arkansas, records show." The classic implicit message was that Governor and Mrs. Clinton were somehow knowledgeable about or involved with James McDougal's "failing savings and loan" and that there was something wrong with Bill Clinton being involved with a "business partner" "subject to state regulation." In the last half-dozen paragraphs of the story, the story suggested that Mrs. Clinton might have done something personally improper. The reference was so subtle, and so buried in the story, that one wonders whether the *Times* debated mentioning it or not. The story ended by referring to the state banking regulator, Beverly Bassett Schaffer, to whom Mrs. Clinton, as a partner in the Rose Firm representing Madison Guaranty in 1985, had "twice applied . . . asking that the savings and loan be allowed to try two novel plans to raise money." Mrs. Schaeffer approved the ideas (one of which involved the sale of special preferred stock) and said: "I never gave anybody special treatment."[6]

The inference that many, if not most, people drew from this passage was that Mrs. Clinton's limited communication with the regulator was somehow improper, i.e., that it was wrong for her to lobby a regulator, regardless of the merits, simply because she was the wife of the Governor. Over a period of time, however, Mrs. Clinton's role became more controversial, and there were more and more attacks on her "improper" activities representing Madison bank.

The undisputed fact remains that the preferred stock and capital-raising proposals briefly supported by Mrs. Clinton in correspondence and brief calls to Ms. Schaffer had merit as a means of raising new equity from outside investors in the troubled bank. And Ms. Schaffer, from day one, insisted that she had reached her opinion on those merits. It is hard to see what Mrs. Clinton had done wrong by advocating these proposals. Of course, spokespersons for the culture of ethics and appearances would argue that it looks bad for the wife of a governor to practice law and then make a call to a state regulator on behalf of her client, regardless of the merits of the matter.

Hiding Something or Not?
Pressures to Appoint Whitewater Special Counsel

Looking back, there were three incidents in 1993 that created excessive, even unbearable, media and political pressure on President Clinton to make the biggest mistake of his presidency, appointing a "special prosecutor" to investigate Whitewater. (The Independent Counsel Act had expired under its five-year automatic sunset provision in 1992, but it was still possible for the attorney general to appoint a "special prosecutor" who had a mandate to conduct an "independent" investigation outside the Justice Department.) Each one made it seem as if the Clintons had something to hide regarding Whitewater even though, at the end of the day, they really did not.

First, there was White House Counsel Bernard Nussbaum's judgment, in the immediate aftermath of Vincent Foster's suicide on July 20, 1993, to prevent FBI agents and Justice Department investigators from searching Foster's office the night of the suicide and from reviewing and retrieving files that might have shed light on his tragic suicide. At the same time, Nussbaum reportedly allowed White House aides to enter the office and search through documents. Nussbaum was (and is) a brilliant senior litigator from one of New York's great law firms; and he had legitimate concerns to review his friend Vincent Foster's personal notes and files to see if any privacy rights needed to be protected, including whether there were any problematical documents relating to Whitewater, the Travel Office and the Clintons. However, he probably should have given greater heed to the issue of appearances, especially in the scandal culture then dominant in Washington. It looked like he was hiding something.

Second, there was the strange decision not to turn over documents requested by the Clinton Administration's own Justice Department. It was strange because the White House was treating the Justice Department as if it were an adversary, rather than part of the same Executive Branch. It was not until President Clinton's own senior political appointees at the Justice Department threatened to issue a subpoena that the White House finally turned over the Foster papers. Again, the resistance unnecessarily created the impression that there was something to hide in the Foster files that might implicate the Clintons in Whitewater wrongdoing. Instead, as it turned out, there were only some personal notes of Mr. Foster, apparently written in the days leading up to his tragic suicide, concerning Foster's anger toward the "blood sport" of the media and innuendo destroying lives in Washington—something both entirely valid and worth being depressed about.

Third, there was the effect of a series of stories in the *Washington Post* in the summer and fall of 1993. These stories reported that an investigator for the Resolution Trust Corporation (RTC), which supervised the failed Madison Guaranty Savings & Loan after its collapse in 1989, had made a "criminal referral" about the Clintons to the U.S. attorney in Little Rock. The U.S. attorney, who had been appointed by President Clinton, had looked into the evidence presented by the RTC investigator and decided there was no criminal case to prosecute or even to investigate. The investigator smelled a cover-up and, somehow, news of her referral, the U.S. attorney's rejection, and intimations of wrongdoing made it into the *Post*'s stories. There were no hard facts to suggest that the U.S. attorney had done anything other than make a decision on the merits, and the facts were not enough to warrant a criminal investigation against the Clintons then or at any time in the future.

However, when word leaked that a senior Treasury Department official had tipped off the White House about the RTC criminal referral, it reinforced the impression that the White House was worried about something related to this case. The leak led to another round of public controversy, accusations of misleading testimony before a congressional committee, and the resignation of that official. Subsequently, the RTC investigator's testimony in public congressional hearings raised serious questions both about the investigator's credibility and apparent political bias against the Clintons.[7] This was way after all the harm had been done, however, by the *Washington Post* stories and the innuendo in them about a politically motivated cover-up.

So, the fires raged higher and higher; the scandal machine was now in full gear. Leaks were feeding headlines, which fed partisan attacks feeding leaks. And politicians, in this case Democrats as well as Republicans, could not resist. Public statements by leaders of both parties called on President Clinton to appoint a "special prosecutor" to "clear the air," air that apparently (in this over-heated scandal machine culture, at least) could not be "cleared" if the investigation were conducted by career professionals at the Justice Department.

The *Washington Post* editorialized on January 5, 1994, just before President Clinton made his fateful decision to yield to the pressure. The editorial's words—and logic, if you can call it that—are emblematic of the post–Watergate legacy of the emphasis on appearances over reality: " . . . [M]urky though most aspects of this case still are, it represents precisely the kind of case in which an independent counsel ought to be appointed. . . . We say that even though—and this should be stressed—*there has been no credible charge in this case that either the president or Mrs. Clinton did anything wrong.*" (Emphasis added.) In other words, in the perverse logic of the post–Watergate appearances culture, the *Post* editorial board managed to turn what is supposed to be the purpose of the criminal justice system on its head. Rather than a prosecutor seeing evidence of a crime and prosecuting it, the appearances culture would say that the very fact there is *no evidence of a crime* but negative appearances (created in large part by the media itself) means an independent counsel is needed to go look for some evidence. Only if he does not find some—with unlimited money, resources, and time—can the "public interest" have confidence that justice has been served. What kind of logic is that?

So, under pressure from leading congressional Democrats, the liberal establishment, and virtually all of his political advisers in the White House (including his top political aide, George Stephanopoulos, but with a vehement and prescient dissent by White House counsel Bernard Nussbaum), President Clinton reluctantly asked Attorney General Janet Reno to appoint an independent counsel to investigate whether any crimes were committed "relating to" the Whitewater Development Corporation and Madison Guaranty Savings & Loan. In mid-January, Attorney General Reno appointed Robert B. Fiske as "special counsel," with public assurances of "independence" and non-interference from the Justice Department.

Fiske immediately announced, in an ominously broad interpretation of the words "relating to," that he would also investigate the Vincent Foster suicide just in case it had anything to do with knowledge of the Clintons' wrongdoing on Whitewater.

The Billing Records Controversy

A final frenzied round of Whitewater coverage followed in early 1996, when Mrs. Clinton's billing records from her work at the Rose Law firm in 1985 were found. They were found on a table in a little attic-type room, called the "book room," located above the White House second-floor residence. The Clintons had used the room to store boxes they had packed up from the governor's mansion. The records were first found by Carolyn Huber, an assistant and friend from Little Rock, in August 1995, among the various unpacked boxes. She said she took them out and left them on a table because she did not realize their significance. They had actually been subpoenaed by both the independent counsel (then Kenneth W. Starr) as well as the Senate Whitewater Committee.

When word went out that the billing files had suddenly been found, and under such suspicious circumstances, the "gotcha" crowd went into overdrive once gain. Cries of "cover-up" and "obstruction of justice" filled the air from Republican partisans, right-wing talk show hosts, and cable TV news shows. The media frenzy was intense.

Four days later, William Safire weighed in with a column attacking the First Lady personally, a new first for Safire (and perhaps in the history of U.S. opinion journalism to date). Even before all the facts were in, Safire connected various unsubstantiated instances in which he claimed that Mrs. Clinton had been untruthful in a column headlined, "Blizzard of Lies." They concerned her involvement in other scandals, from the Travel Office to Whitewater to the billing files, and Safire concluded that all of them showed a pattern: the First Lady was "a congenital liar." (A personal note: I was so infuriated with that Safire column and its lack of factual basis that I spent a week investigating all the facts underlying all of Safire's charges. I wrote an op-ed piece for the *Times* to document that his piece was pure character assassination with no facts to back it up. The *Times* rejected the piece, but instead, my piece was circulated widely by friends of the First Lady. This lead me to be invited to defend Mrs. Clinton, an old friend from Yale Law School, on various TV shows, which ultimately contributed, I am told, to the White House's invitation for me to become in December 1996 "Special Counsel to the President." My primary responsibility was to represent the White House in responding to all questions on "scandals" from the scandal-oriented White House press corps. So, over lunch one day with the one and only William Safire, months after I left the White House in 1998 to return to private life, I was able to tell him that the only good thing I could say about his awful column on Mrs. Clinton was that it triggered a chain of events that led to my opportunity to work for President and Mrs. Clinton in the White House.)

Two weeks later, Independent Counsel Kenneth W. Starr (who succeeded Robert Fiske) decided to add fuel to the already raging fire by subpoenaing the First Lady's personal appearance before the Whitewater Grand Jury at the D.C. Courthouse, rather than avoiding the media circus and allowing her to testify in the White House. Later that month, the First Lady walked calmly out of the grand jury room—the first time the wife of a sitting president had been subpoenaed, much less called to testify before a grand jury. She simply explained that she did not know why or how the billing records had been lost and certainly had no reason to disbelieve her friend Carolyn Huber as to why and how they had been found.

The reason why the "billing records" controversy died down relatively quickly was because the facts spoke louder than the media storm created by Republican politicians and columnists. The billing records, in fact, verified Mrs.

Clinton's original assertion that she had done "minimal" work for Madison Guaranty Savings & Loan. Mrs. Clinton's diary entries showed she had billed *only 60 hours over 15 months,* or about *one hour a week.* Even the most partisan Republican lawyers admitted that for an attorney working on a client matter, it constituted a minimal amount of time. So, what would have been Mrs. Clinton's conceivable motive for covering up these billing records when they vindicated the fact she had done so little for Madison, as she had repeatedly said?

The Replacement of Robert Fiske with Kenneth Starr: Perceptions vs. Perceptions

Before then–"special prosecutor" Robert Fiske had completed his investigation of the Vincent Foster matter, he concluded that it was, in fact, a suicide and provided no evidence of wrongdoing regarding the Clintons and Whitewater. This was contrary to the latest conspiracy theories of the right-wing Clinton-haters, some of whom openly—and recklessly—speculated that Foster had been murdered by the Clintons to keep secret his knowledge of Whitewater wrongdoing. Representative Dan Burton, who chaired the House Committee on Government Reform, even tried to prove that Foster could not have committed suicide, apparently by shooting a pumpkin. The pumpkin did not survive, but no one could figure out what that proved about Vincent Foster's suicide.[8]

After the new Independent Counsel Act took effect on June 30, 1994, the Special Division of the D.C. Circuit Court of Appeals needed to appoint and supervise a Whitewater "independent counsel" since there was no statutory authority to do so. Everyone expected that the panel would simply appoint Robert Fiske, changing his title from "special prosecutor" to "independent counsel." After all, he was a distinguished and highly regarded attorney, and he had already spent eight months investigating both the Whitewater matter as well as the Vincent Foster suicide. He had assembled an impressive team of deputies and young prosecutors to work with and for him.

Instead, to most everyone's utter surprise, the panel announced that it had replaced Fiske with Kenneth W. Starr, a former D.C. Circuit Court judge and Solicitor General under President Reagan. The panel explained that the intent of the new independent counsel statute was to be "protected against *perceptions* of conflict" of interest (there is that word again from the appearances culture). Because Fiske had been appointed by the president's attorney general, Janet Reno, there could allegedly be such a perception of conflict if Fiske was named independent counsel.

The problem was, replacing Fiske with Starr also ignored the appearances of a political conflict of interest surrounding Starr's appointment itself. Judge Sentelle, who headed the judicial panel with authority to appoint Fiske's replacement, had met with the two conservative Republican (and Clinton-hating) senators from North Carolina, Jesse Helms and Lauch Faircloth, just prior to Starr's appointment. Faircloth had been particularly critical of Fiske for failing to endorse his well-publicized view that the Vincent Foster suicide, if it was a suicide, had something to do with the Clintons and wrongdoing in Whitewater. In addition, Senator Helms had been Judge Sentelle's sponsor for his appointment to the bench by President Reagan. Thus, it seemed that Judge Sentelle was more conscious of concerns about "perceptions" regarding Robert Fiske than those regarding his own role and responsibility as a judge on the panel selecting the independent counsel.

Then, there were questions of appearances regarding Starr's prior activities that seemed to align him with the Paula Jones team in their lawsuit against President Clinton. For example, Judge Starr had publicly supported the legal theory advanced by Paula Jones' attorneys that a sitting president was not constitutionally protected from being sued and required to testify while still in office. Starr considered filing a friend-of-the-court brief in the case just before he accepted the independent counsel appointment. Moreover, Jones' lawyers subsequently admitted that during two or three phone calls Starr had provided them with legal advice concerning their Supreme Court argument.[9]

Of course, Starr supporters legitimately argue that he was taking a principled constitutional position, not taking sides in the *Jones* case. In addition, his legal position was vindicated when the Supreme Court held in May 1997 that a sitting president was not immune from compulsory testimony in a suit filed against him during his presidency.[10] Nevertheless, Starr seemed insensitive to involvement with anti-Clinton partisans. In October 1996, while serving as independent counsel, he spoke at a law school run by religious broadcaster Pat Robertson, who had been publicly vicious in his criticism of Clinton.

After his appointment, Judge Starr did not confine his investigation to the "original mandate" issued by the Attorney General and the judicial panel, i.e., to investigate whether any federal laws had been broken by the Clintons and the McDougals in any way "relating to" their "relationships with Madison Guaranty Savings & Loan, Whitewater Development Corporation, or Capital Management Services, Inc."[11] Shortly after accepting the appointment in August 1995, Attorney General Reno requested, and the three-judge panel agreed to, an enlargement of Starr's mandate. It was now to include investigating possible legal violations regarding the firing of Travel Office employees, the Vincent Foster suicide, and the unauthorized access to raw FBI files by certain White House employees. One final addition, the Monica Lewinsky matter, was an enlargement of the original mandate requested first by Kenneth Starr in January 1998 and granted by the attorney general as a separate new investigation.[12]

Outcome of All the Whitewater Criminal and Congressional Investigations

On September 20, 2000, after seven years and over $50 million spent, Robert W. Ray, Kenneth Starr's successor, announced that the Whitewater investigation had closed without bringing any charges of wrongdoing against the Clintons. Rather than leaving it at that, however, Mr. Ray chose to characterize the evidence regarding the Clintons. He said that there was "insufficient evidence" to convict the Clintons "beyond a reasonable doubt." This volunteered opinion bordered on unethical and beyond Ray's legal authority. In fact, as noted earlier, the Independent Counsel Act does *not* require the independent counsel to offer opinions on the evidence. Instead, the independent counsel is supposed to be limited to describing fully and completely his "work, including the disposition of all *cases brought.*"[13]

Most newspaper headlines regarding Ray's final report indicated that Ray had "declined" to "clear" the president—rather than stating that the Clintons were found to have committed no wrongdoing—even though that evidence was insufficient to warrant bringing an indictment. A good example of the headlines caused by Ray's behavior was a lengthy one in the *Los Angeles Times* on September 21, 2000: "The Whitewater Case: Whitewater Case Ends; Clintons Not Charged; Independent Counsel Ray Declines to Clear the President and First Lady but Finds 'Insufficient' Evidence To Criminally Charge Them at the Close of a Six-Year Investigation."[14]

The *Washington Post*, which, it should be recalled, had urged the appointment of a "special prosecutor" for Whitewater from the start, described Mr. Ray's own editorial comments as a "snide parting shot" and "shabby." It further wrote: "Special investigators chosen and instructed by the courts and clothed with the majesty of the law should be required to pronounce the words 'innocent' or 'not guilty,' however painful they may be. . . ."[15] The *Los Angeles Times* wrote: " . . . [I]n writing an end to the complex investigation, Ray pointedly did not exonerate the Clintons, ensuring that their political opponents will continue to tar the couple with allegations of scandal and corruption."[16] Perfect, no indictment, no conviction, just political opponents ready to "tar" with allegations of "scandal and corruption." How emblematic of the ugliness of the guilt-by-innuendo with which the Clintons (and many other victims of the scandal machine in the 1980s and 1990s) were "tarred."

The fact is, Whitewater may be the best example of the statement—much smoke, no fire. Four White house lawyers who brilliantly saw Whitewater as nothing more than a partisan opportunity to attack the Clintons—Harold Ickes, Jane Sherburne, Mark Fabiani, and Chris Lehane—deserve much credit for working to get the facts out (as few as they were), fighting the scandal machine, and, ultimately, winning the media–legal wars on the Whitewater issue.

The Final Whitewater Tally by Independent Counsel Robert W. Ray

Four years later, on March 23, 2004, almost ten years after Kenneth Starr's appointment, Ray issued a press release announcing that the Whitewater/Madison Guaranty Office of Independent Counsel had "terminated all operations." He went on to state that Whitewater prosecutors had won "*sixteen convictions of individuals for violations of criminal laws. . . .*"[17] (Emphasis added.)

But Mr. Ray did not break down the number "16" convictions—which was touted repeatedly by supporters of Judge Starr and his Whitewater prosecutors team, and picked up and repeated uncritically by more than a few reporters, as evidence of Starr's impressive record on the Whitewater investigations. If Mr. Ray had provided more details concerning these 16 convictions, it is likely the record would have seemed less impressive. Mr. Ray could have noted that of the 16 convictions, 9 were, by any reasonable interpretation, "bit" players in the Whitewater controversy. Most of the 9 were guilty pleas to minor offenses. It is likely that none of these 9 would have been prosecuted under ordinary circumstances but for being caught up in the high-profile net of the Whitewater independent counsel.[18]

That leaves seven convictions involving people who became relatively well known as part of the Starr "Whitewater" prosecution. Of these seven, only two directly involved Whitewater—the trial and conviction of James and Susan McDougal on May 28, 1996. Two other convictions (one a guilty plea, the other at the same trial as the McDougals) involved the then-Governor of Arkansas, Jim Guy Tucker—for fraudulent actions having nothing to do with the Clintons or Whitewater. The fifth was a guilty plea to two felonies by David Hale for fraud involving misuse of Small Business Administration funds—again not involving the Clintons or Whitewater. As mentioned earlier, Hale subsequently tried to implicate the Clintons in the SBA fraud case but was unsuccessful, given serious questions about his credibility. The last two convictions involved Webster Hubbell—which will be described in further detail in chapter eight—again for actions having nothing to do with Whitewater or the Clintons.

Ray also omitted from his press release the additional fact that there were seven prosecutions by Kenneth Starr that resulted in acquittals or failed to result in convictions. The most prominent was the trial and acquittal of Herby Branscum, Jr., and Robert M. Hill. These two local bankers were indicted on February 20, 1996, with great fanfare and huge media attention, for 11 felony counts involving alleged illegal use of bank funds to make campaign contributions to the gubernatorial campaign of Bill Clinton. This was the first indictment that directly connected an alleged crime that might have involved Governor Bill Clinton, since the charges were linked to campaign contributions to him. An added dose of media attention concerning this case was Judge Starr's naming Bruce Lindsey, a close friend and Deputy White House Counsel to President Clinton, as an "un-indicted co-conspirator." The coverage of the indictment was so over-the-top that many in the media missed the possibility that naming Lindsey an "un-indicted co-conspirator"—meaning, not enough evidence to indict but to be named with only the innuendo of guilt—was arguably a tawdry tactic by the Starr prosecutors to turn the screws on Lindsey and to show the media how close they were getting to the President. President Clinton himself was forced to testify, through a video deposition, and his deposition was played before the jury during a six-week trial—again, with huge media coverage.

On August 1, 1996, however, in what was then regarded as a huge setback for Judge Starr (and should have been an indication of the poor judgment he and his over-zealous team had exercised, at least in this case), the jury acquitted Branscum and Hill on four counts, and a mistrial was declared on seven counts. A month later, Judge Starr's team seemed to recognize the weakness of their previously heavily publicized case when they he decided not to retry the two.

OTHER PRE-LEWINSKY
"SCANDALS" BESIDES WHITEWATER

Travel Office Firings

The Travel Office "scandal" should have been a non-story from the start. In May 1993, the White House, allegedly influenced by a Clinton friend who had business interests in a travel agency, terminated seven employees in the travel office that arranges the White House press corps' travel plans. Though not a smart move, it was not illegal. The uproar led to multiple congressional inquiries, media rampages, and a White House investigation by senior aide John Podesta, who concluded that the matter had been handled clumsily. At one point, Mrs. Clinton was accused of being primarily behind the firings, but the absence of motivation and her categorical denials weakened the argument that she had done anything wrong.

On November 19, 1998, Kenneth Starr announced he had found no criminal wrongdoing in connection with the Travel Office "scandal," and his successor Robert Ray confirmed the same conclusion in his final report on June 22, 2000. Needless to say, the determination by Judge Starr that there was nothing to it did not receive much media attention—despite all the previous hype of "Travel-gate" for weeks and months on the front pages, before Republican congressional committees, and on right-wing radio talk shows.

Vincent Foster Suicide

Mentioned earlier, the media frenzy this personal tragedy created helped push the Whitewater independent counsel into being. However, this was, purely and simply, a tragic story of a man who suffered from deep depression, who was caricatured and falsely accused in *Wall Street Journal* editorials and took it too much to heart, and who ended up shooting himself after writing a note stating that he could no longer stand the "blood sport" of Washington, D.C.'s politics of personal destruction. The scandal machine was spurred on by hater die-hards on the right and reckless speculation by the likes of Rush Limbaugh and his fellow right-wing talk show hosts. In addition, certain Republican members of Congress kept up a constant barrage of innuendo questioning whether Foster was actually murdered to protect the Clintons, despite the hurt this caused the grieving Foster family.

In late 1994, special counsel Robert Fiske found that the Foster death was, in fact, a suicide. Because so many on the fringes of the right-wing had developed a theory that Foster had been murdered by the Clintons to cover up their crimes, many of these people were furious at Fiske. As discussed, there is some basis for believing that Republican criticism of Fiske over the conclusion he reached on Vincent Foster's suicide was behind the pressure to replace Fiske with Kenneth Starr in August 1994. However, on July 15, 1997, independent counsel Kenneth Starr—no pawn of the vast left-wing conspiracy, that is for sure—agreed with the earlier conclusions reached by Mr. Fiske and declared that Foster had committed suicide. The right-wing conspiracy theorists, including those who shot pumpkins to prove their theories, did not accuse Judge Starr of being a member of the vast left-wing conspiracy for his conclusions that agreed with Robert Fiske's three years before.

FBI Files

The story of a Clinton staffer in possession of FBI "raw" (i.e., unsubstantiated) background reports that broke on May 26, 1996, is emblematic of the excesses of the scandal media corps covering the Clinton White House. The White House acknowledged that during the first four months of the new administration a lower-level White House staffer in the White House Personnel office, had somehow inadvertently obtained hundreds of raw FBI background reports. The reports were not only on Democrats under consideration for appointment but also on some prominent Republicans from the Reagan and Bush Administrations. Raw FBI files contain lots of unverified and false anecdotal information. Why or how the FBI allowed these files to go to the White House at the request of a mid-level White House staffer is a mystery to this day. Certainly then FBI Director Louis Freeh never took responsibility. It was embarrassing, but, from all accounts, it was nothing more than a major screw-up on someone's part.

Predictably, the scandal machine went into overdrive on this issue. The White House press corps clamored for answers. Republican congressional leaders held hearings and called for the appointment of an independent counsel. Cable TV talk show hosts had guests shouting at each other. Right-wing radio talk show hosts spoke darkly of a Clinton-orchestrated smear campaign against Republican senior statesmen. Once again, the Attorney General found herself forced to yield to naked political demagoguery by Republican congressional leaders and requested the enlargement of Kenneth Starr's jurisdiction to investigate what was quickly referred to by William Safire, and then everyone else, as "Filegate." On November 19, 1998, Kenneth Starr announced that no legal violations were found, and Robert Ray confirmed the same conclusion almost two years later. (But Safire never apologized for over-hyping the episode as another "-gate.")

1996 Democratic Campaign Finance "Violations"

The "campaign finance scandal" charges began to build in the summer and fall of 1996. There were complaints from the Republican presidential candidate Bob Dole and others that the Clinton campaign was running "informational ads" funded by corporate (or unlimited) "soft" money.

This was seen as a loophole around, if not a violation of, the limitation on individual contributions (so-called hard money) imposed by the campaign finance laws.

That Bob Dole admitted to an audience of ABC television executives that he and the Republican National Committee had also run the same "informational" ads using soft money seemed to go unnoticed. The rumors were further energized by leaks and a statement from FBI Director Louis Freeh that these "soft money" expenditures should lead to the appointment of an independent counsel. Freeh, however, never did get around to explaining the Dole comment or the fact that the law and the Federal Election Commission regulations did not ban such soft money expenditures.

By the fall of 1996, the issue expanded to include rumors about Asian friends of Clinton supporters, money from Chinese government companies, and a Clinton meeting with an Indonesian businessman who had family in Arkansas. One story reported that Vice President Gore had attended a function at a Buddhist temple in California that was organized as a fundraiser by Democratic National Committee officials. Apart from the tackiness of holding a fundraiser at a Buddhist temple, the brouhaha seemed typically overwrought. It ended up becoming an emblematic story that lived on and on, carrying all the way through to the Vice President's presidential campaign in 2000. One thing that gave the Buddhist Temple story additional journalistic "legs" was the unlucky fact that there was video coverage showing the Vice President schmoozing among the robed Buddhist monks in their temple, which ended up as a fund-raising event.

MEDIA HYPE AND CONGRESSIONAL INVESTIGATIONS

Shortly after the 1996 campaign ended and Clinton had won by a substantial majority, Republican committee chairs in the House and the Senate issued broad subpoenas for virtually every document at the DNC and at the White House. The Clinton campaign and DNC had generally refused to answer questions about the campaign finance issue during the presidential campaign, and this strategy simply led to increased pressures to break new stories and dig up information. By January 1997, the White House press corps was in an investigative journalism frenzy. Everyone in both print and broadcast was working to scoop everyone else on the latest DNC fundraiser engaging in tacky campaign fundraising techniques that arguably were common to both parties. The *Washington Post*, for example, organized a special investigative team of reporters singularly dedicated to "finding another Watergate story"—as the head of the team told me shortly after my arrival at the White House in December 1996. I had joined the administration as "Special Counsel" in charge of responding to the press inquiries on the campaign finance "scandal" and any other scandal that might break out.

All this negative scandal mongering of course led to more leaks, more headlines, more calls for independent counsel, and more stories. Then came the unsurprising announcements by Republican Senator Fred Thompson, chair of the Senate Committee on Governmental Affairs, and Representative Dan Burton, chair of the House Committee on Government Reform, that they would hire staff, issue new subpoenas for documents, and conduct what they expected would be nationally televised hearings on the Clinton "campaign finance scandal" issue by mid-summer 1997.

There was a scent of another Watergate in the Washington air that year. The excitement was apparent in the Republican cloakrooms, in the newsrooms of the nation's leading newspapers, and among producers and hosts of TV and radio news shows. All saw huge opportunities for finding serious campaign finance legal violations and, incidentally, other benefits, such as ratings increases and higher revenues on the back of new "scandals" breaking virtually every day and an almost endless series of unforgettable characters that had raised or contributed huge sums to the Democratic National Committee. Many of the more controversial campaign finance stories seemed to suggest possible criminal conduct that, if substantiated and proven, could have been devastating for President Clinton's presidency. Three of these appeared, on the surface, to hold the most danger for Clinton, thus producing some of the more strident and high-decibel headlines. These stories form the core of what are described generically as the "Clinton campaign finance scandal" that dominated the news virtually every day throughout 1997.

John Huang. The first of these concerned John Huang, a Chinese American who had lived in Little Rock, Arkansas, and who raised money as a DNC finance committee official during 1995 and 1996. It turned out that Secret Service entry-exit records that track White House visitors showed that Huang had visited the White House "hundreds" of times. The headlines and stories about all of those visits generated even more negative energy for the scandal machine, as if more was needed. Only months later were White House lawyers belatedly allowed to disclose to the press that virtually all of Huang's visits were at White House social receptions where there were hundreds, and sometimes thousands, of people also in attendance.

At one point there were anonymously sourced stories, of course, that Huang was "under investigation" for "possible links" (a favorite innuendo of the press corps) to the Chinese government. Stories suggested, but never demonstrated, that Huang was a conduit for feeding Chinese government money into Democratic campaigns. Some said that he might even be a Chinese government spy.

Rumors had it that the FBI, allegedly encouraged by its director Louis Freeh, a former Republican, had shared information about a Chinese government "plan" to funnel money into U.S. political campaigns with Senator Thompson's committee investigating campaign finance abuses. Senator Thompson chose to rely on this rumor and focused on that charge at the outset of his nationally televised hearings in June 1997. As things turned out, the hearings turned up nothing to support the charges that Huang, or any other Democratic fund-raiser, was involved as a conduit for the Chinese government. The Thompson hearings were thus deemed a failure by much of the conventional wisdom within the Beltway—some blaming the FBI hype and leaks more than Senator Thompson for the failure.

The Lincoln Bedroom Overnights. One night I clearly understood just how big of a problem the Lincoln Bedroom story had become. My own mother, who loved President Clinton and worked hard in Miami Beach for both of his presidential campaigns, called me to complain, "How come President Clinton lets rich people who give money to the campaign sleep overnight in the Lincoln Bedroom, and not me?"

The story was that the Clintons had invited, among many other social, political, and family friends, certain DNC-sponsored donors to stay overnight in the Lincoln Bedroom and that these donors had given substantially to the DNC before and after their overnights at the White House. The news broke after a memo was found in White House Deputy Cheif of Staff Harold Ickes' White House files. It contained the President's handwritten note to his personal secretary—"Yes pursue all and promptly—and get other names at $100,000 or more—$50,000 or more"—referring to a list of big DNC donors suggested for Lincoln Bedroom overnights.[19]

Those of us at the White House working with the press corps knew this would be a nasty story on appearances alone. But, you would think, from the huge front-page print coverage and TV network news coverage—including an entire edition of *Nightline* devoted to this topic alone—that something bordering on an impeachable offense had occurred. Even after putting out documented evidence that President George H. W. Bush had invited plenty of big campaign donors to the Republican Party stay overnight at the White

House and that President Reagan had actually pitched for money during a White House gathering of fat cats called the Republican Eagles, the story raged on.

White House Coffees. The fact that the Democratic National Committee used the White House, with a Democrat as President, as a fundraising vehicle in 1995 and 1996 should not have been a particularly controversial or shocking story. Indeed, White House Press Secretary Mike McCurry could have issued a press release that this was being done (that is, had the White House political operation or lawyers told him about the fundraising aspects of these "coffees"—which it did not). When the inevitable cries came from Republicans that the Clintons were misusing the "people's house" for fundraising purposes, McCurry could have trotted out the number of instances when Presidents Reagan and Bush had invited Republican donors for just that purpose. Indeed, the Clinton lawyers working this story found a videotape of President Reagan pitching the big donor "Republican Eagles" for money during a pep talk in the East Room of the White House.

Instead, the dozens of White House morning coffees were kept secret, even from McCurry. Each meeting included about 20 to 25 potential big Democratic donors each having a fundraising target of $50,000 (to be raised before or after but not at the White House event). When videotapes were discovered of the various coffee appearances by President Clinton, the media storm focused on two controversies. The first was the "propriety" of holding "fund-raising events" at the White House. The second was the fact that the materials relating to the coffees were accidentally discovered in the White House basement by a White House lawyer, despite having been subpoenaed by various congressional committees.

The hunt was on, and the scandal machine once again went into overdrive. When there was a "viewing" of the dozens of boring videotape excerpts of President Clinton circulating and shaking hands at the coffees, the Executive Office amphitheater was standing room only. "This is better attended than a showing of *Debbie Does Dallas* [a classic pornography film of the 1970s]," quipped one White House lawyer.

The important thing to remember, after all the stories written and produced about these "scandals," is the virtual lack of wrongdoing. There were no indictments or convictions involving anyone from the Clinton campaign or any senior officials from the DNC concerning any campaign finance violations. A few minor fundraisers, however, pled guilty to minor campaign finance violations.

The Bogus "Scandals" of Clinton Cabinet Investigations

When President Clinton and the Democratic Congress reenacted the independent counsel statute in 1994, it was Democrats who mainly tried to expand the jurisdiction of the attorney general to appoint an independent counsel. These efforts were defeated, ironically, by Republicans who were still angered about the misuse of the statute by Lawrence Walsh.

However, once the act was renewed, the roles reversed and some partisan Republicans playing "gotcha" chose to pressure the attorney general to appoint independent counsels to investigate senior administration officials. Unfortunately, under the political circumstances, she could not resist the pressures. Even though in most instances the allegations of wrongdoing were insubstantial or from highly questionable sources, Attorney General Reno appointed six independent counsels to investigate five Clinton Cabinet members and one senior official. The outcomes proved beyond a doubt how senseless and unnecessary these investigations were. They caused the individuals who were the targets and their families much suffering.

The first of those investigated during the five-year period from 1994 to 1999 was Secretary of Agriculture Mike Espy. He was accused of accepting football tickets and other gratuities from people who had business before the Agriculture department. Donald Smaltz was appointed as independent counsel on September 9, 1994. In the end, Espy was acquitted. HUD Secretary Henry Cisneros, was next, accused of making false statements to the FBI during his background interviews prior to his confirmation as secretary. David Barrett was appointed on May 24, 1995. Cisneros ended up pleading guilty to a misdemeanor and paid a $10,000 fine. Commerce Secretary Ronald H. Brown was accused of improper business relationships, so Daniel Pearson was appointed on July 6, 1995. The investigation was subsequently dropped upon Secretary Brown's tragic death in a plane crash over Croatia in April 1996. The fourth cabinet member investigated was Interior Secretary Bruce Babbitt, for supposedly making false statements during congressional testimony about contacts with a lobbyist. Carol Elder Bruce was appointed on March 19, 1998, but no charges were ever brought forward. Labor Secretary of Labor Alexis Herman was accused of improper involvement with a lobbyist, so Ralph I. Lancaster was appointed on May 26, 1998. Again, like Babbitt, no charges were brought. Finally, the late Eli Segal, the CEO of Americorps, was accused of not having disclosed a conflict of interest during background vetting. Curtis Emery von Kann, appointed November 27, 1996, did not bring charges against him, either. The more abusive of these investigations will be further explained in chapter eight.

It is hard to recall (much less appreciate) the personal impact and pain to the individuals and their families of the blaring headlines these investigations created. Each of these senior officials faced accusations in the national media of criminal conduct and an independent counsel with unlimited time and money seeking to bring charges against them and put them in jail. Did these investigations serve a higher good? It seems very unlikely. In the end, each of the individuals mentioned above were victims of the scandal culture stuck in high gear—payback time for Republicans in the 1990s for the misuse of the independent counsel by Democrats in the 1980s against Reagan and Bush Administration officials. It is a sorry record and one that should not be repeated, regardless of which party wields power.

Summary of the Pre-Lewinsky Clinton "Scandals"

Clearly, there was not much substance to all of these so-called scandals. That being said, politics is ultimately about the public trust—and the standard for conduct in politics must be higher than "not convicted of a crime." Ethics standards may be elusive, and reporters and ethicists may overuse subjective terms like "inappropriate" or "improper." But that does not mean politicians should not consider such words, as fuzzy as the standards are, when they decide how to conduct themselves. And had there been more concern about appearances in the Clinton White House, especially in the early years, it is possible many of the pseudo-scandals, such as the Travel Office, FBI files, Lincoln Bedroom controversies, and some of the campaign finance unseemly practices, could have been avoided.

THE MONICA LEWINSKY SCANDAL

And so, after a nearly endless stream of headlines, inquiries, and investigations throughout his two terms, Clinton finally faced the full fury of the scandal machine over a regretful personal indiscretion. One can hardly be critical, or surprised, that the media jumped on the Lewinsky story. It was, after all, probably the biggest story, from a sheer journalism standpoint, involving a President of the United States since Watergate. The Lewinsky matter represented the final simultaneous nuclear-like implosion of all the elements and negative energy of the scandal machine that had evolved since the 1960s and

Watergate: the scandal-hungry press corps; an independent counsel who op-
erated within *both* the criminal system and the political process; hyper-partisanship; the telecommunications revolution; and, most sadly from President
Clinton's vantage point, the final chapter in the termination of the "gentleman's agreement," leaving the mainstream media free to report not only
about the private relationship of a sitting president but the salacious details as
well.

Of course, no one forced President Clinton to have the relationship with
Ms. Lewinsky or to put the country through eight months of denial until he
told the truth during his grand jury testimony in August 1998. Mr. Clinton
was his own harshest critic in acknowledging his wrongful private behavior
and the harm he had done to his family and the nation. Worst of all, probably
from President Clinton's perspective as well, was his nationally televised, fin-
ger-pointing denial of the relationship on January 22, 1998—the second day
after the scandal story broke. That denial was false and a serious breach of
trust that any president owes to the American people. The videotape of that
denial, played and replayed seemingly ad infinitum, will tragically never be
deleted and is probably the most painful moment of his presidency.

There were many sincere Republican House and Senate members, including Republican House impeachment managers, who sincerely believed
that false sworn testimony by a president was an impeachable offense, regardless of the circumstances. That being said, when historians consider the
Lewinsky scandal, they hopefully will put it into the context of the role the
virulent scandal machinery played in the impeachment process in two key
phases: first, in creating the trap President Clinton walked into in the *Jones*
case leading to his false testimony; and second, in energizing the hyper-
partisanship to even a higher level, if that was possible, which dominated the
House Republican impeachment process.

To start with, it has long since been documented that there was, in
fact, an extensive network of ultra-conservative, Clinton-hating lawyers
and activists (subsequently dubbed the "elves") who served as links between the Paula Jones attorneys, Linda Tripp (who surreptitiously and
treacherously taped her "friend" Monica Lewinsky), and the Starr prosecutor team. All the strands of this network came together late on the
evening of September 16, 1998. Earlier in the day the Starr prosecutors
had wired and supervised Linda Tripp as she induced Ms. Lewinsky to
speak further about her relationship with Mr. Clinton during a lunch at a
Virginia hotel. Then late on the evening of the 16th, it was an FBI agent
working for the Starr prosecutors who drove Ms. Tripp to her home in

Columbia, Maryland. There she met with the Jones legal team. She briefed them on the Lewinsky relationship with President Clinton. Thus, she prepared them to set up Mr. Clinton to deny that relationship under oath the next day, which both the Jones attorneys and the Starr prosecutors fully expected him to do. And of course they were right.[20]

In light of the importance attached to the Clinton deposition in the *Jones* case in leading to the historic impeachment crisis, two facts about that deposition and his testimony must be understood by future historians trying to put all this in perspective. First, the fact that Mr. Clinton might have had a relationship with Ms. Lewinsky, even if true, was found by the presiding federal judge on January 29, 1998, less than two weeks after the deposition, as "not essential to the core issues" of the *Jones* case.[21] Then, on April 1, 1998, the judge held that the Jones' allegations were so meritless as a matter of law that the entire case should be thrown out without the need for a trial.[22]

The second phase of the scandal machine's critical role in leading to President Clinton's impeachment was the hyper-partisanship by certain House Republicans that dominated the House impeachment process. This was the case despite the fact that there were many sincere Republican conservatives and moderates who genuinely believed impeachment was justified, as noted earlier. The Republicans allowed the scope of the investigation to go well beyond the immediate issues involving alleged perjury and obstruction. They allowed Judge Starr to testify and, in effect, advocate his position in favor of impeachment—the ultimate manifestation of the fatal combination of the criminal and political processes.

Then came the November 1998 elections. The Democrats made surprising gains in both houses of Congress. This was seen as reflecting most Americans' general disgust with the impeachment process. Nevertheless, Republican House leadership insisted on moving ahead with impeachment after the election, even though that meant allowing "lame duck" partisan members to vote for impeachment. Those insisting on pursuing an impeachment vote were unconcerned about general voter sentiment. (Another manifestation of gerrymandered congressional districts, which has allowed members to pander to a narrow partisan base without the need to temper their stance to win over a more moderate electorate.[23])

Historians might also debate whether President Clinton missed at least two opportunities to avoid impeachment—opportunities that are easier to see with the wisdom of hindsight. The first opportunity, which is highly debatable, is whether he would have been better off confessing his relationship with Ms. Lewinsky early on rather than waiting eight months until the federal grand jury testimony in August. Surveys taken shortly after the story broke showed that the American people did not think the President should have to resign, even if he had a sexual relationship with an intern, by a two-to-one margin; independents felt the same way.[24] Clinton's former adviser, Dick Morris, had offered advice to Clinton (based on a quick overnight poll) shortly after the Lewinsky story broke that he could not afford to admit to the relationship with Lewinsky. The subsequent polling data at least casts some doubt on the validity of this overnight data.

The second real opportunity to avoid impeachment occurred at the very moment of victory after the November 4, 1998, congressional elections. Had President Clinton chosen that moment—a moment of maximum strength—to reach out to Judiciary Chair Henry Hyde and other House Republican leaders and offer to accept a toughly worded joint congressional censure resolution, he might have avoided impeachment. This is certainly the view of many Republicans I have talked to, including at least two of the key House Republican impeachment managers. Such a tough resolution would likely have been passed by an overwhelming bipartisan majority in both houses. President Clinton would have signed the resolution himself, thus satisfying those who wanted him to take public responsibility and would have set a historical precedent that his conduct was unacceptable for future presidents.

When Mr. Clinton's supporters offered a censure resolution on the eve of the impeachment vote, it was too late. It was ignored by House Republican leaders. Led by majority whip Tom DeLay, they would not even allow their Republican colleagues the right to an up-or-down vote on such a resolution. The obvious reason was that it would have passed overwhelmingly.

Instead, the Republicans plowed ahead knowing that the vote in the House would end up almost entirely partisan. The situation seemed more reminiscent of the partisan House vote to impeach President Andrew Johnson in 1868. Also notable was the fact that the Republican House managers had such a weak legal and political case that they could not convince a majority of the Senate controlled by Republicans 55–45 to support either of the two impeachment counts. Voting against one or the other impeachment counts were moderate and conservative Republican Senators Olympia Snow and Susan Collins of Maine; Arlen Specter of Pennsylvania, a former district attorney; Fred Thompson of Tennessee, a former criminal-defense attorney and Watergate committee minority counsel; and Slade Gorton of Washington state, a former state attorney general.

Finally, there is one crucial event in the dominoes that led to the Clinton impeachment that had nothing to do with the scandal machine: the decision by the Supreme Court, on May 27, 1997, that allowed a president to be compelled to testify in a civil case filed against him while he was still in office.[25] That decision was remarkably unanimous (with Justice Breyer issuing a more narrow concurring opinion). It must now be regarded as one of the most ill-advised decisions in the Court's history. The Court reached the constitutionally defensible conclusion that there was no absolute immunity preventing a president from being sued while in office based on the separation of powers doctrine.[26] But the Supreme Court did not have to address this issue under the separation of powers doctrine. It could have reached a factual conclusion that such testimony by a sitting president could be deferred until he left office without prejudicing the plaintiff. In this case, the court could have reached such a conclusion or remanded to a lower court to make a finding on the prejudicial effect of a two-year delay to taking President Clinton's testimony.

Instead, the court concluded, in words that must be embarrassing when read today by at least some of the Justices:

> "As for the case at hand, if properly managed by the District Court, it appears to us *highly unlikely to occupy any substantial amount of petitioner's time.*"[27]

Obviously, that turned out to be an incorrect assumption, to say the least.

One can only hope that the court's prediction that its decision would not likely lead to a "deluge of such litigation" against future presidents[28] proves more accurate than its prediction that the *Jones* case would not occupy a "substantial amount" of President Clinton's time.

It is certainly possible to view the Lewinsky episode as unique and not comparable to the prior abuses of the scandal machinery seen in the previous two decades. One conclusion cannot be avoided, however. When all was said and done, there was no criminal sanctions for his conduct in the Lewinsky matter and the rest of the so-called Clinton scandals were mostly smoke and little fire. Appendix I at the end of this chapter illustrates how much media smoke there was about all the so-called Clinton Scandals—and demonstrates once again the mathematical truism that no matter how big the number, if you multiply it by zero, you still get zero!

Regardless of one's personal views about Bill Clinton, the fact remains that during his two terms as president, he turned deficits into surpluses, provided record years of consecutive national prosperity, repositioned the Democratic Party to be competitive in national elections for the first time in more than 25 years, and left his second term, despite all the Lewinsky problems, with one of the highest approval ratings for a second-term president since modern day polling was invented a half-century ago. Those are the stubborn facts of Bill Clinton's two terms as president that historians must ultimately view as the big picture.

SUMMARY OF GOOGLE "HITS" AND NEWS STORIES REGARDING WHITEWATER AND VARIOUS CLINTON SCANDALS

"Scandal" Topic	Google Hits	NY Times articles mentioning	WashPost articles mentioning	LA Times articles mentioning
General				
"Clintons"/"Scandal" (Bill/Hillary/White House) (1993–98/Pre-Lewinsky)	8,390,000	1,503	1,358	1,699
Specific "Scandals" By Name				
1. Clintons/Whitewater (1993–01)	1,490,000	2,920	3,175	1,895
2. Non-Whitewater (1993–01)				
• Travel Office	597,000	431	312	553
• Vincent Foster/suicide	72,000	218	262	445
• FBI Files	964	57	46	107
3. Campaign finance "Scandals" (1993–01)				
• John Huang (Clinton fundraiser)	90,100	386	287	339
• Lincoln Bedroom Sleepovers	98,700	204	176	250
• White House Coffees	62,800	671	542	1,065
4. Lewinsky	1,990,000	4,428	2,472	3,322

DEATH OF THE
INDEPENDENT COUNSEL
STATUTE—AND GOOD RIDDANCE

O n midnight, June 30, 1999, the Independent Statute Act was allowed to expire. As CNN reported: "Blame Richard Nixon, if you like, for the birth of the independent counsel. Blame Ken Starr, if you choose, for its death. From Watergate to Whitewater, the Independent Counsel Act has prompted 21 [*sic*] investigations and 21 years of controversy."[1]

In fact there were 20 (not 21) separate investigations over 21 years involving 25 separate individual independent counsels between 1978, when the independent counsel was first created (called "special counsel" then), and 1999, when the statute was not renewed.[2] Collectively, these 25 independent counsels spent more than $175 million—more than 40 percent, estimated at between $70–$80 million, was spent by Kenneth W. Starr and Robert W. Ray alone.[3] If you add in the six-year Lawrence Walsh Iran-Contra probe of $40 million, the $23.7 million spent by Donald Smaltz on the probe of former Agriculture Secretary Mike Espy, and the $21 million, 11-year probe of former HUD Secretary Henry Cisneros by independent counsel David M. Barrett, nearly 80 percent of all the money spent in 21 years was for just these four probes.

For all that money, time, and effort, as well as all the legal, political, and constitutional havoc wrought, it is surprising how little these investigations tangibly produced. It is an understatement to suggest that these 25 independent counsels, who spent over $175 million of taxpayers' money over more than two decades, had, at best, a thin record of convictions of serious crimes. On at least 14 occasions, investigations by independent counsels were dropped without filing any charges. Three of the high-profile convictions were reversed after trial. Only one of the many individuals among all who were prosecuted, convicted after trial, or pled guilty over Iran-Contra–related offenses ever went to jail.[4] Never has so much money, spent by so many prosecutors, with so much unlimited time and unlimited budgets, produced so little.[5]

THE WORST OF THE INDEPENDENT
COUNSELS FROM THE 1990s

As we have seen in chapter four, certain independent counsels and the investigations they conducted clearly stand out to earn the label of being the worst for the 1980s. The 1990s had equally notorious independent counsels appointed during that decade. It was a close competition, but three independent counsels stand out above all the rest for exercising the worst judgment and abuse of their prosecutorial powers.

The Outrageous Donald Smaltz

First, there was Donald Smaltz. There is simply no word other than outrageous to describe his conduct, especially after his victim, former Clinton Secretary of Agriculture Mike Espy, was acquitted. He was appointed as independent counsel as a result of pressure, largely from Republicans in Congress, to investigate Espy. The Agriculture Secretary had allegedly had accepted various gifts or "gratuities" (including sports tickets, meals, and travel) from individuals or companies that were, directly or indirectly, subject to Agriculture Department regulation.

Smaltz ended up investigating Espy for more than four years and spent $23.7 million.[6] He managed to obtain a *38-count* indictment of Mr. Espy, though eight were dismissed by the judge before trial (reminding any objective observer of the old saying, "a prosecutor can indict a ham sandwich if he wants to"). The case Smaltz put on regarding each of the 30 counts was so ludicrously weak that Espy decided to put on no defense at all. Smaltz put on an extensive case presenting *70* witnesses over seven weeks, while Espy and his lawyer decided to tell the jury what they thought of Smaltz's case by *putting on no case at all*. They rested as soon as Smaltz finished his case. After deliberating for less than eight hours, the jury acquitted Espy on all 30 counts.

Smaltz then made a public statement that the indictment itself had social value, even if the defendant was acquitted. "The actual indictment of a public official may in fact be as great a deterrent as a conviction of that official," he was quoted as saying. "The *appearance of impropriety* can be as damning as bribery is to public confidence."[7]

If that is not incredible enough, Charles Lewis, a leader of the Center for Public Integrity, to this day one of the best reform-oriented organizations of the post–Watergate era, for some reason thought it appropriate to re-state the charges against Espy, despite his acquittal: "Call me old fashioned, but I think when a cabinet secretary receives tens of thousands of dollars in gifts and favors from people regulated by that secretary it should be investigated and, if proven, prosecuted."[8] The legacy of the post–Watergate ethics and appearances cultures is apparent. Unfortunately Donald Smaltz's attitude was all too typical and continued long after he was thankfully allowed to retire and end his unfortunate reign of legal terror on Mike Espy.

The Over-the-Top David Barrett

David Barrett was appointed on May 25, 1994, to investigate whether Henry Cisneros made false statements to FBI agents checking on his background prior to his confirmation as HUD secretary. Cisneros was accused of not being honest in an unsworn interview with the FBI describing the nature of payments he had been making to a female friend who was not his wife.

Attorney General Reno could have resisted pressure to seek appointment of an independent counsel on such a relatively trivial offense but she did not—such were the media and political pressures at the height of the scandal culture America found itself in.

After four years of an investigation costing more than $11 million, Barrett indicted Cisneros on *18 felony charges* arising out of that one relatively trivial allegation. The next year, in 1999, Cisneros finally decided to end the torture and pled guilty to a single misdemeanor of making false statements, paid a $10,000 fine, and the 18 felony-count indictment was dismissed. (He was later pardoned by President Clinton in January 2001.)

And that should have been the end of that, but in 1995 Barrett sought and obtained authorization from Attorney General Reno to expand his investigation into Cisneros' 1992 tax returns. He kept going . . . and going . . . and going. The three-judge panel, vindicating Justice Scalia's earlier concerns in his 1988 dissent, refused, or was politically unable, to fire him. Barrett went on for *six more years* spending *nearly another $11 million*.

Finally, into his *eleventh* year—more than six years after obtaining the misdemeanor plea from Cisneros—Barrett concluded his investigation and issued a final report of *474 pages* on January 20, 2006.

The Barrett report remarkably alleged that officials from *both* the Clinton *and* Bush Justice Departments, as well as Internal Revenue Service, "resisted our efforts" to investigate tax violations by Cisneros. Rep. Henry Waxman (D.-Cal.) referred to this Barrett hyper-conspiratorial accusation as "delusional." Barrett referred darkly to a "cover-up at high levels of our government" preventing him from bringing tax charges against Cisneros and possibly others. Here is the *only* instance in the history of the independent counsel over 21 years where there was a bipartisan denunciation of the excessive zealotry of an independent counsel. "Mr. Barrett conjured up a far-fetched theory of a wide-reaching government conspiracy to justify his tenure for another six years," wrote Susan J. Park, a trial lawyer in the Bush Administration's Department of Justice. "He has nothing to show for his efforts. If Mr. Barrett is serious about exploring the issue of integrity, he should examine his own."[9]

At least one could take some solace that the three-judge panel actually tried to prevent the final report from including accusations related to the Clinton Administration officials, but was "overruled," according to the *Washington Post*, by congressional Republicans.[10]

Kenneth W. Starr: The Unjust Prosecutions of Susan McDougal and Webster Hubbell

Whether or not Independent Counsel Kenneth Starr exercised poor judgment in many aspects of his investigations of the Clintons has been much debated, with partisanship often affecting the way people answer this question. On many occasions, he certainly exercised poor judgment, so poor that many attributed it to his conservative Republican biases, his lack of experience as a prosecutor, and his willingness to assume the worst about the Clintons. In the final accounting of what he accomplished, putting aside the Monica Lewinsky episode for a moment, the legitimate question is why he could not have wrapped up the Whitewater investigation of the Clintons much earlier than he did.

With the benefit of hindsight, it is legitimate to point to three of Judge Starr's prosecution decisions as prime examples of his worst judgment that seemed to equate to prosecutorial abuse and miscarriages of justice. Two concerned former Associate Attorney General Webster Hubbell, and the other regarded Susan McDougal. As one lawyer who had extensive dealings with Starr's prosecutors at the time told the *Washington Post*, "[Starr and his prosecutors] had an attitude of intimidation and nastiness that maybe you treat the Mafia and paid Mafia lawyers that way."[11]

The Cruel Second Indictment of Susan McDougal

A Little Rock jury convicted Susan McDougal in May 1996 of being involved with her husband James B. McDougal in committing various felonies relating to Whitewater and the Madison Bank. Sometime after this, Kenneth Starr and his Little Rock prosecutor team decided that Susan McDougal had information that could incriminate the Clintons. When they decided this and on what factual basis has never been revealed.

At first they began the traditional prosecutorial process of trying to convince her to testify as to what she knew concerning wrongful conduct by the Clintons relating to Whitewater. She told them she knew nothing. They did not believe her. So, they began to threaten her to testify to what they believed she knew. Normally prosecutors who have already won a conviction would try their best to pressure the convicted criminal to testify against a higher-up, and then let it go. However, Starr and his prosecutors were anxious to turn the screws to the maximum extent to get McDougal to testify before the grand jury. They granted her immunity but she still refused to testify, convinced that if she did so truthfully, they would indict her for perjury and obstruction.

The Starr prosecutor dealing with Susan McDougal, Ray Jahn, had reportedly applied pressure to McDougal to testify by causing the OIC to issue subpoenas to two of Susan's brothers, both previously cleared of wrongdoing in connection to Madison Guaranty and by threatening her with an IRS investigation. Susan never claimed Jahn asked her to lie about the Clintons. She recalled that he had said, "you know who the investigation is about and you know who we want." (Under oath, Jahn denied making those statements).[12]

When McDougal was sentenced to two years after her fraud conviction along with her husband, Jim McDougal, concerning Whitewater and Madison Guaranty, she was shackled hand and foot and led past TV cameras to a waiting prison van. At the Pulasta County Jail, she was stripped naked, given a full body search, and doused with delousing chemicals.[13]

Does this look like prosecutorial excess?

On September 4, she appeared before the Little Rock Whitewater grand jury and, despite being given immunity, she refused to answer any questions. As a result, she spent 18 months in jail for civil contempt of court. At one point, during a subsequent criminal trial she faced in Los Angeles for alleged embezzlement (she was acquitted), she was transported to and from jail in leg irons and kept inside a cage in the van surrounded by hardened criminals.

There may be some prosecutors who defend these techniques to force an immunized witness to testify. But once her contempt sentence was completed, Starr and his team took another step, and this seemed one step too far. On May 4, 1998, they indicted Susan McDougal on two more counts of criminal contempt and one count of obstruction of justice. The trial did not take place for another ten months, but when it did the jury acquitted McDougal of obstruction of justice, and there was a hung jury on the criminal contempt charges. Starr decided not to retry the case.

The Shameful Webster Hubbell II and Hubbell III Prosecutions

It is amazing that even to this day few people are aware of the facts regarding the second and third prosecutions of Webster Hubbell by Judge Starr and his team of prosecutors. More than any other example, it demonstrates the loss of judgment and perspective by prosecutors accountable to no one and nearly obsessed with scoring the Big One. Namely, that meant finding President Clinton guilty of something in Whitewater—no matter what it took. After re-reading the facts about these two prosecutions and verifying them again and again to be sure they were right, including several telephone interviews with Mr. Hubbell himself, one is left with a sense of disbelief and an overwhelming feeling that not much more than sheer venom and vindictiveness were significant factors in the prosecutorial decisions to seek and obtain these two indictments.

How did the media basically miss these gross injustices done to Webster Hubbell—which is why so few people know about them? A typical reference to these two convictions, without further explanation, is the *Los Angeles Times* story at the close of the Whitewater investigation. The *Times*, a great newspaper that should have done much better, reported simply that as a result of these two indictments, Hubbell had pled "guilty to a felony and a misdemeanor."[14] Well, that is not exactly the whole story.

Hubbell I

First, there was what I shall call "Hubbell I"—the prosecution of Hubbell for fraudulent billing practices while he worked at the Rose Law Firm in Little Rock, Arkansas. (Hubbell had included personal expenses on many bills he had sent to clients.) This prosecution had nothing to do with Clintons or Whitewater and involved conduct that occurred before he accepted an appointment as associate attorney general. On December 6, 1994, Hubbell pled guilty to two felony counts: mail fraud and tax evasion. He was sentenced to 21 months imprisonment and ordered to pay $135,000 restitution to his law firm, as well as undergoing three years of supervised release and 48 hours of community service.

Webb Hubbell had made a tragic mistake, committed a serious crime that he pled guilty to, and did his time. Up to then, Hubbell had been a leader of his community, a former football star at the University of Arkansas, a judge, an outstanding attorney, and most of all—known by all who knew him—a kind and good man. He entered prison in August 1995 and was not released until February 1997. He had paid about $85,000 of the $135,000 back to the law firm.

During his prison term and after, FBI agents called him to testify many times before the Watergate Grand Jury and before various congressional committees. The Starr prosecutors suspected that Hubbell knew about wrongdoing by the Clintons in the Whitewater matter and was remaining silent to protect them. What they thought he knew and what wrongdoing they thought he was covering up were never stated and remain unclear today.

The Illusory "Hush Money" Conspiracy

When Hubbell got out of prison in February 1997, his nightmare should have been over. But instead, it was about to begin all over again. First, during the months after his release from prison, reporters nearly jumped over each other to report on stories about Hubbell. They were especially interested in Hubbell's various friends in high positions in the Clinton White House and administration who had helped him obtain work and income as an attorney in the seven months between his resignation as associate attorney general and his guilty plea in December 1994.

I was serving as White House special counsel at that time, responsible for dealing with reporters on all potential "scandal" stories. For several months in the late winter and spring of 1997, there were "breaking" stories about Hubbell's friends trying to help him get legal work. Many stories played on the front page of the *New York Times* and *Washington Post* and were about each of Hubbell's friends who had made these calls. The innuendo was that these calls were the functional equivalent of "hush money," in compensation for Hubbell keeping quiet about what he knew about the Clintons and Whitewater. There were suggestions on the editorial pages and on the cable TV talk shows of a possible obstruction of justice case against these individuals.

The explanation at the time, which was never disputed, was that these calls were pure and simple acts of friendship. Hubbell was not a wealthy man and was without an income after his resignation. Whenever I asked these reporters, "What information do you think Hubbell is covering up?" they would tell me that their "sources" at the Office of Independent Counsel were "convinced" that "Hubbell knew a lot and wasn't talking."

Such was life in the scandal culture of the 1990s, where innuendo and anonymous suspicions were reportable, and when repeated enough times, started to seem like the truth. On one occasion, I called an editor at the *New York Times* who suggested in an editorial that these calls might constitute an orchestrated cover-up by the White House and asked him whether he had any factual basis for making that suggestion. "No, but it sure looks that way," he said. What a perfect, emblematic comment for the appearances culture of the post–Watergate scandal machine.

I remember being amazed that this "hush money" story about Hubbell had such legs. Even ABC's Ted Koppel thought it important enough to devote an entire *Nightline* show to it. I appeared on the program to offer the simple explanation that these calls were acts of friendship. Koppel kept insisting that there had to be another explanation. I reminded him that at the time the calls were made to help Hubbell, no one knew that Hubbell would end up pleading guilty to fraud.

In retrospect, all this media hype about the calls made to help Hubbell was proven to be much ado about nothing.

Hubbell II

As we now know, however, it had a significant effect on Starr's prosecutors. If mainstream news organizations thought it might be credible that Hubbell had been paid to cover up what he knew about the Clintons concerning Whitewater, then there was little reason why Starr's prosecutors would not share the same perceptions. So, it is no surprise that they decided to turn the screws on Hubbell to see if he could be pressured to "tell all"—which, they assumed, would somehow incriminate the Clintons.

Each time Hubbell testified they were disappointed, however, because he insisted that he had no information that suggested the Clintons had done anything wrong in Whitewater or anything else for that matter. As Hubbell said in 2006, almost ten years later, "I simply refused to lie about the Clintons to protect myself from Ken Starr's prosecutors."

So what did Starr do to try to pressure Hubbell to offer up testimony that might incriminate the Clintons? On April 30, 1998 (recall that this was three months into the Lewinsky investigation), Starr indicted not only Hubbell but *his wife, his accountant, and his attorney* on *ten felony counts* alleging income-tax evasion and filing a false tax return. (They also threw in the usual related felonies, such as conspiracy, "impeding and impairing" the IRS, mail fraud, wire fraud, etc. I will call this indictment "Hubbell II" and will refer to it generically as the tax-indictment.) Starr issued a press release announcing the ten-count indictment but little factual information at the time.

Now we know the reason: Starr was charging Hubbell with filing a false tax return (assisted by his wife, accountant, and attorney) because he had not yet paid the back taxes he owed as a result of his guilty plea in the Rose Law firm case. He also had not paid other taxes for income he received in 1994 before he pled guilty. In other words, Starr charged Hubbell for not paying the IRS the money he owed in federal taxes (estimated to be less than $100,000) while he was in federal prison earning ten cents an hour doing his prison job. Also, Judge Starr sought and obtained an indictment of Hubbell's wife for co-signing an allegedly fraudulent tax return, and his accountant and lawyer for helping to prepare that return. Just after Starr announced the Hubbell II indictment, the *Washington Post* reported that, "choking up as he and his wife talked to reporters outside their Washington home, Hubbell said the new indictment was intended only to pressure him to lie about the president. 'I will not do so, and my wife would not want me to do so. I want you to know the office of independent counsel can indict my dog, they can indict my cat, but I'm not going to lie about the president, I'm not going to lie about the first lady or anyone else. My wife and I are innocent of the charges brought today.'"[15]

If there was any debate about whether this tax indictment was an example of prosecutorial overzealousness and poor judgment by Judge Starr, the stinging, personal rebuke contained in the decision handed down by U.S. District Court Judge James Robertson on July 5, 1998, should have resolved it.

Judge Robertson granted Hubbell dismissal of this entire Hubbell II indictment as a matter of law and most of the counts applicable to his wife, accountant, and attorney. Judge Robertson described the indictment against Hubbell as the "quintessential fishing expedition."[16] He criticized Judge Starr and his prosecutors for illegally expanding the scope of the investigation beyond matters "relating to" or "arising out of" Whitewater and Madison Guaranty. Judge Robertson then mocked the Starr team's argument in terms that attempted to justify their bootstrapping of the original grant of jurisdiction into their tax-evasion indictment of Hubbell: "[Starr's] argument is that, so long as the independent counsel is investigating obstruction, he may prosecute whatever crimes he may come across, committed by whomever he may come across, regardless of whether the charges or the individuals are demonstrably related in any substantive way to the Original Grant, and regardless of whether he has found any [actual evidence of] obstruction."[17] The court, sounding very much like Justice Scalia dissenting in the case that upheld the independent counsel law some ten years before, agreed with the defense counsel that Starr could not be allowed to "stray in as many directions and . . . as far in any given direction as [his] energy and zeal might take him."[18]

Hubbell III

Despite, or perhaps because of, this unusual public humiliation of Starr and his team—an indictment is rarely thrown out of court within two months of it being handed down—and reprimand by a U.S. federal judge, Judge Starr and his deputies did not give up. They seemed unconcerned about an appearance of overzealousness. So, less than five months later, they served up another indictment ("Hubbell III"). On November 13, 1998, Starr announced a new *15-count indictment* against Hubbell. On its face, this one seemed even more serious than the tax-evasion case. Hubbell was accused of perjury, making false statements, mail fraud, and other crimes related to misleading and impairing the Federal Deposit Insurance Corporation and the Resolution Trust Company in connection with the collapse of the Madison Guaranty Savings & Loan Bank. It appeared that Starr could not be accused of enlarging his jurisdiction beyond the matters contained in his "original grant" to investigate Whitewater and Madison Guaranty. But then again, what was really the crime Starr was accusing Hubbell of? Did it have anything to do with Whitewater? No, it did not.

In fact, it had very little to do with . . . anything. As things turned out, and what few people knew at the time, Hubbell was accused of not disclosing an alleged conflict of interest when he represented the FDIC and the RTC in the late 1980s. Apparently, his *law firm* also represented an accountant in one of the firms that the FDIC and RTC was suing for fraud. That was the crime Hubbell was being charged with? That was what Starr's office announced with huge fanfare as a "15-count indictment" for perjury and fraud relating to "Madison Guaranty?"

Starr must have had his doubts about this indictment, because it was not soon after that negotiations commenced for a global plea bargain that would take care of both Hubbell II and III. Hubbell finally agreed to make a deal with Starr but not to lie about the Clintons. He agreed to a plea bargain that would clear his wife, attorney, and accountant, since some of the counts in their indictment in the Hubbell II tax case had not been dismissed by Judge Robertson. Starr, on his part, wanted a chance to appeal Judge Robertson's (and the D.C. Court of Appeals') decision to the U.S. Supreme Court. This related to the issue of whether Starr's office had violated their promise of documentary immunity to Hubbell when they indicted him for tax evasion.

So, the deal was struck on June 30, 1999. First, Hubbell would plead guilty to a felony in Hubbell III of making a false statement (i.e., failing to disclose the alleged conflict of interest to the Federal Deposit Insurance Corporation). He would also pay a $100 "special assessment" and accept one year's probation. In turn, Hubbel III's 15-count indictment would be dismissed by Starr's office. Second, the indictments of Mrs. Hubbell, Hubbell's attorney, and his accountant in the Hubbell II tax case would be dismissed. Lastly, Hubbell would agree to plea to a "conditional" misdemeanor in the Hubbell II tax case so that Starr could take his appeal to the Supreme Court. Without the plea, Starr would not otherwise be able to do so, given the unfavorable decisions by the D.C. District Court and the Court of Appeals.

The final chapter concerning the fiasco of Starr's misguided second and third attempted prosecutions of Webster Hubbell was the repudiation of his legal position by the United States Supreme Court. On June 5, 2000, the Supreme Court vacated Starr's indictment of Hubbell, and on October 20, 2000, it vacated the "conditional plea and misdemeanor tax charge." So that was the end of that.

At the end of the day, for all the headlines that Starr generated in Hubbell II and Hubbell III, plus the ten-count and 15-count indictments, respectively, all he and his team got was a $100 fine, a misdemeanor plea by Hubbell, and a dismissal of everything else. The nightmare for Webb Hubbell was finally over. To this day, no one, not Kenneth Starr, not the columnists, editorial writers, or hundreds of reporters who all virtually declared that Webster Hubbell was guilty of a cover-up on behalf of the Clintons, has ever apologized for what they put him through. You see, in the world of the scandal machine and the appearances culture, if there is enough "out there"—suspicion, leaks, investigations, media stories—apologies are not necessary. Two of the best reporters who covered the Hubbell "hush money" story from the *New York Times* and the *Washington Post* gave almost identical comments in defense of their actions: "All we were doing was reporting on what was out there."

Speaking more than eight years after the nightmare of the Starr team's bogus Hubbell II and Hubbell III had so terrified him, his wife, his attorney, and accountant (but not his dog), Webb Hubbell told me: "I hold no anger any longer. Mr. Starr and his prosecutors thought they could roll me like I was a mobster, who would lie about others to save myself. I just refused. It was as simple as that."

DIRTY HANDS FOR ALL

In the final analysis, the worst legacy of the independent counsel was how it served as the most destructive ingredient of the gotcha culture. As the Republicans rightfully claimed in the late 1980s in reaction to the excesses of Lawrence Walsh, it literally "criminalized political differences." Both major political parties have dirty hands here. Speaking for myself, I do too. I certainly cheered on all the Democrats who called for independent counsels investigating the Reagan and Bush White Houses in the 1980s, and rooted for all of them to bring home indictments that would do damage to the Republicans politically. I certainly recall feeling no doubts about the merits of the various investigations of Raymond Donovan. I am ashamed to say all this today—but I was just as much caught up in the gotcha culture as partisans on the Republican right.

All partisans on the left and right, if we can be honest with each other for just a moment, share this much in common: sanctimony when it is the other guy getting the heat, outrage when it is your guy getting the heat; and enough hypocrisy to spread around evenly across the spectrum in both parties.

Just as Kenneth Starr's Whitewater investigation was getting started, two law professors wrote of the dangers in mixing politics and the criminal justice system: "Instead of purifying our governing institutions, special prosecutors play into a pathology that thrives on an appetite for scandal and a distrust for our system of government."[19] Another writer expressed his concerns about actions taken during the independent counsel era this way: "Rather than allowing voters to decide whom they want to represent them, politicians are increasingly calling on the FBI, the courts and special investigators to determine the outcome of partisan battles. It's politics by legal brief, not by the ballot."[20]

Even Kenneth Starr, whose arguably poor judgment and prosecutorial excesses helped kill the Independent Counsel statute, strongly advocated its death. He told a Senate Committee that the law that gave him his job was "structurally unsound" and "constitutionally dubious." He stated that it should not be renewed: "The statute tried to cram a fourth branch of government into our three-branch system."

Fortunately, in 1999, Congress recognized the dangers of the independent counsel and refused to renew the act on a bipartisan basis. Under regulations published soon after the expiration of the act, the attorney general was given the ability to appoint a "special prosecutor" whenever the "public interest" requires it, whatever that meant. This special counsel would investigate wrongdoing in the White House and the Executive Branch, but the attorney general would retain supervisory or a "veto" power over indictments, appeals, and other major investigative steps. According to a Justice Department official, a veto would be used only under "extraordinary circumstances," and the special counsel's judgment would be given "great weight."[21] In fact, this brought things closer in line with history. Prior to the enactment of the Ethics in Government Act in 1978 that first created a "special prosecutor" independent of the Executive Branch, there had been six such special prosecutors authorized in the previous hundred years or so—the first during the presidency of Ulysses S. Grant.[22]

Even with the elimination of the independent counsel as a "fourth branch" of government, the danger of political pressures causing the appointment of too many "special prosecutors" outside of the Justice Department still remains. Only if the attorney general has the political fortitude to resist partisan pressures can we avoid repeating the excesses of the independent counsel era of the 1980s and 1990s.

So, what is to prevent politics from compromising the Justice Department if it is called to investigate a senior member of the Executive Branch? Well, just as the adage says "fight fire with fire," the answer here is politics.

It was politics that caused Richard Nixon's attorney general, Elliot Richardson, to appoint a special counsel outside the Justice Department, Archibald Cox, to investigate Watergate in 1973. It was politics that caused the Nixon Justice Department to appoint another Watergate special counsel, Leon Jaworski, after the Saturday Night Massacre. It was politics that caused President George W. Bush's attorney general, John Ashcroft, to recuse himself from the investigation into the White House leak of Valerie Plame's identity as a CIA operative. And, it was politics that drove James Comey, Ashcroft's deputy, to appoint Patrick Fitzgerald as special prosecutor to continue the Plame investigation.

The lesson is that our political process usually works, sooner or later. Grassroots pressure from the American people forces the government to do the right thing, eventually. In the end, the political process is more trustworthy and less dangerous than depending on extra-constitutional criminal prosecutors who can be appointed *but not removed* because of politics.[23]

THEY WERE NOT ALL BAD

Joseph diGenova, a former Republican U.S. attorney under President Reagan, made what is perhaps the best comment on the prosecutorial excesses and poor judgment exercised by so many independent counsels in the 21 years of their existence. It was a response to the decision by independent counsel Larry Thompson to accept a misdemeanor plea from former Interior Secretary James Watt for making "inaccurate and misleading statements" to an FBI agent.[24] It should be recalled that some five years before, Watt had been indicted on 25 alleged felonies by Thompson's independent counsel predecessor, Arlin Adams. Mr. diGenova, not known for being bashful, said:

> I've always believed that these pleas say something about the nature of the investigation. I don't think any reasonable people can look at that plea and say anything other than, what gives? . . . When a 25-count felony indictment gets pleaded down to a misdemeanor, it raises serious questions about the original indictment and its probity. This is not what the process is supposed to be about. It's not about personalities. It's about evidence. . . . Indicting someone is a very serious matter. This type of plea makes it look as if it isn't."[25]

These are words that are equally applicable to the questionable independent counsel investigations of Ted Olson, Ed Meese, and Raymond Donovan in the 1980s. They also capture the mostly fruitless, excessive investigations of Caspar Weinberger, Mike Espy, Henry Cisneros, and especially Webster Hubbell and Susan McDougal.

Despite these long lists of questionable investigations, we cannot forget that there were also a few independent counsels who should be regarded as heroes, not for what they did but for what they decided not to do. Mr. diGenova is one of them. He was appointed an independent counsel on December 14, 1992, to investigate whether certain Bush State Department officials illegally examined Democratic presidential candidate Bill Clinton's passport records for political purposes. Again it is debatable whether an independent counsel should have been appointed at all. This case was clearly an example of what were, at best, questionable political activities that hardly warranted serious criminal prosecution conducted independently of the Department of Justice. In any event, diGenova practiced what he preached. After a thorough investigation that took three years to complete, but stayed within a limited budget, diGenova indicted no one.

Kurtis Von Kann, the independent counsel who investigated the Americorps director, the late Eli Segal, also exercised prosecutorial discretion and restraint, as did Carol Elder Bruce (Interior Secretary Bruce Babbitt) and Ralph I. Lancaster, Jr. (Labor Secretary Alexis Herman). All three conducted thorough investigations over a limited period of time, spent a limited amount of money, and stopped when they found no basis for indictments. Alexia Morrison, of whom I was critical in chapter four for her prolonged investigation of Ted Olson, at least had the intellectual integrity finally to give up and not indict Mr. Olson. That is not to say that heroes do not indict and bad guys do. But as we have seen, the public is all too prone to assume guilt whenever anyone is accused of wrongdoing, much less headlined in an indictment. As a result, prosecutors who recognize their awesome powers and appreciate that their obligation is to do justice not only to the public but to the person accused, should be valued today more than ever.

CHAPTER NINE

THE
BOOMERANG EFFECT:
GINGRICH AND LIVINGSTON

"And I want to say to you bluntly: You live today with the most corrupt Congressional leadership we have seen in the United States in the 20th Century. You have to go back to the gilded age of the 1870s and 1880s to have anything comparable that we've lived through."

—Rep. Newt Gingrich, February 1992.[1]

Among partisan Democrats, there was a sense of some sort of poetic justice in what happened to Newt Gingrich and Bob Livingston just at the peak of conservative Republican sanctimony. This was marked by their moralizing about the Clinton White House "scandals" and "corruption" and aggressively moving to impeach President Clinton over the Lewinsky matter. Democrats willing, or able, to take a longer view, however, saw the danger in the gotcha cycle. They recognized that the boomerang that knocked down Gingrich and Livingston could come back just as quickly to hurt Democrats when it was the Republicans' turn—once again—to get even. That is not to say that Democrats did not relish the moment. Gingrich had made so many enemies, and had acted so viciously during his campaign that forced Speaker Jim Wright's resignation in May 1989, that Gingrich's own ethical crash in 1998 was unapologetically celebrated by House Democrats.

The delicious irony, of course, was that Gingrich's first signs of trouble began right after his resounding victory in the November 1994 elections. Two weeks before he took over as speaker, the story broke that Gingrich had signed a two-book deal in which he would be paid a cash advance in excess of $4 million, to be published by HarperCollins. That publishing house, which was known for publishing a number of volumes by conservative figures, just happened to be owned by News Corporation at the time. This is the media company controlled by Rupert Murdoch, who also owns the Fox Broadcasting Company. Murdoch, it turned out, had strong commercial interests, which he made no effort to disguise, in several regulatory matters before the federal government. These included a case filed by NBC and the NAACP, which claimed that as an Australian company, News Corporation's ownership of Fox Broadcasting was in violation of federal restrictions on foreign companies owning U.S. broadcast licenses.

Democrats lost no time in suggesting that Murdoch's publishing company was attempting to buy influence with the Speaker-to-be through this extraordinarily large advance. News coverage compared it to the $7 million paid to President Ronald Reagan for his memoirs. There was also no time wasted in recalling how Gingrich had helped to bring down Speaker Wright over using bulk sales of his books to lobbyists. Gingrich had claimed that Wright used an unusually high royalty rate of 55 percent as an indirect method of allowing lobbyists to purchase access and influence with the then-Speaker. So it was fair game for Democrats to immediately attack the Gingrich book deal on the same grounds.

Since there were no bars on demonizing the political opposition in the scandal culture of the times, Democrats quickly depicted Gingrich as, well, greedy. "This is the first guy who tried to cash in before he was sworn in," Democratic and Clinton campaign strategist James Carville told the *Washington Post*. "It certainly seems like Representative Gingrich is out to capitalize on the office of the speaker before he even enters the job," Fred Wertheimer, president of Common Cause, also told the *Post*.[2]

Nor was there much sympathy when Newt Gingrich, who had called Speaker Jim Wright "the most corrupt Speaker in the 20th century," suddenly cried foul at Democrats using bad words about him. Commenting about the personal criticisms of his $4 million book deal, Gingrich complained that "there is a small group of people so bitter about losing control of the House that they have decided that any device which destroys me is legitimate."[3] One House Democrat, Representative Carrie Meek, had the temerity to suggest on the floor of the House that Gingrich's book deal would allow him to earn "a whole lot of [gold] dust." The remark, somewhat tame when compared to Gingrich's comments on the House floor about Speaker Wright, nevertheless provoked an uproar among Republican House members. They insisted that Meek's remarks be stricken from the House official record after a two-hour partisan shouting match. This was an indication of the significant increase in personal venom and partisanship in the

House of Representatives in the aftermath of the Gingrich-led Republican takeover.[4]

Just two years later, on January 21, 1997, Gingrich was reprimanded and fined $300,000 by the bipartisan House Ethics Committee for his own ethical lapses, which may have escaped punishment in a less viciously partisan era. Gingrich admitted publicly that he had brought discredit to the House and broke its rules. He failed to ensure that financing for two projects (teaching a college course and developing materials for the course) would not violate federal tax law and he gave the House ethics committee false information.

That made Gingrich the first Speaker in the House's 208-year history to be disciplined for ethical wrongdoing. (Speaker Wright was never disciplined for ethical violations, but he did resign under pressure as Speaker thanks to Gingrich's two-year campaign against him.) The vote to reprimand Gingrich was overwhelming and bipartisan, 395–28, following a 7–1 vote of the 50–50 bipartisan House Ethics Committee.

Comments made by Republican leaders at the time of the vote to reprimand Gingrich were both interesting and ironic. "If our action today fails to chasten this body and bring a halt to the *crippling partisanship and animosity that has surrounded us*, then we will have lost an opportunity," said Representative Nancy L. Johnson of Connecticut, chair of the Ethics Committee.[5] None other than Tom DeLay, the new Majority Whip of the Republican-controlled House, weighed in on the issue, as well. Calling the penalty imposed on Gingrich unwarranted, DeLay, who prided himself on being known as the "Hammer" for his not-to-gentle political style, opined: "The highest possible standard does not mean an impossible standard no American could possibly reach." In an impassioned floor speech defending Gingrich, some nine years before he would face an indictment and series of ethical charges himself, he closed—and I am not making this up: "Let's stop this madness, let's stop the cannibalism." It seems he said this with no apparent understanding of the delicious hypocrisy of the comment.

Of course, the reference to "cannibalism" evoked memories of virtually the exact phrase used by Speaker Jim Wright in his poignant and eloquent resignation speech. When he surrendered to the two-year campaign waged against him by Newt Gingrich eight years earlier, he urged House members "to bring this period of mindless cannibalism to an end." Could it be that the Hammer did not realize he was using the same words that Wright had used? This is the man who just a year later insisted on pushing forward the impeachment resolution and vote against President Bill Clinton. This is the man who insisted on an impeachment vote *after* the Republicans had suffered unprecedented losses in the November 1998 elections and *before* the new members could be sworn in. DeLay did so despite every single opinion poll indicating more than two-thirds of the American people opposed the impeachment of Bill Clinton over the Lewinsky matter. Was there no limit to the hypocrisies of gotcha politics?

THE BOB LIVINGSTON RESIGNATION

There was definitely a difference in the reaction to the downfall of Gingrich compared to the downfall of Bob Livingston over a sexual affair. The joy and satisfaction that most Democrats, even those not overly partisan, took in Newt Gingrich's downfall was not present when Bob Livingston faced his day of reckoning.

A big reason for this was because Livingston was forced to resign due to the outing of his extramarital sexual affairs by Larry Flynt, publisher of *Hustler* magazine. Flynt, seeking revenge on the determined effort of House Republicans to impeach President Clinton over the Lewinsky matter, offered an award of up to $1 million for sexual dirt on members of Congress. Flynt disgusted even the most partisan Democrats by this tactic.

On December 17, 1998, Livingston, who had become the heir apparent to the office of the Speaker in the wake of the resignation of Newt Gingrich, preempted what he knew was going to be Flynt's announcement of evidence of the affairs. He admitted to the House Republican Caucus that he had had these affairs and asked for understanding and forgiveness. (Again, Clintonites and Democratic members had some appreciation of the irony when they heard that Mr. Livingston received a standing ovation from the Republican caucus after confessing his affair. *Washington Post* columnist Mary McGrory had it right when she wrote: "Republican adultery is apparently quite different from the Democratic kind. Livingston got a standing ovation from the people who were sharpening their axes to behead Clinton for much the same transgression. . . . Did Moses add, 'Don't get caught' or 'you can lie about it if you have to, but for God's sake don't raise your right hand over the Bible.'") Then two days later, as the House debate of the impeachment of President Clinton started, Livingston took the floor to explain why he believed, in principle, that President Clinton should be impeached for lying under oath.

His first comment certainly was greeted sympathetically by a broad segment of the public fed up with the hyper-partisanship that had enveloped the political process. It seemed at odds, however, with the Republican leadership's partisan decision to press for an impeachment vote and to block an alternative censure resolution that many Republicans and most Democrats favored. He said:

> I very much regret the enmity and the hostility that has been bred in the halls of Congress for the last months and year. I want so very much to pacify and cool our raging tempers and return to an era when differences were confined to the debate, not to a personal attack or assassination of character. . . . When given the chance, we often find that aside from political and partisan differences, we have much in common with one another. But we never discover that common ground may be with the gulf between the sides of this narrow aisle.

Livingston explained that he supported impeachment because of his strong belief that the president had committed perjury, and that that was an impeachable offense no matter what the circumstances, even if it was about false testimony in order to avoid disclosure of a private relationship. That, he said, was his principled position. He also said he was opposed to a censure resolution in lieu of impeachment, which he genuinely believed was not provided for by the Constitution. He never explained, though, why members should not be allowed to *vote* on a censure resolution. The cynicism of stating his opposition to censure while blocking members of his own party *a right to vote* on it should have been obvious. Also, he (or any other House Republican who opposed allowing a vote on censure) never adequately explained the logic of preventing colleagues from having an opportunity to vote. The obvious reason, which everyone knew but few were willing to admit openly, was that had such a vote occurred, it would have passed substantially. (I know this because two of the key Republican House managers independently told me months later that "several dozen" Republican House members would have voted for censure rather than proceed to impeachment had they been permitted to do so.)

Livingston in his speech then asked President Clinton to resign, and the reaction was boos and shouts from the Democratic side of the aisle. Still, there was no sign of the surprising announcement to come.

He seemed to grimace at the sound of the booing, took a deep breath and continued to announce his startling decision:

> I was prepared to lead our narrow majority as speaker, and I believe I had it in me to do a fine job. But I cannot do that job or be the kind of leader that I would like to be under the current circumstances. So I must set the example that I hope President Clinton will follow. I will not stand for speaker of the House on January 6th, but rather, I shall remain as a backbencher in this Congress that I so dearly love for approximately six months into the 106th

Congress, whereupon I shall vacate my seat and ask my governor to call a special election to take my place.

The shock in the House of Representatives and to the millions of people across the country watching this first day of the historic impeachment debate was powerful. The Democratic Minority Leader, Richard A. Gephardt, drew thunderous applause from both sides of the aisle when he stood and asked Livingston to reconsider his decision, saying passionately: "The politics of smear and slash-and-burn must end."

The sympathetic reaction was not unanimous, however; certainly not among some of the more sanctimonious moralists on the religious right. Richard Land, president of the Southern Baptist Ethics and Religious Liberty Commission, said: "A man who will break his oath to God, his wife and the assembled witness is likely to break his oath of office." At least one conservative member of the House Republican caucus, Rep. Mark Sanford of South Carolina, said on CNN's *Crossfire* what a lot of the more conservative religious-right members were saying privately within the caucus: "The bottom line is Livingston lied. He lied to his wife."[6]

THE SCANDAL MACHINE SUMMED UP

The next day, the *Washington Post*'s highly respected media affairs reporter, Howard Kurtz, wrote a powerful piece on scandal, sex, and the politics of personal destruction. "There's virtually no zone of privacy left for any public official," Sanford Ungar, dean of American University's School of Communications, told Kurtz. "And there are many co-conspirators in creating that situation—politicians themselves, the media, the Internet. . . . This town has gone nuts."

Kurtz noted that the media no longer followed the old rules when it came to covering a politician's private life and sexual conduct. "There are no gatekeepers anymore," said Tom Rosenstiel, director of the Project for Excellence in Journalism. "These things are no longer vetted by the press. They're vetted by the public."

Kurtz cited other victims of the sex-scandal culture, a culture with none of the traditional restraint shown by the mainstream media. The *Indianapolis Star and News* demonstrated such a disregard when it reported that Representative Dan Burton had fathered a son out of wedlock; and the *Idaho Statesman* disclosed that Representative Helen Chenoweth had had a relationship with a married man; or the liberal-leaning Web site, Salon.com, reported that Representative Henry Hyde, in charge of the impeachment proceeding, had had an extramarital affair 30 years before.

Kurtz compared the changed rules to the different understanding between the media and politicians that existed earlier. "It was a rare day in 1976 when the *Washington Post* reported that then-Representative Wayne Hays was having an affair with a staffer, Elizabeth Ray, who famously declared that she could not type."

Finally, Kurtz seemed to sum up the shifting rationale among the media and elements of the scandal machine alike: "No news organization *says* it is delving into sexual matters simply for salacious effect, or to sell newspapers or grab ratings share," Kurtz wrote perceptively. "The investigations are generally attributed to the importance of some larger value, such as character, dishonesty, or hypocrisy . . . it's not about sex, it's about perjury. But that in turn has emboldened some journalists to ask whether those judging the president have sexual skeletons in their own closets."[7]

Kurtz had nailed it: The gotcha culture had finally erased all boundaries. This included not just the gentlemen's agreement between the media and politicians that had prevailed from George Washington at least through the Reagan years but also the boundaries of what is, or is not, legally and rhetorically appropriate ways of attacking the opposition.

The politics of healthy debate have been replaced by the politics of personal destruction, and the media, politicians, lawyers, and the Internet revolution are all complicit. Most complicit of all are the American people. While expressing their disgust and repulsion for the hyper-partisanship and no-holds-barred attack politics inside the Beltway, they are still prone to reward those politicians who use them to destroy their opponents. They continue to buy more newspapers and watch more nightly cable TV shows, boosting ratings whenever the topics include sex, lies, and videotape.

A BRIDGE TO THE TWENTY-FIRST CENTURY?

As the twentieth century drew to an end, after the final votes were cast acquitting President Clinton on impeachment, there was some faint hope that the scandal machine would lose some of its energy. With luck it might actually be replaced by a new kind of politics in the dawn of the new millennium.

Unfortunately, despite the brief time after September 11, 2001, when the country actually seemed to pull together in common support of President Bush in his war against terror, this did not happen. The language of hate and the habit of accusing someone of being evil or a liar rather than of being wrong or exercising poor judgment re-appeared. Except this time, the hateful words were used by the left to attack President Bush rather than from the right aimed at President Clinton. With the invasion of Iraq and the misstatements concerning weapons of mass destruction, the personal venom between left and right only got worse.

As we will see, those caught in the middle of this vitriol have grown increasingly fed up with this kind of politics in this country, seeing through the hypocrisies on the left and the right, and their numbers are increasing.

PART IV

THE REVOLT
OF THE CENTER

CHAPTER TEN

HYPOCRISIES ON
THE LEFT AND RIGHT

On a spring day in 1968 while serving in Vietnam, Max Cleland had both his legs and an arm blown away by a hand grenade. He came home to a life in a wheelchair, but he refused to give up on the system that had sent him to Vietnam. He ran for the State Senate in 1971 and was elected. Then he ran for the U.S. Senate in 1996 from that same wheelchair. He won and compiled a moderate voting record known, in particular, for his support of a strong national defense.

A little more than 34 years after the loss of his three limbs in battle, Senator Cleland was in the midst of his reelection campaign when his Republican opponent, four-term congressman Saxbe Chambliss, ran a television ad. It started by showing four photographs—Osama Bin Laden and Saddam Hussein in two of them and U. S. GIs in the other two. The voice-over then stated that Senator Cleland had voted "11 times" against pending legislation to create a Department of Homeland Security. A photograph of Senator Cleland followed, and the voice-over questioned Senator Cleland's "courage to lead."

The ad's intent was factually misleading in several ways. First, Senator Cleland had consistently supported the establishment of a Department of Homeland Security, but the ad omitted that fact. In fact, it falsely suggested that he had opposed the new department. Second, the ad omitted the fact that the Bush Administration had initially opposed the establishment of a separate department after 9/11 and had only in the last year supported it. Third, it did not explain the "11 votes," leaving only the impression that they were either for or against the establishment of the department. In fact, Cleland (and many other Senate Democrats, plus some Republicans) had voted against Republican-sponsored amendments to the bill that would have deprived employees of the new department of the labor rights enjoyed by other federal employees. Finally, and worst of all, there can be no dispute that the decision to include photos of Bin Laden and Hussein in the ad's opening along with raising the question whether Cleland had the "courage to lead" was intended to associate Cleland with being soft on the war against terror or on Saddam. Both were the worst kind of innuendo.

The effect of the ad was slow-building. Cleland decided to ignore it and not to dignify it with an attack ad of his own. He thought Georgia voters would have no doubts that a man who served in Vietnam and was so tragically injured in battle had the "courage to lead." He also thought that they would be smart enough to know that votes to protect labor rights were not the same as opposing the establishment of the Department of Homeland Security. Most certainly, it did not mean he was soft on Bin Laden or Hussein. When the ad started running, Cleland was comfortably ahead in the polls. After the ad started running, his polls began to slip. By Election Day, he lost by a narrow margin, which most people attributed to these ads.

At the time, Democrats immediately condemned the ads as outrageous and demanded that they be stopped. Conservative Democratic Georgia Senator Zell Miller, who was a co-sponsor of the legislation and later switched to become a Republican and supported President Bush for reelection in 2004, denounced the ad: "It's disgraceful for anybody to question Max Cleland's commitment to our national security." He attacked Representative Chambliss personally for sponsoring the ad. He declared that Chambliss "should be ashamed."[1] Other leading Democrats called on Chambliss to pull the ads, as well as two leading Republican Vietnam War veterans—Senator John McCain of Arizona and Senator Chuck Hagel of Nebraska.

Where was the rest of the Republican Party leadership? They were silent, including those who were so critical of what they regarded as the distortions of the media campaign run against Robert Bork.

Richard Cohen, a columnist for the Washington Post, *wrote about the Chambliss ad on Election Day, November 5, 2002, before the results were in:*

> *Where is the outrage? Where are the national politicians willing to stand up and actually denounce these ads? . . . The thinking in Washington and elsewhere is that these ads are disconnected from politics as practiced the rest of the year or from government in general. That, though, is not the case. . . . If they sold out during the campaign—signed off on some scurrilous ad—we can hardly be surprised if they sell out while in office. Virginity is not retroactive. . . . So today, if I could, I'd vote for everyone who was targeted by an intellectually dishonest attack ad. It's personal. After all, the insult to their character was nothing compared to the insult to our intelligence.[2]*

The evening after this column appeared in the Post, *it was official: Max Cleland was defeated. Exit polls and anecdotal evidence suggested that just enough voters had doubts about his courage and commitment to homeland security directly as a result of the Chambliss ads—despite his loss of two legs and an arm in battle—to cost him the election.*

Nearly three years to the month after these outrageous and misleading ads against Senator Cleland began to run, another series of ads aired. This time they were put out by a pro-choice group that liberals have long supported, including me.

On August 12, 2005, I first saw a 30-second TV ad sponsored by the National Abortion Rights Action League (NARAL), an organization with which I had a great deal of sympathy. The ad was aimed at defeating the nomination of Judge John Roberts for the U.S. Supreme Court. With ominous music playing in the background, the ad visually depicted protesters and violence in front of an abortion clinic. It implied that Judge Roberts did not support prosecuting violent protesters, including a notorious anti-abortion criminal who attempted to bomb abortion clinics.

I knew as I watched the ad that it was misleading, at best. I had previously read that when Mr. Roberts was a principal deputy solicitor general in 1991, he prepared, as part of his job, a legal memorandum concerning what the Bush Justice Department's response should be to a lawsuit involving protests at a Virginia abortion clinic. It was based on the valid view that the plaintiffs were misusing a 140-year-old federal statute as the basis of the lawsuit. It did not mean that he was at all sympathetic to violent protests or the bombing of abortion clinics, as the ad strongly implied.

Senator Arlen Specter, Republican chairman of the Senate Judiciary Committee, was furious and expressed himself immediately. He publicly called on NARAL to stop running the ad. It should be recalled that Senator Specter, at his political peril, was a leader in the Republican opposition to Judge Bork's confirmation and a pro-choice supporter of NARAL. He said: "Judge Roberts has unequivocally stated that those individuals who violently target abortion clinics 'should be prosecuted to the full extent of the law.'"[3]

What made the ad even more indefensible was that the violent protests used as footage in the ad had occurred almost 15 years after Roberts wrote the Justice Department legal memorandum.

It was clear to me that this ad hurt the cause of making strong and clear arguments concerning Judge Robert's conservative philosophy and record as a jurist. Why damage the credibility of opposing Judge Roberts for the Supreme Court on a reasonable basis through a misleading ad?, I asked myself. Apparently, enough pro-choice NARAL supporters felt the same way as Senator Specter and communicated their concerns. Within a day, NARAL announced that it had decided to pull the ad. "We regret that many people have misconstrued our recent advertisement about Mr. Roberts's record," said a NARAL leader in a letter to Senator Specter.

The problem was that the ad had not been "misconstrued." The ad was, simply, false and misleading, so taking it down was the right decision. If the goal was to raise legitimate doubts about whether Judge Roberts should be confirmed, running false ads would only hurt, not help, their cause. The next morning, however, there were still Democrats trying to justify the ad. Several leading Democratic consult-ants seemed unhappy that Democrats were not willing to run false ads the way Re-publicans were, as if it showed a lack of some form of toughness. "Republicans don't mind running an ad that's entirely false, but Democrats have never learned and I'm not sure many of them want to learn how to play that kind of politics," said one. Another, who wished Democrats were better at playing "hardball politics," said, "We Democrats bring a well-thumbed copy of Marquess of Queensbury Rules while the other side unsheathes their bloody knives, with a predictable outcome." This ex-pert said the NARAL ad was "great" without disputing that it was completely mis-leading.[4] There were no other national Democratic Party leaders included in the Post *article denouncing this misleading and unfair ad—although it appears that allies and supporters of NARAL also quickly and quietly phoned to convince the or-ganization that the ad was counterproductive and should be taken down.*

Senator Cleland was badly hurt by the outrageously misleading ad run by Con-gressman Chambliss. This, however, was because Senator Cleland did not immediately go on TV to denounce it personally and challenge Congressman Chambliss to meet him face-to-face in the same TV studio to defend them. The Kerry campaign made the same mistake in the delayed response to the smear and misleading statements in the ads run by the so-called Swift Boat veterans. It is fair to ask whether Senator Kerry could have decisively turned the Swift Boat ads issue to his advantage by going on national TV and demanding that President Bush, who did not serve in Vietnam, personally denounce these ads. He could have continued to run his own TV ads with an empty chair chal-lenging President Bush to fill it and to condemn those ads. It is important to note that in the case of the Swift Boat ads, at least Republican senators like John McCain and Chuck Hagel responded with outrage and called on the sponsors to take them down—in contrast to the GOP's leaders' silence on the slimy Chambliss ads.

If there is any doubt that this is not about being tough but, rather, about win-ning elections, contrast the way the 2004 Virginia Democratic gubernatorial candi-date Timothy M. Kaine responded to a sleazy and misleading TV ad sponsored by his Republican opponent, Jerry Kilgore. Kilgore had been running what seemed like round-the-clock repeats of this ad accusing Kane of not being willing to execute murderers because he was morally opposed to the death penalty.

Instead of listening to the often conventional wisdom that you should not respond to negative ads, thus giving greater publicity to the other side's agenda (apparently the advice that Senator Kerry and Senator Cleland followed), Lieutenant Governor Kaine went on TV immediately with his own ads. In the ad, he stood alone, looked into the camera, and said the Kilgore ad was false. He said he would abide by the death penalty laws of Virginia, while still repeating his unpopular position of personal and moral opposition to it. He repeated this ad at the expense of staying on his "own mes-sage," as traditional political consultants might have advised him.

In fighting back, himself, Mr. Kaine brilliantly made Kilgore's character the issue, as well as his own character—not only his moral convictions but also his willingness to fight back when he was smeared by his opponent. Editorialists and columnists throughout Virginia, as well as the Washington Post, *which influences the heavily populated areas of northern Virginia's suburbs and exurbs, responded by condemning Kilgore and praising Mr. Kaine's candor.*

In the end, Timothy Kaine was elected Governor of Virginia, one of the reddest of the Red states, succeeding his Democratic predecessor, Governor Mark Warner.

I was quoted in the August 13, 2005 Washington Post *story on the NARAL ad, criticizing it as misleading and hurting what needed to be a serious effort to examine Judge Roberts's record. I also indicated the importance of Democrats separating themselves from such distortions of the facts, especially when it occurred on our own side of the ideological divide.*

The next day, the reaction from at least some liberal Democratic friends of mine was fierce. It was as though I had signed up with the Republican Party or, at the very least, I had lost my manhood. "You're just in favor of wimping out. That's why we lose elections," one said. My response was that we get hurt when we get caught distorting the facts, and we should fight back when the other side does it. Then I asked, "How can we attack what happened to Cleland and Kerry and defend using a false ad against Roberts? Don't we lose credibility?"

"Well, that's different," was the answer. "We are right and they are wrong."

There it was—the double standard, without apology, and without realizing that by being as bad as they are, we lose—not win—elections.

So it hit me once again. There was something increasingly sick in our politics. Good people were moving further and further out of the mainstream. They were willing to justify and use distortions and half-truths not because they could defend them ethically or morally but because the other guy was doing it, so why not us? As former President Jimmy Carter commented: "The best way to win an election is totally destroy the character of your opponent."[5]

THE HYPOCRISIES ON THE LEFT

The Presumption of Innocence and the Double Standard of the Left

Civil liberties, due process, and the presumption of innocence—these are, or at least should be, fundamental principles of liberalism. Indeed, as long as I can remember, my dad, an unapologetic ACLU member and FDR liberal, always reminded me about the importance of these principles. He hated the demagogic and dangerous Senator Joe McCarthy precisely because McCarthy helped to destroy so many lives by his innuendo-based accusations. Those accusations of being a "communist" or a "pinko" immediately made headlines, and most people believed such accusations were as good as being guilty.

We have seen the danger of the scandal culture in the 1980s and 1990s, with too many journalists trying to get the story first before necessarily getting it right. The public reads headlines of accusations of wrongdoing and then is too quick to conclude, "where there's smoke, there must be fire." We also have seen how outraged Democrats were over the word "scandal" or "corruption" being associated with the Clintons and the Clinton Administration due to those headlines.

Yet some liberals today, despite their ideological commitment to civil liberties, seem too willing to ignore the presumption of innocence when applied to Republicans. One example (and there are many) could be seen on a liberal blog site, the Daily Kos, on October 17, 2005. Someone with the screen name "lorelynn" posted this comment about corruption in the Reagan Administration: "Challenged by a conservative to present evidence that Reagan ran the most corrupt Administration of the 20th Century, I assembled *this list of convicts* from Reagan's ranks [emphasis added]." "Lorelynn" then listed 21 alleged "convicts" who held positions in the Reagan Administration, including three—White House official Lynn Nofziger and Iran-Contra figures John Poindexter and Oliver North—whose convictions were overturned on appeal. Under the Constitution, these three individuals whose convictions were overturned are once again innocent until proven guilty. (In all three cases, the government never chose to re-try them.) Yet this did not bother "lorelynn," who still included them on the list of "convicts."[6]

Moreover, this liberal blogger began the list of Reagan Administration "convicts" with the following quote: "By the end of his term, 138 Reagan Administration officials had been convicted, had been indicted, or had been the subject of official investigations for official misconduct and/or criminal violations. The record of his administration was the worst ever."[7] This blurring of the crucial distinction between convictions vs. indictments/investigations is yet another scary symptom of today's presumption of guilt culture, to which partisans on the left and right both contribute.

Mike McCurry, former press secretary to President Clinton, recognized the danger of the over-use of the word "corruption" and failure to make these important distinctions: "We're now calling 'sleaze' and 'corruption' matters so insignificant that they would have gone unreported in earlier years. The best way to report on this is case by case. There's a rush to lump everything together."[8]

Of course, that could now apply as equally to the way Democrats have characterized Republicans, including most recently the Bush Administration.

This is scary stuff. The fact that this broad use of the word "corruption" without proof of guilt comes from an allegedly liberal blogger who should be more ideologically concerned about civil liberties, due process, and the presumption of innocence than people on the right makes it even scarier. The fact that this blogger has such a following among readers who also call themselves liberal and do not see the hypocrisy makes it scarier still.

Here's what the traditionally liberal *New Republic* wrote about another posting on the Daily Kos in early 2006:

> A regular writer at the Flagship liberal blog "Daily Kos" . . . quickly declared that "the real purpose of [Senator John] McCain's bipartisan task force [on lobbying reform] . . . is to whitewash a purely Republican scandal." Is it really? That's peculiar, given that McCain's hearings into the Abramoff scandal were—as [Democratic Senator Barak Obama] put it—"instrumental in promoting public awareness" of Washington corruption . . . *Don't try explaining that to the liberal bloggers. For them Good and Evil are always reducible to D and R.*[9]

We live in a dangerous presumption of guilt culture—and of all people, liberals, whose ideological values are supposed to emphasize civil liberties and due process rights, should be the first to blow the whistle on the rush to judgment. This should be the case whether during the McCarthy era of the 1950s, the Clinton scandal machine of the 1990s, or during the Bush Administration. To do otherwise invites not only a perception of a double-standard, but also opens Democrats up to charges of hypocrisy when a Democratic official also gets accused or indicted of lobbying corruption, as has occurred as recently as the spring of 2006.

In the case of former Republican House Majority Leader Tom DeLay, it is perhaps understandable that the Democrats could not resist holding his feet to the fire after his indictment by a grand jury in Texas. After all, his was the loudest voice of hate and partisanship when it came to declaring President Bill Clinton "guilty" and "corrupt," and he was now actually criticizing those who were not giving him the benefit of the doubt. Talk about chutzpah! This is the same man who unmistakably threatened the Florida state judges who would not reverse their decision on the Terry Schiavo case, saying: "The time will come for the men responsible for this to answer for their behavior."[10]

The same instinct to defend the presumption of innocence rather than accept the presumption of guilt should be applied by liberals to corporate CEOs post-Enron. Instead, most people, including too many otherwise civil-liberties minded liberals, are quick to assume that any CEO accused in the headlines of accounting fraud or insider trading must be guilty—until proven innocent. This is unfortunate and inconsistent with long-held liberal values.

Democrats may try to score short-term political gain by arguing that Republicans are generally more corrupt than Democrats, but this will not work. It does not work any better than when post–1996 Republicans tried to argue that the Democratic fundraising practices were any worse than what the Republicans had done. History still demonstrates that the American people can smell hypocrisy pretty quickly. For a Democratic Party that denounced these innuendo attacks on Bill Clinton's "corruption" so vociferously now to be so quick to do the same thing cannot be a good thing politically in the long run.

Democrats do have some leaders who are courageous and intellectually honest and willing to take responsibility when partisan excesses on their side occur. For example, Senator Harry Reid, the Democratic minority leader, learned that a Democratic press release had been issued, titled: "Republicans cannot be trusted to end the culture of corruption." It included the statement, "The idea of Republicans reforming themselves is like asking John Gotti to clean up organized crime." Senator Reid immediately took responsibility and apologized. The document, he wrote, "went too far, and I want to convey to you my personal regrets."[11]

WHERE ARE THE SMALL "D" DEMOCRATS?

Recently, I asked what I thought would be a provocative question at a dinner table peopled with liberal Democrats, who presumably believed in democratic values: "Why shouldn't we let voters in each state decide the legal definition of marriage and where the line should be drawn in regulating abortions? Why do we prefer trusting lifetime appointed judges to make these decisions?"

I looked around, waiting for a response. I assumed the democrats (as opposed to the Democrats) at the table would at least grapple with the problem of opposing democracy and preferring judicial decisions when the democratic results turned out differently than what we wanted. The response was quick—and fierce. I got killed. I was shouted down, called a homophobe, a male chauvinist pig, and a right-to-lifer.

It seemed as though some issues have become incapable of an honest give-and-take discussion, even among like-minded liberals who believe in free speech and open debate as fundamental values.

I decided that being provocative on this subject was not such a good idea.

The double standard on the issue of democracy versus judicial power practiced by some liberal purists has become increasingly apparent over the years. Of course, there are basic Constitutional rights that protect the individual from the democratic tyranny of the majority and that guarantee equal rights for all Americans. Liberals rightfully turned to the courts in the 1950s to bar segregation in public schools. This was not only because national as well as southern democratic institutions were unable to end segregation, but also because "separate but equal" was inherently unequal and, thus, violated the Fourteenth Amendment. It was also the fundamental individual liberty and privacy rights implicit in the Fourteenth Amendment that served as the basis for the Supreme Court decision in *Roe v. Wade* overturning state statutes prohibiting all abortions.

However, liberals also should believe that, whenever possible, democratic values and decision making should be preferred over fiats by federal judges appointed for life. Yet this much-needed debate within the Democratic Party over judicial power versus democratic processes has been thwarted by the purist left. It is not just that they reject any suggestion that reasonable abortion regulation or the legal definition of marriage are better left to democratic processes that reflect local mores and culture than the courts. Even such giant liberal jurists as Archibald Cox, Ruth Bader Ginsberg, and Stephen Breyer (the latter in his recently published highly regarded book, *Active Liberty*) question whether liberals have gone too far in seeking judicial fiats in areas better reserved to democratic processes. Of all people, liberals should prefer mobilizing voters over litigation to achieve their goals. The Democratic Party should remain faithful to its historic tradition of trusting the people, which runs back to Jefferson and Jackson.

It is ironic that the New Left in the 1960s developed the mantra of "power to the people" and "participation democracy" and "empowering neighborhoods." Yet, in the twenty-first century, purist liberals and some pro-choice activists fear fighting the battle for choice at the precinct level and would rather rely on nine people sitting in Washington as the U.S. Supreme Court (especially if *Roe v. Wade* is effectively overturned by a more conservative Supreme Court by allowing burdensome regulations that do not risk the life of the woman). Whether they like it or not, however, if Democrats do not win the presidential election of 2008, Democratic liberals will have no choice but to start doing the hard work of democracy to persuade a majority of voters, one voter at a time, of the correctness of their position on abortion.

RELIGIOUS TOLERANCE BE DAMNED

It was 1992, and I was hanging out on the floor of the Democratic National Convention as a delegate. The rumor had spread that the Pennsylvania delegation was thinking of walking out. That would ruin the unanimous nomination of then-Governor

Bill Clinton as the presidential nominee. The Pennsylvanians reportedly were angry because their Democratic governor, Robert Casey, had been barred from delivering an anti-abortion, "pro-life" speech to the convention.

I returned to the area where my Maryland delegation was seated. I asked a few of my fellow liberal Marylanders to join me in a resolution supporting Governor Casey's right to speak. "Aren't we in favor of freedom of expression and tolerant of dissent?" I asked. I was shouted down. "What are you, a pro-lifer?" a female Maryland delegation member asked me. I felt intimidated, and I shut up.

Eight years later, in 2000, Senator Joseph Lieberman, Democratic candidate for vice president, talked about God and his deep faith in his acceptance speech at the Democratic National Convention and in his early speeches on the campaign trail. As an orthodox Jew for the more than 30 years I have known him, Joe Lieberman lived his life as a religious man of faith. This was not an invention for the political occasion or words chosen for political effect.

Yet, virtually every one of my liberal friends, who knew of my long-time friendship with Senator Lieberman, told me they were not only uncomfortable with Joe Lieberman's frequent references to God and religion—they were certainly entitled to feeling that way—but were critical of him "bringing up God too much."

Shortly after, I happened to come upon and read the famous Farewell Address by Abraham Lincoln as he boarded the train in March 1860 from Springfield, Illinois, to start his inaugural journey for Washington, D.C. Ahead of him was war, death, and what he knew would be perhaps the most painful experience that any President in U.S. history had faced since the founding of the nation—a civil war between Americans, between states, between families, and brothers. And these were his final words as he said goodbye to his friends:

> *"Without the assistance of the Divine Being . . . I cannot succeed. With that assistance I cannot fail. Trusting in Him who can go with me, and remain with you, and be everywhere for good, let us confidently hope that all will yet be well. To His care commending you, as I hope in your prayers you will commend me, I bid you an affectionate farewell."*

I wondered: Would my liberal friends have regarded Abraham Lincoln as "bringing up God too much?" Could liberals really reconcile intolerance for people of deep religious faith who speak of their faith in personal and authentic terms as Abraham Lincoln did—even though they do so without proselytizing to others that they must accept their faith or, indeed, any faith—with the fundamental liberal value of tolerance?

"Why is there a Religious Right but not a Religious Left?" my oldest son, Seth, now age 36, once asked me. I thought about that and realized that there is, well, at least used to be, a prominent and outspoken religious left. They used religion, God, and the pulpit to preach social justice and—often *from* the pulpit—the duty and obligation of everyone to help the oppressed and the needy.

The first leader of the religious left was, at least in the view of many Christians I have talked to, Jesus of Nazareth. One thousand nine hundred and fifty-five years or so later, Reverend Martin Luther King and other religious leaders continued the work of Jesus in the early days of the Civil Rights movement. They spoke from the pulpit, preached about God, and quoted from the Scriptures over and over again. I wonder if there were liberal Democrats back then saying they were "uncomfortable" with politicians who referred to their Judeo-Christian faith while supporting Dr. King's dream of racial and social justice because they "talked about God too much."

In the 1960s, there was the inspiring Jesuit Catholic priest, Father Robert F. Drinan, who as a matter of moral conscience spoke out against the Vietnam War. He ran for and was elected to Congress while a priest on the platform that the War was morally wrong and needed to be ended. Robert Kennedy knelt in prayer with César Chávez in the Napa Valley grape vineyards seeking social and economic justice for the impoverished Chicano migrant workers. Then, there was the magical moment in February 2006, when rock icon Bono addressed the National Prayer Breakfast—3,000 members of Washington's business, civic, religious, and political establishment, most of them political and religious conservatives. Here is what Bono said:

> It is not a coincidence that in the Scriptures, poverty is mentioned more than 2,100 times. It is not an accident. . . . You know the only time Christ is judgmental is on the subject of the poor. "As you have done it unto the least of these my brethren, you have done it unto me." . . . *It is very easy, in these times, to see religion as a force for division rather than unity. . . . This is not a Republican idea. It is not a Democratic idea.* It is not even, with all due respect, an American idea. Nor is it unique to any one faith. "Do to others as you would have them do to you." Jesus says that.[12]

How would Bono have been greeted if he had made this speech at a Democratic National Convention? Perhaps it would have stirred memories of that tradition of a religious left not uncomfortable with mentioning God or faith in the context of a political speech. You cannot have a religious left without a religious right, however. You cannot believe in Bono's words without being tolerant of those whose religious faith leads them to political views vastly different from that of a pro-choice Democrat.

That is why an emblematic and soul-searching memory for liberals should be what the Democratic Party did to Governor Bob Casey of Pennsylvania when he asked to address the convention to explain his views opposing abortion on moral and religious grounds. By opposing Casey's ability to make a pro–right-to-life speech, the party acted in a way that is simply and starkly antithetical to liberalism by any definition. It is consistent only with intolerance and a need to divide the world into good and evil rather than right and wrong. Anyone who disagrees is on the wrong side of the line. It is not just the intolerance of many on the left of the Democratic Party to dissenting conservative Democratic views on issues like abortion, gay rights, prayer in school, and religious displays in public places. It is contempt or disrespect for the deeply religious and those who believe in the power of prayer.

That sneering attitude is not only felt within liberal circles over dinner table conversations but more acutely within wide swathes of America whose constituents do hold strong religious views. It is no wonder that the Democratic presidential candidates in 2000 and 2004 had to travel so far and wide to find anyone in the great middle and southern regions of this country who had any likelihood of voting for a national Democrat. If you are a Democrat and truly care about winning back the presidency and the Congress to bring back two-party government in this country, something is clearly wrong with that picture.

Bill Press, formerly the liberal co-host of CNN's Crossfire and now a talk show host on Sirius satellite radio, made the right distinction in his important book published in 2005 on religion in politics, *How the Republicans Stole Christmas*. Press articulated the distinction between speaking authentically of one's own faith in God and belief in religious and moral values versus organized religious groups, such as elements of the religious, evangelical right, to impose one's moral and religious values on others. This is precisely the distinction made by Madison and the Framers in the First Amendment: between barring the "establishment" of religion by the state—the famous "separation" between Church and State doctrine—versus honoring and guaranteeing the "free exercise" of religion. As Bill Press wrote:

> We are a secular nation . . . we are also the most religious nation on earth . . . 81% of Americans say prayer is an important part of their daily life . . . Our Founding Fathers had the wisdom, foresight, vision and courage . . . to make the United States the first nation on earth with a clear line of demarcation between religion and the state. . . . This was their great, double gift to the American people and to the world: the freedom to practice our faith, without having it undermined by the state; and the freedom to exercise our government without having it undermined by religion."[13]

Intolerance is just as unacceptable whether exhibited by someone on the left toward Governor Bob Casey or Senator Joe Lieberman or the religious right trying to impose their religious views on those who do not share them.

THE HYPOCRISIES ON THE RIGHT

"We took a strong stand in 1994 to make clear the Republican Conference would live by a higher standard than our Democratic colleagues. We won the election in '94 because we were going to be different, and what I continue to see is a slow but continual erosion in what made us different."

—*U.S. Rep. Chris Shays (R.-Conn.), Nov. 19, 2004.*[14]

The Silence of the Moralists

For those among Republican leaders who might claim that the slime campaign run against Senator Cleland was exceptional, or only happens to Democrats, it is important not to forget what happened to John McCain in March 2000 at the hands of Republican supporters of then-Governor George W. Bush. John McCain had just surprised everyone, especially then-Governor George W. Bush, and won the New Hampshire primary. His momentum seemed to be carrying him into South Carolina. If he won that state's primary, he could have been on his way to the Republican nomination. Then supporters of the Bush campaign began a classic smear campaign against Senator McCain. As the South Carolina campaign manager for McCain wrote subsequently, the "most effective smears are based on a kernel of truth. . . ." It seems that Senator McCain and his wife Cindy had adopted a daughter from an orphanage in Bangladesh. The child happened to have darker skin than a Caucasian.

Bush supporters—most likely organized by the South Carolina Bush campaign or its affiliates—started "push polling." This means making calls to undecided voters asking them leading questions that plant negative impressions about the opposing candidate. In this case, the question reportedly was whether a voter would be more or less likely to vote for John McCain if he or she knew that he had fathered an illegitimate black child. A Bob Jones University professor Richard Hand reportedly sent out an e-mail to "fellow South Carolinians" stating that McCain had "chosen to sire children without marriage." The mainstream media picked up the charge and publicized it. CNN interviewed Hand, confronting him with the fact that McCain did not have children out of wedlock. His answer should be made a classic in the moral hypocrisy of the religious right: "Wait a minute, that's a universal negative. Can you prove that there aren't any?"[15]

This was not the only example of the smears that hurt John McCain, a man of unquestioned integrity who was a POW and hero in Vietnam. After this, Governor Bush reportedly stood on a platform while a Vietnam veteran, Thomas Burch, who had previously accused Governor Bush's father, President Bush, of abandoning veterans, denounced Senator McCain as a POW who "came home and forgot us." Also, Bush supporters distributed leaflets describing McCain as "pro-abortion" and the "fag candidate" (because he was the only Republican candidate to have been endorsed by the gay Republican group, Log Cabin Republicans).[16]

Where was the moral leadership of the religious right and national Republican leadership denouncing these tactics?

Double Standards of the Religious Right

Let me get this straight. The self-proclaimed conservative Republican Party—the party of individual rights and states rights versus an intrusive federal government—rams a bill through Congress that would override a state legislature and state court? The Republican Party would attempt to interfere in a family's agonizing, private decision about what to do about Terri Schiavo, who was both a daughter and a wife, and who had been in what seemed to be a nonreversible vegetative state for ten years?

The same conservative Republican Party describes its commitment to the "right to life" as so strong that it opposes abortions of a one-minute-old fertilized cell even in the case of rape and incest (a position endorsed unanimously by numerous Republican National Conventions over the decades). If you doubt this, look at the position Republican Senator Tom Coburn took during his successful campaign in Oklahoma in 2004. He actually came out in favor of the death penalty for physicians who performed abortions except when the woman's life is in danger. Surely a majority of mainstream conservative Republicans would not support this position, indeed, probably a majority of pro-life Republicans. Not one national Republican leader, however, has criticized or publicly separated himself or herself from Senator Coburn's position on this issue, then or now. Indeed, the Republican National Committee continued to direct campaign contributions to Mr. Coburn even after he had taken this position.

Is this the same "pro-life" Republican Party that supports the death penalty? Is it the same party that supports the banning of stem cell research—in other words, putting a higher value on the "life" of a frozen embryo than on the millions of lives that might be saved through that research?

Former Republican Senator John C. Danforth, also an Episcopal minister, perhaps best summarized the alienation of traditional Republican conservatives in a June 2005 *New York Times* op-ed piece on the dominance of the religious right in today's Republican party:

> Republicans have transformed our party into the political arm of conserva-
> tive Christians. The elements of this transformation have included advocacy
> of a constitutional amendment to ban gay marriage, opposition to stem cell
> research involving both frozen embryos and human cells in petri dishes, and
> the extraordinary effort to keep Terri Schiavo hooked up to a feeding
> tube. . . . As a senator, I worried every day about the size of the federal
> deficit. I did not spend a single minute worrying about the effect of gays on
> the institution of marriage. Today it seems to be the other way around.[17]

Another take on this shift within the Republican Party comes from Kevin Phillips, a very influential Republican conservative writer. In 1969, Phillips published the seminal political work, *The Emerging Republican Majority*, which presciently predicted the tectonic realignment leading to a new conservative national majority that won the presidency for the Republicans by landslide margins in four out of the next five elections (1972, 1980, 1984, 1988). He correctly predicted that the movement of people and resources from the Northern industrial states into the South and West (apparently inventing the famous expression, the "Sun Belt") would create an enduring conservative Republican majority for decades to come. However, in his new best-selling book, *American Theocracy*, published in the spring of 2006, Phillips warns about the takeover of the Republican Party by what he describes as a "radical" Christianity theocratic movement.[18] Phillips writes ominously that the Republican Party's national leaders have allowed the "mingling of theology, popular culture and theocracy" which has "brought about aspects of an American Disenlightenment, to employ a descriptive antonym." He continues: "Effects can be seen in science, climatology, federal drug approval, biological research, disease control, and not least in the tension between evolution theory and the religious alternatives—creationism and so-called intelligent design."[19]

Phillips cites the hypocrisy of the moralistic Christian right and its obvious double standard—one example being their different attitude when it comes to women's sexual health concerns versus males and Viagra: "While the Christian right and the U.S. Food and Drug Administration blocked sexlinked medications for women—a vaccine to prevent HPV, the virus responsible for most cervical cancers, and Intrinsa, a testosterone patch intended to raise libido in women whose ovaries have been removed—male use of Viagra was encouraged."[20]

It is still debatable how numerous these religious extremists are and how much they influence Republican Party mainstream conservative leaders.[21]

Nevertheless, where are the Republican leaders speaking out against this theocratic shift within the Republican Party? Keeping silent as the far right hijacks
the party's agenda does not seem like the way to build a stronger America.

Judicial Conservative Liberals

> *I read the Supreme Court's decision overturning the 1994* Violence against
> Women's Act *with the same disbelief as when I read the opinion in* Bush v. Gore,
> *which overruled Florida state courts and elections procedures. These people call
> themselves judicial conservatives?*
>
> *The need for national uniform standards to deter wife beaters and batterers
> was so obvious that the final bill passed the House and the Senate virtually unani-
> mously. Liberals, conservatives, Democrats, Republicans, the president—it did not
> matter. All supported it. It was not even a close decision.*
>
> *The Supreme Court, then led by the late Chief Justice William Rehnquist,
> heard a challenge to the constitutionality of this legislation on the grounds that vio-
> lence against women is a state issue. The "commerce clause" argument being made
> to overturn a congressional statute seemed a stretch at best—that battering a
> woman within a state could not potentially effect interstate commerce, and thus
> could only be legislated at the state, not the congressional, level. It was natural to as-
> sume that a Supreme Court with seven of nine justices appointed by conservative
> Republican presidents would defer to Congress's legislative policy judgments. It
> would not be prone to "legislating" from the bench, as conservative Federalist Soci-
> ety members would say it. It was a logical conclusion, but wrong. Led by the so-called
> judicial restraint conservatives, Antonin Scalia and Clarence Thomas, the court
> held that the Violence against Women Act was unconstitutional by a 5–4 vote. The
> next day I tweaked a conservative Republican friend of mine about the decision.
> "Well, this is different," he said. "Congress shouldn't be dictating issues involving
> marital relationships—that should be left to the states."*

The Republican Party has made political hay over the years—really ever
since the Warren Court of the 1950s and 1960s—that there is something
wrong with "judicial activism." "Strict construction" of "original intent" was
preferable to "liberal" interpretations of the U.S. Constitution to "legislate"
from the bench. *This was and is the central tenet of Judge Robert Bork's philosophy.* During his Senate confirmation hearings, Chief Justice John Roberts
strongly endorsed the need for judicial "modesty" and "restraint" in deference to democratic policymaking.

Yet, the willingness of the conservative judges on the U.S. Supreme Court (and on lower courts as well) to overturn liberal social legislation has been breathtaking. The silence of the conservative leaders of the influential Federalist Society is equally surprising. It makes glaringly clear that there is a "good kind" of legislating from the bench and a "bad kind" (depending on what you agree or disagree with philosophically).

The Supreme Court in 1867 described declaring an act of Congress unconstitutional as an act "of great delicacy, and only to be performed where the repugnancy is clear and the conflict irreconcilable. Every doubt is to be resolved in favor of the constitutionality of the law."[22] For example, between 1790 and 1858, only two such invalidations occurred. This is because, as Professor Paul Gewirtz of Yale Law School and Chad Golder, a Yale Law graduate, wrote in a brief law review article: "Declaring an act of Congress unconstitutional is the boldest thing a judge can do. That's because Congress, as an elected legislative body representing the entire nation, makes decisions that can be presumed to possess a high degree of democratic legitimacy."[23] These are words that could be taken directly from a George W. Bush speech or the key note speech at the latest Federalist Society convention.

That is not to say that there are not and have not been very good reasons to strike down laws enacted by Congress. They may make good politics or good policy but are outside the boundaries of the Constitution and the federal system. Still, since the Supreme Court assumed its current composition in 1994, it has struck down 64 Congressional provisions. You would expect that the most conservative members of the court would have voted to strike down acts of the national legislature the least number of times, but this is wrong. In fact, it was Justice Clarence Thomas—who prides himself on being a "strict constructionist"—who had the largest percentage of votes in Supreme Court decisions overturning acts of Congress during this period: 65.63 percent. Justice Antonin Scalia was third, at 56.25 percent. The least likely to overturn congressional legislation was Justice Stephen Breyer, appointed by President Clinton and known as a liberal jurist—consistent with the views he expressed in his book, *Active Liberty*, which emphasizes respect for democracy.[24]

True judicial conservatives in the Republican Party must recognize the cynical double standard at work here. Judicial activism seems to be acceptable if it is in the name of conservative outcomes, unacceptable if it supports liberal ones. It is no surprise that many true conservatives are alienated and angered by hypocritical activist judges placing their political judgment over the democratic process in the name of "judicial conservatism."

Borrow-and-Spend Conservatives

"Reagan proved deficits don't matter. . . . We won the midterms. This is our due."[25]

—*Vice President Dick Cheney, shortly after the 2002 elections.*

From the earliest days, Republican conservatives have stood for fiscal responsibility, balanced budgets, and squeezing waste and pork out of federal spending, and the Democrats have been depicted as standing for the opposite. Somehow, something has happened to turn this picture upside down.

A Republican president and a Republican-controlled Congress took a trillion dollar surplus bequeathed by the Clinton Administration and have turned it into the greatest accumulated deficit and national debt in this country's history. In March 2006, President Bush asked and obtained from Congress a measure raising the debt ceiling of $8.184 *trillion* another $781 billion. This means that during his term in office, President Bush presided over a 46 percent increase in the federal debt (from about $5.6 trillion to $8.124 trillion). In contrast, during President Clinton's two terms, the increase was 28 percent, but during the last few years of his presidency, Mr. Clinton actually began to pay down the country's "real" debt, the debt held by the public.

In short, under a supposedly "conservative" president, the new debt accumulated during President Bush's years in office has been greater than the entire debt amassed by the United States from George Washington through Ronald Reagan's last term. Conservative author Kevin Phillips deplores the "national-debt culture" that spans both Republican and Democratic administrations, but he notes how Bush Administration policies have exacerbated things.[26] This is a truly radical shift in philosophy, in practice, and, as Vice President Cheney's remark (quoted above) indicates, in fundamental attitude. What Vice President Cheney is basically saying here is that it's okay to use credit cards today to enjoy the good life (as in getting reelected), and let our children and grandchildren worry about paying the bills.

In addition, the corruption and pork barrel politics that Gingrich Revolutionists accused the Democratic congressional majority of practicing has now been embraced, to say the least, by Republican conservatives. The so-called small government right has presided over a 29 percent rise in nondefense spending since 2001. In 1987, Congress passed a highway bill that contained around 150 pork projects. In the summer of 2005, Republicans passed a $275 billion Transportation Appropriations bill that contained more than 6,000 pork projects—including Vermont snowmobile trails, Virginia horse trails, decorative trees for the California Ronald Reagan freeway, and an Alaskan "bridge to nowhere." Referring to the Transportation Appropriations bill, Representative Young of Alaska, chairman of the House Transportation and Infrastructure Committee, bragged to his fellow conservative Republicans: "I mean I stuffed it like a turkey."[27] Republican Senator John McCain of Arizona described the legislation as "so laden with pork as to betray the party's principles."[28]

Since the Bush presidency began in 2001, the number of lobbyists has more than doubled. As *New York Times* columnist Frank Rich observed, "Conservatives who once aspired to cut government 'down to the size where we can drown it in the bathtub' . . . had merely outsourced government instead to the highest bidder." A Republican conservative columnist, Andrew Ferguson, put it more bluntly: "It's the end of the Republican Revolution. Slaying a corrupt, bloated Democratic establishment was out, gluttony for the GOP and its fat cats was in."[29]

Meanwhile, President Bush and congressional Republicans are now borrowing and spending more than $6 billion per month to pay for the war in Iraq. They do not even bother asking the wealthiest Americans who benefited from their tax cuts to give up, or even just delay, any of them. The Bush Administration's tax cuts, which overwhelmingly benefited the wealthiest 1 percent of America—amounted to $225 billion *in 2005 alone*. This would be more than enough to pay for hurricane reconstruction in Louisiana and Mississippi, as well as the schools the Bush Administration is building in Baghdad rather than in America. It is no wonder that traditional conservatives no longer recognize the Republican Party or the radical, tax-cutting, pork-barrel spending wing that has come to dominate it in recent years.

CONCLUSION: THE HATE WORDS ARE STILL WITH US

With the hypocrisy so visible on both sides of the aisle, it makes sense that there are vast numbers of people who consider themselves traditional Democratic liberals or traditional Republican conservatives who no longer understand where their parties are heading. Growing numbers of Americans across the spectrum are starting to see through the hypocritical justifications of leaders of the left and right who say: "what is good for us is wrong when they do it. What hurts us is okay to use against them."

We have seen the destructive power and hyper-partisanship of the scandal culture and gotcha politics. It has continued virtually unabated from the late 1970s until today, with a brief hiatus after 9/11. It is true that the independent counsel is no longer with us, thank goodness. Also, we have seen the good works Presidents Bill Clinton and President George H. W. Bush have carried out together as bi-partisan senior statesmen. They have reached across the political spectrum to teach the important lesson of how much good can be accomplished when two leaders from opposite parties can rise above politics. Silence is not forgivable when Democratic and Republican leaders allow those on the left and right to equate "corruption" with people who have yet to be convicted of any wrongdoing. Nor is it acceptable when Democrats and Republicans remain silent about, and sometimes even play up to, the hate-mongering talk show hosts, bloggers, and commentators who spew hate and filth every day.

Some, such as Vice President Cheney, actually still call into the *Rush Limbaugh Show*, without taking any pains to separate their own positions from Limbaugh's distortions and hate. (Of course, Mr. Cheney is more than happy to criticize certain equally irresponsible voices on the left for doing the same thing.) For example, Limbaugh has called abortion activists "feminazis," has told an African American caller to "take that bone out of your nose," has referred to prisoner abuse at Abu Ghraib as "blow[ing] some steam off," and has declared that "what's good for Al Qaeda is good for the Democratic Party." Through his silence and his apparent interest in supporting Limbaugh's show, Vice President Cheney tacitly endorses this hate speech. Either that, or he lacks the intellectual and political integrity to call him on it. Limbaugh regularly touts his close friendship with President Bush and that he "got a big hug" from him during a 2004 White House visit.[30]

Decent Republican conservatives and leaders also stay silent about the many other vicious right-wing talk show hosts and commentators. The most notorious, other than Limbaugh, are conservative extremists Ann Coulter and Michael Savage. Coulter thinks it is funny to state that "my only regret with the [Oklahoma City bomber] Timothy McVeigh is he did not go to the *New York Times* building" or to describe the Democratic National Convention as a gathering of the "Spawn of Satan convention." (For the latter comment, she was unceremoniously disinvited by *USA Today* as a columnist during the Democratic Convention.) Her obscene and hateful public comments about all Muslims must have made the Bush White House and responsible conservatives cringe, but still no one spoke out to denounce her. Coulter has said that all of Islam is a "car-burning cult." After she published another book filled with a continuing tirade of bigotry, lies, and hate, she was interviewed on *Hannity and Colmes* on October 4, 2004. Here is what she said to co-host Alan Colmes:

Colmes: Would you like to convert these people [Muslims] to Christianity?

Coulter: The ones that we haven't killed, yes.

Colmes: So no one should be Muslim. They should all be Christian?

Coulter: That would be a good start, yes.[30]

Then in early June 2006, Coulter published another book filled with hate ravings, this one accusing liberals of being "Godless." If it's possible, this time she was even more despicably vicious: She actually criticized widows of husbands who died in 9/11 of exploiting their husband's deaths to accomplish their own political agendas. The overwhelming silence of Republican leaders about Coulter's hate who have been so quick to exploit 9/11 and the security issue themselves—including the sanctimonious Rudy Giuliani, who uttered not a word of criticism of this hate-filled right-wing extremist—was nothing short of shameful.

Then there is Michael Savage. Here is a typical sample of Savage rhetoric that went unchallenged by Republican Party leaders during the time of the Terri Schiavo debate:

> The radical Democratic left is an army of soulless ghouls . . . they can engage in such anti-life abominations . . . because they have no souls. They have said that the tears of Terri Schiavo are mechanical. They have said that her smile is reflexive. They can rip an emerging child from the womb, murder it, and call this a compassionate act. Like [Josef] Mengele—the doctor of death from the Nazi concentration camps—the radical, soulless Democrats keep referring to "the doctors," as if a medical degree guaranteed humanity.[32]

Of course, these extremist remarks cannot be attributed to most responsible Republicans or conservatives. They find them as offensive and reckless as Democrats do.

But it remains a sad fact of political life in America that comments like these are usually greeted with a wall of silence from Republican Party leaders. This is the same wall that Democratic leaders display when extremist hate words come from some elements of the Democratic left. It is as if there is a different kind of tacit "non-gentlemen's agreement," i.e., not only do political leaders avoid offending the most extreme voices in their bases, but they also dignify them by appearing on their shows or reading their blogs.

Partisanship, hate words, venom, gotcha politics; it seems we have seen this all before, and it just keeps going and going. The *New York Times* published a full-page ad on January 20, 2006, signed by well-known liberals who have frequently been on the front lines fighting for social justice and liberal values. It called on President Bush to "step down and take your program with you. . . . This regime is immoral, dangerous, and criminally indictable. Bush Lied. Bush Spied. Bush Step Down."[33]

With memories of the haters of Bill Clinton, whom we liberals used to regard as so excessive as to be scary, we somehow seem to give a pass to the hate-Bush industry that has become rampant with the bloggers of the left. A *Washington Post* article in the spring of 2006 was devoted to a lengthy portrait of a woman who created a popular Bush-bashing blog and who proudly signs her posted comments, "if I can't rant, I don't want to be part of your revolution." On her blog was posted the following comment about George W. Bush:

> It was rather thoughtless of me to compare the most asinine, brutal, criminal, disgusting, enraging, felonious, gross, horrendous, incompetent, jaundiced, kleptocratic, lazy, malicious, nefarious, objectional [sic], psychopathic, quarrelsome, repulsive, sanctimonious, treasonous, unfit, vindictive, wasteful, xenophobic, yahooish, zealotic piece of [expletive] inhabiting the White House and the planet to persons suffering with a neurobiological disorder.[34]

Hate by the alphabet; trying to be cute with hate words doesn't mean this writer is not as scary as the Clinton-bashing fanatics were during the 1990s.

These are voices who are impatient with the hard work of politics and democracy. They seem to prefer using hate speech to win their argument over hard facts, knocking on doors, and trying to persuade the great middle of this country—both ideologically and geographically—to vote for candidates who agree with their liberal values.

On the other hand, the Republicans face the same challenge or worse on the fringes of their own party. The venom and blind hatred of Rush Limbaugh, Ann Coulter, and Michael Savage should be embarrassing to mainstream conservative Republicans. They should not get a free pass by being indifferent to their words, either. They should be willing to do what Senator Harry Reid did when he saw excessive Democratic partisan rhetoric and what Senator John McCain and Senator Chuck Hagel did when the shameful Chambliss ads were broadcast. They need to step up to the line and say this is wrong and we need to stop it.

President Bush did not help set an example of distancing himself from the haters and smear artists on the right wing fringe of his party when he appointed Karl Zinmeister in June 2006 as his top White House policy adviser. Zinmeister over the years had an extensive published record of hurling intemperate personal epithets not only at President Bill Clinton, of whom he seemed to have possessed a personal hatred that appeared to border on the pathological, but also Hillary Rodham Clinton, for "dubious personal morality." He had even attacked President Bush for showing "an eerie lackawanna when it comes to actually keeping a lid on the federal [spending] Pandora's box," neglecting to mention the borrow-and-spending pork barrel "conservative" Republican congress also had some responsibility. Also Zinmeister exemplifies the hypocrisy of the sanctimonious right (shared, as mentioned earlier, with elements of the purist left) by pronouncing moral judgments on the Clintons (and other liberals) while being guilty himself of inflating his resume and tampering with one of his more embarrassing quotes in the *New York Sun* by revising it (without disclosure) in the American Enterprise Institute Website. And this is the man President Bush appointed to the highest position in the White House advising on domestic policy![35]

Both parties face the challenge of standing up to the voices of hate on the left and right. In particular, the Democrats face the challenge of not resting on the unprecedented low job-approval ratings of President Bush and the disenchantment with the war in Iraq. Democrats have an opportunity in 2006 and 2008, but they must define an affirmative program going forward to address the real problems facing most Americans. Republicans cannot rest on the old tactics of dividing the country on bogus social issues like gay marriage constitutional amendments—as they did once again in June 2006. Both parties face the challenge of reaching across the center to forge a new governing majority.

CHAPTER ELEVEN

THE NEW CENTER

"The 1800 elections revealed, for the first time, the powerful centrist pull of American politics—the electorate's tendency to rein in anything perceived as extreme."

—*Ron Chernow*, Alexander Hamilton[1]

F atigue with the scandal culture and with the viciousness of personal destruction that has marked the country's politics for the last 30 years is an important catalyst in the growing revolt of a New Center in this country. As noted in chapter ten, increasing numbers of traditional liberals and conservatives see hypocrisy in the ranks of the Democratic and Republican parties, respectively, with traditional values and positions turned upside down and a double standard shamelessly practiced by both sides.

The dramatic decline in favorable impressions of *both* parties in 2006 cannot be denied. "A pox on both your houses" is the most common attitude across the political spectrum. The result of this growing center is a political majority positioned in the center-left and center-right who see more in common with each other than with the purist political extremes. If a leader steps forward ready to present an affirmative program to solve America's problems, whether Republican or Democrat, holding the mixed positions of this New Center, a majority is there to claim as early as 2006 or 2008.

The philosophical positions of people who find themselves in this New Center are nuanced, mixed, and unable to fit into the neat ideological pigeonholes that the press and the pundits love so much. The pundits on the left and right are used to reacting to such centrists with the almost robotic putdown that they are "wishy washy," "follow the polls and political winds," "have no vision or core values," or all of the above.

But they are absolutely wrong. The New Center has a simple idea about the role of the federal government that those pundits looking for neat ideological pigeonholes will have difficulty grasping: the federal government is a friend of the average American, not the enemy (a liberal idea), but that the federal government must be limited, pro-market, and committed to fiscal responsibility and balanced budgets (a conservative idea).

Note that this simple idea is a rejection of *both* the conservative orthodoxy that depicts government as the enemy and the liberal orthodoxy that government intervention and regulation are the only answer. Or, as Sebastian Mallaby wrote in an op-ed piece in the *Washington Post* in the fall of 2005, "the small-government right and the big-government left are equally exhausted."[2]

The New Center also responds to John Kennedy's memorable call for public sacrifice and service in his 1961 inaugural speech, to national public service at home and abroad, such as the Peace Corps or Teach for America, and looks for leaders ready to call for their involvement. The *Post*'s Mallaby also credited Republican Senator John McCain during his 2000 presidential campaign with reminding Americans of the "virtue—and more than that, the satisfaction—of committing to a cause larger than oneself: to the nation, to its system of values, to common ideals of honesty and decency. This appeal lays the emotional basis on which to build a better government."[3] Eight months later, in May 2006, a liberal Democratic writer, Michael Tomasky, amplified in detail on this concept of public interest over special interests by calling for what he described as a return to traditional liberal government that rises above focusing on individual or group "rights" and, instead, acts for the "common good."[4]

So, the New Center begins with a definition of government that is both responsible and limited, that calls on Americans to respond to a government acting in the public interest, and that calls on each American to contribute to the community and not just demand government benefits. Now the question is: What are the specific policy goals and values of such a government or, as former Democratic Vice President Walter Mondale asked during his 1984 presidential campaign regarding his then Democratic opponent for the nomination, Senator Gary Hart: "Where's the beef?" Here are the four core policy goals and values that would be the first priorities of a New Center government, reflecting its unique ideological mix:

1. Fiscal conservatism: paying our bills with current revenues and paying down the deficit, and thus ensuring economic growth and job creation rather than mortgaging the future of our children and grandchildren;

2. Social liberalism: new government programs that better help average Americans meet their most important needs—such as education, health care, protecting the environment, and achieving energy independence—paid for with new specially dedicated taxes that are protected in "trust funds" that cannot be raided for other purposes;

3. Cultural moderation: promoting family and moral values by returning to conservative, Jeffersonian values of a government that respects
individual liberty, privacy, and democratic choices at the state and
local level; and

4. Strong national defense: increased resources for military and intelligence capabilities to find and destroy terrorists wherever they are and
to prevent terrorist attacks; and a return to requiring all U.S. presidents, regardless of party or ideology, to obtain a formal *and explicit*
congressional declaration of war before committing U.S. forces to
wage war for any significant period of time.

This is not a crass effort to pick "two from column A and one from column
B" based on polling data in order to create an illusory political majority in the
center that tries to appeal to everyone. This is a mix of policy positions that are
both right for the country and also happen to be where a substantial portion of
the American people are and want their national political leaders to be.

Critics on the left and right hate the isolation this New Center approach
creates for each of them, so their instinct has been and will be to attack this
broad bipartisan philosophy as wrong and even dangerous for the Democrats
and Republicans, respectively. For example, President George H. W. Bush in
1990 and President Bill Clinton in 1993 were courageously willing to stand
up to their political bases, at great political cost, to raise taxes and cut spending in order to stop hemorrhaging deficits. This worked to build the foundation for the record-breaking surpluses and prosperity that occurred in the
later 1990s.

Critics on the right have to this day never forgiven President Bush I for
this. Nor have the purist voices of the Democratic left forgiven President
Clinton for holding the center on fiscal and cultural issues. For example, despite the fact that he was the first Democrat to win two terms in the White
House since FDR, there are still strident voices on the Democratic left who
blame the loss of Congress in 1994 and the last two presidential elections to
George W. Bush on Bill Clinton's centrist policies. One of the most strident
liberal bloggers, Markos Moulitsas, actually wrote in May 2006 that President Clinton was "complicit" in the Democrats' failure to win more than
50.1 percent of the vote since 1964—a year when Bill Clinton was a college
student at Georgetown University! He continued: "Despite all his successes—and eight years of peace and prosperity is *nothing to sneeze at* . . . Democrats held fewer congressional seats at the end of his presidency than
before it. The Democratic Party atrophied during his two terms, partly because of his fealty to his 'third way' of politics."[5]

As we saw in the 1960s, the left and the right seem to have more in common with each other, expressing contempt for those who are not ideologically pure by their definitions, than with those Democrats and Republicans who tend toward the center.

Being in the cross-fire between the hard ideological bases of the left and right would mean that the New Center is doing something right. So now let us examine each of the four policies and values that would constitute the first priorities of a New Center government and that would address the most divisive and important issues of the last several elections.

PAY YOUR BILLS ON TIME— AND TARGET MY TAXES

Fiscal Responsibility

The New Center starts with an old idea of the government paying its bills on time as well as a new idea for raising money to pay for investments in our future. First, the New Center would return to fiscal conservatism and pay-as-you go government, with the objective of reducing the national debt and returning to balanced budgets. That means no new spending without increasing taxes and/or specific cuts in other government programs.

Liberal Democrats learned the moral and economic value of conservative economics under President Bill Clinton and his Treasury Secretary, Robert Rubin. Reducing deficits and balanced budgets are fair to future generations, who should not be left to pay the bills while their parents and grandparents enjoy the benefits of living on credit. More importantly, however, the Clinton-Rubin team proved that government restraint in borrowing to finance deficits leads to lower interest rates and the unleashing of private capital and investments. That, in turn, produces new industries, jobs, and substantial new tax revenues for public investments.

A renewed version of the "Gramm-Rudman" budget act that makes it even more difficult for Congress to bust budget caps is one answer for this. It means no tax cuts without spending cuts to match them and no new spending programs without spending cuts or tax increases to match those as well. In addition, there needs to be a follow-on version of the 1990 and 1996 congressional budget rules forbidding the raising of budget ceilings. This time, however, it should require supra-majorities in both houses of Congress, not just the Senate, to raise the limit.

The reality is that to achieve such budget discipline, there needs to be bipartisan support. There is a substantial centrist consensus on such a policy. What is missing is the political leadership to execute it.

The Targeted Tax

Additionally, this approach supports the policy of using the "targeted tax" to raise new revenues. Another way of saying this is to call it a dedicated or "earmarked" tax. However, instead of borrowing to spend on pork like bridges that lead to nowhere, the tax revenues *must*, by statute, *only* be used for the designated purpose. One practical way to insure this is to create special "trust funds" into which revenues from that tax must be deposited. These would have statutory prohibitions (carrying steep sanctions applicable to federal appointees in the department to which the funds are assigned) against spending those funds on anything other than the legislated targeted purpose. An extra-majority—such as a two-thirds or four-fifths majority vote by both houses of Congress—would be required before Congress could re-direct the targeted tax revenues to anything other than what is specifically designated under the law.

Actually, the idea of a targeted tax is not new, but the expansion of the concept to fund new government programs and investments is. Since President Eisenhower in the 1950s, the Highway Trust Fund has received billions of dollars of gasoline tax revenues that for most of its history could only be used to construct the interstate highway system. Only in recent years, overcoming intense opposition from the highway lobby, have some of the Highway Trust Fund revenues been made available for mass and public transportation investments.

Once the American people trust that these targeted tax revenues cannot be raided by law, it is likely that support for these new types of taxes should dramatically increase. These could include a targeted, special "Value Added" or national sales tax (made progressive through lower-income rebates), as well as special targeted income tax surcharges weighted toward wealthier taxpayers.

LIMITED GOVERNMENT FIGHTING FOR US

The New Center starts with the proposition that, in a democracy, government is the friend, not the enemy, despite a quarter century of Ronald Reagan and his followers proclaiming that government is the problem, not the solution. The core values of liberal government remain those most eloquently expressed by former Senator and Vice President Hubert H. Humphrey: to provide a social safety net for children in the dawn of life; the elderly in the twilight of life; and to the poor, in the shadow of life.

This pro-government—albeit limited government—philosophy, however, must be tempered with an appreciation and protection of the workings of the private market and business enterprise. *The New Center must be prepared to challenge the anti-business left as well as the anti-regulation right,* just as Republican Theodore Roosevelt did in the beginning of the twentieth century and Bill Clinton did at century's end.

As Robert Kennedy stated and re-stated in urging support among liberals for his Bedford-Stuyvesant redevelopment package of tax incentives and business subsidies, there is nothing inherently anti-liberal about being pro-business and pro-market. History proves that job creation and economic opportunity can be sustained in the long-term only by growth in the private sector. And private sector growth requires profits to generate new investments.

At the same time, Republican Presidents such as Theodore Roosevelt, Dwight Eisenhower, and Richard Nixon demonstrated that there is nothing inherently anti-conservative about supporting reasonable regulation of the excesses of the private market. These center-right presidents—and many other traditional limited-government conservatives—recognized that, at times, the private market needs to be regulated and balanced by public interest considerations.

SETTING FOUR PRIORITIES

Once the New Center program has established "pay as you go" fiscally responsible economic policies and targeted new taxes that can win broad support in the country, the most important next step is to find the leadership discipline to set priorities and stick to them. There must be a guarantee to taxpayers that under the targeted tax system the money will go into "trust funds" that cannot be raided by anyone, including Congress, other than for the designated purpose of the targeted tax revenues.

Here are four potential targeted-tax "trust funds" that reflect the priorities of most Americans. First, the EDUCATION TRUST FUND would be specifically targeted to build new schools, fund higher teacher salaries, expand "Head Start" tutorial attention for the poor and the underprivileged, and provide tax breaks for the middle-class for college tuition. The HEALTH

CARE TRUST FUND would guarantee minimal access to insurance and health care for all Americans, with focus on those at the lowest end of the economic ladder. It would also use tax and other market incentives to reward private medicine for cutting medical care costs. The MASS TRANSIT AND ENVIRONMENTAL TRUST FUNDS would focus on transportation and environmental infrastructure. It could be used to rebuild our decaying bridges and highways, expand mass transit and public transportation alternatives, and to subsidize investments in technology to ensure cleaner air and water. Finally, the ENERGY INDEPENDENCE TRUST FUND would be for developing clean energy alternatives to achieve independence from foreign oil, including synfuels (using new synthetic fuel technologies to convert coal into gasoline, diesel, jet fuel, and other petroleum products, as Montana Governor Brian Schweitzer has argued is now both economic and practical at today's price of oil), safer and environmentally clean nuclear energy, electric powered cars, as well as solar, wind, and water power technologies. As Tom Friedman has written, unless America can be weaned away from dependence on foreign oil, this country will not be able to regain its economic and political independence that has been so compromised.

Of course, there are other priorities and public investments that can be paid for by new targeted taxes, such as restructuring Social Security, a massive "Marshall Plan" to re-train workers whose jobs are threatened by outsourcing and unfair competition in developing countries, and expansion of President Clinton's national service corps in which all high school graduates can perform some form of national service for one to two years after graduation.

Once the targeted tax is accepted as the governing revenue-raising principle, there is a greater chance for selling tax increases in the future to fund new programs such as these, as well as the ability to address the new problems that are bound to arise.

CULTURE MODERATION AND TOLERANCE— "LEAVE ME ALONE" PROTECTION OF INDIVIDUAL LIBERTY

The conventional wisdom is that Democrats have lost many Red State voters on cultural and moral issues, making the difference in the contested states in 2000 and 2004. Polling data suggests that is true.

What has been missed, though, is that these cultural issues also present dangers to the Republican Party. As the radical religious right comes to dominate the party, the extreme positions they have dictated on these cultural issues have already alienated broad numbers of center-right Republicans. In fact, the extreme ends of both parties have angered centrist liberals and conservatives. These centrists share basic principles concerning these cultural issues: toleration of differences in religious faith and moral values, preferring democratic processes and decision-making to judicial ones, and opposition to excessive government interference in individual liberty and privacy rights. This is how and where the center-left and the center-right can come together.

Applying these principles to the five hottest and divisive cultural issues—immigration and treatment of illegal aliens, abortion, guns, prayer in public places, and gay marriage rights—produces positions that are not very difficult to articulate and offer the best chance of achieving a consensus in the broad center of American politics.

Immigration and Illegal Aliens

The first illegal aliens—or at least the most famous—to arrive in America without permission of Native Americans were the Pilgrims.

Today's debate about what to do about the nation's eleven million or more illegal aliens has a clear, surprisingly obvious centrist solution, which polls show is supported by more than 60 percent of all Americans across the political spectrum. Most everyone agrees that there must be better security at America's borders—not just to protect against a flood of illegal immigrants but potential terrorists as well. America is the land of immigrants—and most Americans are proud of that heritage. The first step, therefore, is not only increasing border security but re-evaluating the quota ceilings for legal immigrants to determine whether they can be gradually increased and improving the procedures for visa issuance so that more *legal* immigrants are permitted, rather than forcing desperate people to sneak over the borders illegally.

In addition, substantial majorities of Americans—with perhaps only the hard-core right wing opposed in what appears to be nothing more than old-fashioned nativism—support allowing America's current 11 million illegal immigrants to *earn* their citizenship over time. If they pay their taxes, are fined for illegal entry, and can earn their citizenship through a probationary period of work, civic responsibility, and possibly a public service requirement, they should be able to become U.S. citizens.

Demagogic and strident opponents of this fair and thoroughly American solution forget we are a nation of immigrants and our diversity is our strength—from the Irish, Italian, and southern European immigrants of the late nineteenth and early twentieth centuries to today's Hispanic and Latino immigrants. The series of impressive grassroots demonstrations recent immigrants carried out by the hundreds of thousands in the spring of 2006, with many families and their children risking INS seizures in order to make their case to be allowed to become American citizens, prove the commitment of these resident illegal immigrants to the American way.

President Bush, living up to the slogan of "compassionate conservatism," has broken with the shrill voices of his Republican base and supports this centrist solution. Wrote John Cassidy, in the April 10, 2006, *New Yorker:* "Over the course of its history, the United States has gained enormously from its image as an open society: open to new commodities, open to new ideas, open to new people. President Bush, to his credit, regularly defends this tradition, and urges voters to reject the rival tradition of insularity and isolationism." Republican conservative leader Grover Norquist sees the political necessities for Republicans to be cultural moderates on this immigration issue. "We can't afford to do to the Hispanics what we did to the Roman Catholics in the late nineteenth century: Tell them we don't like them and lose their vote for a hundred years," he said.[6]

When Grover Norquist, the *New Yorker,* and I agree on something, you know it is part of a strong new center position that should prevail.

Abortion

The New Center balances government's obligation not to intrude on the right to privacy and individual liberty as guaranteed under the 14th Amendment and, wherever possible, respect and deference to democratic processes. This centrist balance is possible without overturning *Roe v. Wade.* Pro-choice liberals must allow states to regulate abortions if their state legislatures, reflecting popular will, stay within the Supreme Court's standard, articulated by Justice O'Connor, that such regulations cannot "unduly burden" a woman's right to privacy. All but the more extreme pro-life conservatives can concede that banning *all* abortions under *all* circumstances (including rape and incest or where the health of the mother is endangered) violates a woman's constitutionally protected liberty and privacy interests.

This could be the real wedge issue that could bring the center-left Democrats and center-right Republicans together—forcing Republican candidates to defend, or denounce, the positions taken by religious right extremists. As pointed out in the previous chapter, Senator Tom Coburn from Oklahoma is on record favoring the death penalty for doctors who commit abortions other than to save the life of a woman, which would include cases of rape and incest. In March 2006, the South Dakota legislature codified Senator Coburn's total ban—in violation of *Roe v. Wade*—hoping a newly constituted Supreme Court would have the fifth vote to overturn it.

With the additions of Justices Roberts and Alito to the U.S. Supreme Court, it is clear that even if *Roe* is not overturned, the court will give state legislatures broader discretion to regulate abortion, such as parental and spousal notification, consent requirements, waiting periods, and counseling on adoption and other alternatives. Thus, Justice O'Connor's "undue burden" standard will likely be increasingly narrowed, perhaps even to the point where it does very little to protect women from oppressive regulations. That will make it very difficult for women to obtain an abortion, at least without traveling to another state. This would end up, as it almost always does, burdening the poor, who will not be able to afford traveling to get an abortion, while the wealthy will buy airplane tickets and make appointments with doctors in pro-choice states.

When and if Justice John Paul Stevens retires, and if he is replaced with an anti-*Roe* justice before the end of President Bush's term, it is entirely possible that there will be a 5–4 majority in favor of upholding the South Dakota statute and overturning *Roe*. Twenty-three states—including such supposedly "Blue" state bastions as Massachusetts, Michigan, Pennsylvania, and Illinois—have laws on the books that have "trigger" laws or an existing ban on the books that would be automatically reviewed on the overturning of *Roe*.[7] The result could be a huge political backlash against the Republicans. Moderates would be caught between placating their religious right, anti-abortion base, and the substantial majority of the American people who believe a woman should be able to get an early-term abortion in some circumstances, such as rape and incest. Pro-choice supporters will have to look to the ballot box and the political process to protect their individual liberties and privacy rights. They will have to knock on doors of voters in contests for the state legislature and convince a majority to vote for pro-choice or at least moderate legislators.

The democratic process must be counted on in the world beyond *Roe v. Wade*. Politics and the power to persuade others of the validity of your viewpoint must once again be the primary instrument to prevent the government from intruding on individual liberty and privacy. This will be especially true for the private doctor-patient relationship concerning the difficult and tragic decision to have an abortion.

An increased understanding of each side's respective moral and personal viewpoints will come about through that rough process of politics and debate. That is what politics produces in its best sense: understanding. Out of that understanding, the great political center will find a nuanced balance on this issue as well. That balance recognizes that abortion is a tragic and difficult decision for women, and that society should do everything possible to make it rare, especially after the first term, and used only when there are no other alternatives. As one pro-choice writer recently put it, commenting on the political difficulty pro-choice Democrats have had defending late-term abortions, "When you look at the trends—more foolproof contraception, more access to morning after pills, earlier and fewer abortions—you can begin to envision a gradual, voluntary exodus from at least half the time frame protected by *Roe*. That's the half the public doesn't support."[8]

Anna Quindlen wrote a column for *Newsweek* in November 2004. It should be required reading for those who genuinely believe that the choice to have an abortion is a fundamental right of a woman as well as those who genuinely believe any type of abortion should be barred by law. Ms. Quindlen, who as a columnist for 15 years has been strongly pro-choice, concludes:

> People will keep on reducing this discussion as best as they can: God and freedom, rights and wrongs. But this will never be an easy issue to parse. It can't be; instead of fitting neatly into black-and-white boxes, it takes place in that messy gray zone of hard choices informed by individual circumstances and conscience. People of good faith need to talk about it just that way, to advance the dialogue even in the face of rigid opposition. We insult women by suggesting that this issue is easily encapsulated in aphorisms. We insult ourselves by leaving its complexities unexamined.[9]

Guns

The conventional wisdom has it that in the last two presidential elections Democrats lost some states, such as Arkansas and West Virginia, primarily on the issue of guns. Democrats failed to use their framing of the gun issue as a wedge to peel off moderate suburban and exurban Republicans. For example, Democrats could have accurately depicted the NRA-dominated Republican Party as opposed to bans on the sale of assault weapons and other weapons of war—an example of an NRA position that is rejected by over two-thirds of the American people in both political parties.

However, when it comes to gun ownership and regulation, the "leave me alone" attitude of the New Center should be applicable. Democratic (small "d") values should generally prevail, with states given greater discretion to protect gun ownership rights as well as to regulate gun usage. Federal legislation is also necessary to ban weapons used for war, not for hunting and recreational purposes. Huge majorities of the American people support such bans—another wedge issue that would appeal to a broad New Center electorate.

Faith and Prayer

Most Americans—left, center, and right—believe in a strict separation of Church and State, a value that clearly traces back to the Founding Fathers. This is not only reflected by the Establishment Clause of the First Amendment but also in the Federalist Papers and other contemporaneous writings. These same Founders, however, publicly spoke and wrote about God and religion frequently.

The Supreme Court since the Warren Court has tried to draw the line between coercive practices and voluntary ones. This draws a line between prohibited endorsement and financial subsidies of religion by government versus noncoercive choices and equal access to public places by people of faith as well as atheists. The Supreme Court will continue to try to find the right line between the First Amendment's ban on the "establishment" of religion by coercive government activities versus the "free exercise of religion" also guaranteed by the First Amendment. Ultimately, democracy will once again become more important under the new Roberts-Alito conservative-dominated Supreme Court. This means that, as in the cases of abortion and guns, advocates will have to turn to politics, the polls, and the political marketplace. More nuanced positions are likely to be present if democratic processes are permitted to prevail at the state level, such as some states allowing for a voluntary moment of prayer or contemplation in public school classrooms and other public events.

Gay Rights and Gay Marriage

On this difficult issue, two competing values must again be balanced. On one side is the need to respect an individual's liberty and right to make private moral and lifestyle choices, including sexual preference and choice of marriage partner. The individual needs to be treated with equal protection and without discrimination as guaranteed to all citizens under the 14th Amendment to the Constitution. On the other side is the democratic value of allowing popular will, preferably acting through state legislatures and local governments, to legally define marriage in a way that reflects that state's cultural mores.

Despite all the alleged divisiveness and apparent polarization surrounding this issue, there should be a broad centrist consensus on this issue. Again this would reflect the "leave-me-alone" attitude and a preference for allowing the democratic process to dominate decision-making at the state and local level. States and communities will be given broad discretion to decide on definitions of marriage, while the Supreme Court and Congress will be expected to ban discrimination and ensure equal Civil Rights for all, whether a gay or heterosexual couple.

Security, Security, Security

As they say in real estate, there are only three important words—except now, faced with a world threatened by terrorists, the word is "security." Clearly on this issue, Democratic liberals are more vulnerable than Republican conservatives. This traces back to the anti-military rhetoric of the protests of the 1960s against the Vietnam War and through support of substantial defense cuts and the "nuclear freeze" in the 1980s. The Iraq War, however, has the potential to change the entire dynamic. If there was ever an issue that has the potential of bringing left and right together into an angry center, Iraq is it. By the spring of 2006 a substantial majority of the American people believed that the Iraqi intervention was a mistake. Increasing numbers also began to realize that more than that, it had actually *increased* the dangers of terrorism, not decreased it, since it diverted our military and financial resources away from finding and destroying Osama Bin Laden and destroying Al Qaeda. It also significantly isolated the United States and diminished its credibility in dealing with greater dangers of WMDs in North Korea and Iran.

The current political atmosphere is more than a little reminiscent of the "fight or get out" mood that brought left and right together in the closing days of the Vietnam War. U.S. soldiers and diplomats today find themselves in a crossfire between warring Kurds, Sunnis, and Shiites. As of the spring of 2006 the United States was spending more than $6 billion per month with no end in sight. More and more Americans are asking why we are borrowing billions to reconstruct Baghdad instead of rebuilding New Orleans and Gulfport, or the bridges, highways, and schools in this country.

Meanwhile, soldiers on the ground whose lives are in jeopardy have no apparent easy way out. Parents back home on the left and right are asking why. A mother of an Ohio marine killed in an August 2005 roadside explosion put it succinctly: "We feel you either have to fight this war right or get out." This is the closing of the circle between the left and right—let's win or get out—that occurred in Vietnam. It clearly is happening now across the country and across the spectrum when it comes to Iraq.

That being said, honorable Senators and Congresspersons in both parties voted for the war resolution because they genuinely believed that removing the murder-thug Saddam Hussein was a good thing and the establishment of a democracy in Iraq could have encouraged the spread of democracy and stability throughout the Middle East. No one wants to leave a "rogue state" in Iraq as a new terrorism base for Al Qaeda and only a few are indifferent to the moral and security consequences of a precipitous withdrawal of all U.S. forces. But if and when U.S. forces are mostly withdrawn, American military power, especially air power, will still be available, as it was to destroy Al Qaeda's bases in Afghanistan. At some point in the not too distant future, though, and it could be as soon as the 2006 Congressional elections, the broad centrist consensus will be that it is time to set a reasonable time table to turn this war over to the Iraqis. No war can be fought if the American people do not support sending its young men and women to risk their lives. That was the lesson of Vietnam. It is now more and more the reality of the decline of popular support for the Iraq War on the left, right, and center.

Even as late as 1972, most Americans abhorred the notion of simply picking up and leaving Vietnam. Most Americans were still concerned then about injuring America's credibility and honor by a "unilateral withdrawal." Those two words were viewed as tantamount to aiding and abetting the enemy. Thousands of American deaths and casualties later, in 1975, a Republican president presided over the final "unilateral" withdrawal of U.S. troops. Americans watched on TV as the last U.S. helicopter took off from the roof of the U.S. Embassy in Saigon, with the Vietnamese who worked for the Americans hanging from the landing runners. This left a generation of Americans asking, "What did those young American heroes die in Vietnam for? To protect the mistakes made by old men in Washington who sent them there?"

So, that difficult decision to get out of Iraq and let the Iraqis decide their own future may yet be inevitable. American military force can still be redeployed in nearby bases "over the horizon," however. They will be ready to react to the appearance of Al Qaeda or any terrorist-harboring government that could threaten America.

Whichever party and political leader is able to take the lead on a position that gets Americans out of harm's way and out of Iraq responsibly, while reinforcing U.S. commitment to seek out and destroy Al Qaeda and their protectors wherever they are, will be supported by a broad center of Americans in this country.

Going forward, there is one lesson learned from the intervention in Iraq that all Americans should support: It is time to require the president of the

United States—*any* president, regardless of party or ideology—to follow the United States Constitution and refrain from making war without a declaration by the U.S. Congress. After Vietnam, Congress tried to enforce the Constitution by passing the War Powers Act, which would require a president to seek such authority or, after responding to an emergency with military deployments, to seek post-facto congressional authority.[10] Now, in the wake of Iraq, more and more foreign policy and constitutional experts are making the case for new and more enforceable congressional action to prevent future preemptive wars by U.S. presidents without an *explicit* declaration of war by the U.S. Congress. It is certainly possible that had there been such a requirement imposed on President Bush, a congressional declaration of war supported by the American people would not have passed. At the very least, the debate and Congressional hearings would have increased the chances that the flaws in the intelligence on WMD would more likely have been discerned.[11]

CONCLUSION

"Look, there's Ted Kennedy, shoulder-to-shoulder with John Mc-Cain, Republican presidential frontrunner, just after the collapse of the immigration deal the pair had brokered. And there he is, again, right behind a beaming Mitt Romney—Kennedy's '94 [Republican] Senate opponent, Massachusetts Governor and, yes, 2008 Republican presidential wannabe—as Romney signs a [state] health care bill."

—*Ruth Marcus*, Washington Post, *April 25, 2006*

In this same column, Marcus questions whether some partisan Democrats regard Kennedy as a "political dinosaur" because of his willingness to engage in "cross-party collaboration" to actually solve problems rather than to play partisan politics. But, she writes, "if Kennedy is a dinosaur, we should all—Republicans and Democrats alike—lament the arrival of a new political ice age in which the ability to legislate is frozen and bipartisanship is extinct."

So, it seems, Kennedy's brand of partisanship—fight for your principles and then reach out to the other side and try to solve the people's problems—may be subject to ridicule in today's polarized political culture. But there is anecdotal evidence everywhere that the voters out there—everywhere, Red States, Blue States, and in-between states—are waiting, ahead of the inside-the-Beltway partisans, for the politicians to catch up or for some leader from one of the two parties to get out in front of the great wave of desire for problem-solvers who can rise above partisanship.

The bad news is that the polarization and hyper-partisanship on the left and right have not disappeared. The hate culture, the politics of character assassination, and the presumption of guilt are still with us. You can still hear the venom on the right-wing radio talk shows or read it on the strident left-wing blog sites.

But the good news is that the New Center is growing, energized by repulsion from these haters and hyper-partisans, ready to revolt and to embrace a party or a politician who can seize the moment and shape a new kind of politics of consensus and civility. And there are places in the United States where it is already happening. Take the redistricting system, for example, established in the state of Iowa. There, with the support of Democratic Governor Tom Vilsack, congressional district lines are drawn not by partisan Democrats trying to roll over Republicans or Republicans trying to roll over Democrats, but rather, through the neutral auspices of a bipartisan commission.[12]

It is entirely possible that a breaking point has been reached. The country may be positioned for a new centrist politics—even a Grand Coalition presidency and bipartisan government—where problem solving is the priority rather than the gotcha politics of personal destruction that we have seen practiced by ideologues dominating both parties over the last 30 years. What is missing is, simply, leadership. As Carl M. Cannon wrote in the January 21, 2006, cover story for the *National Journal:* "It's tempting to invoke Ben Franklin's quip about all hanging together lest we 'all hang separately.' But . . . the real moral of this story might be that if it takes a village to polarize a nation, it may take a president to heal it."[13]

CHAPTER TWELVE

PURPLE NATION
AND THE
"GRAND COALITION"
GOVERNMENT

There may be hope for Washington yet. We may have found a so-lution for reversing the partisan politics of hate that has crippled governance in the nation's capital.

Call it the X Factor. Or more accurately, the "Ex" factor.

The Ex-Factor: While Washington's top Republicans and Democ-rats seem incapable of halting their political food-fight to find compromise solutions for our problems, Washington's most promi-nent ex-officials have been demonstrating that there is nothing in the DNA of elephants and donkeys that prevents peaceful and even constructive coexistence.

—Martin Schram, Scripps Howard News Service,
March 7, 2006

As Martin Schram, one of the great political journalists of our time, points out, our nation's ex-presidents—Gerald Ford, Jimmy Carter, and, most recently, George H. W. Bush and Bill Clinton—have a habit of reaching across the Republican and Democratic Party divide to work together, especially on humanitarian efforts. That in itself is not very un-usual. There is a unique opportunity at this moment in history, however, for current political leaders of both parties to do the same.

There is a strategy that would allow leaders of either party to exploit the anger in the New Center of this country and to turn it into a new *bipar-tisan* consensus for governing. They can do this only if they have the wis-dom to act, the courage to take political risks, and the strength to challenge conventional wisdom. If there are leaders running for president in 2008 from either or both political parties who fit this bill, then it may be at last possible to enjoy a bipartisan Grand Coalition government—even for just one four-year presidential term. More importantly, it may be possible to break the terrible cycle of hyper-partisanship and division facing the country today.

For the experiment to forge a bipartisan Grand Coalition government to be even remotely possible rather than a political scientist's pipedream, the presidential candidate needs to possess two things. First, the candidate must authentically stand for the New Center's ideological mix of fiscal conservatism, social liberalism, and cultural moderation. Second, the candidate must be a political leader with the courage—and thick skin—necessary to take on the left and the right in both political parties. Theodore Roosevelt came close in his nearly two terms as president, but his 1912 third-party campaign ended up leaving him as a caricature of himself. Bill Clinton came close to establishing an enduring "third way" in his second term—having defied the liberal wing of his party on the balanced budget, welfare reform, and NAFTA. Of course, the Lewinsky matter tragically interrupted his historic effort to reposition the Democratic Party as a centrist party.

George W. Bush began his presidency under the banner of "compassionate conservatism" and dramatically brought the country together as it has never been before in the days after 9/11. Then for reasons that are still not clear, he quickly undermined that unity and exacerbated the divisions between Red and Blue states by going strongly to his right on economic and cultural issues to "stay with the base." This has ultimately caused even more division because of the war in Iraq.

There is, in fact, a precedent in our nation's recent history of a politician who reflected both the ideological mix of policies and the brand of leadership willing to take on the left and the right, standing and abiding on his deep convictions. That politician was the late New York Senator Robert F. Kennedy. He had been known, even after his election to the U.S. Senate in 1966, as a partisan Democrat as well as a loyal and sometimes ruthless supporter of his brother, President Kennedy. He slowly evolved, however, into a different person and different kind of leader. This change most dramatically manifested itself in the brief four-month period that he ran for president between March and June 22, 1968, when he lost his life to an assassin's bullet. Those who are ready to seize the moment of history we now face and who are looking for the kind of political leadership that might make it happen would do well to study his example.

THE ROBERT KENNEDY PARADIGM

As the liberal majority coalition of the Democratic Party unraveled in the late 1960s, only one politician at the time seemed to demonstrate the ability to defuse the hate on both sides: Robert F. Kennedy. Most conservatives probably think of RFK as a figure of the left. He was certainly disliked by many conservatives back in the 1960s, particularly during his presidential campaign when he strongly opposed the Vietnam War and challenged President Johnson's policies before he even entered the race. Seeing him as just a liberal, though, is much too simplistic. True, Kennedy was liberal on social issues and came to strongly oppose the Vietnam War, but he was conservative on law and order, religion, and, in many respects, was pro-business. He was also a strong anti-Communist. In fact, during his tenure as New York senator, he was opposed, even hated, by substantial numbers of New York liberals.

For example, when Kennedy announced his Bedford-Stuyvesant redevelopment plan, which used Republican-style market incentives and tax breaks for business to spur jobs in the urban inner city, the liberal writer Robert Sheer wrote disdainfully in *Ramparts Magazine:* " . . . the solutions which [Kennedy] has begun to propose would not be likely to shock even the more conservative members of the Senate. . . . The Kennedy plan . . . [is]more reminiscent of [conservative Republican] Ronald Reagan than [liberal Republican] Herbert Lehman." Michael Harrington, a well-known Democratic Socialist writer, criticized Kennedy for putting "too much trust in private business, which remains motivated by profit, rather than by social and aesthetic goals."[1] When told about this criticism from the left, Kennedy is said to have responded (at least, in paraphrase), "The difference between me and them is I mean what I say."[2]

Meanwhile, the leading conservative author and publisher at the time, William F. Buckley, Jr., had positive words about Kennedy's market approach. He wrote:

> Senator Robert Kennedy was distributing a statement on the poverty program so sensible that it made recommendations I made three years ago. . . . [He recommended] a series of tax inducements to private enterprise to (a) give jobs to the poor and unskilled workers; (b) build and operate plants in ghetto areas; and (c) replenish the capital machinery of those plants by generous tax depreciation schedules. . . . The stock market went up on the day Mr. Kennedy made his poverty proposals. Appropriately.[3]

It is true that Kennedy was increasingly liberal on social issues after becoming a senator and especially during his brief presidential campaign. As stated in chapter ten, he prayed with César Chávez in the grapefields of California to win collective bargaining rights and justice for agricultural workers. Also, he went into the worst neighborhoods of the inner cities, including the night Martin Luther King was assassinated, to reach out to African Americans and other minorities. He spoke out for the underclass and the under-represented. He also appealed to blue-collar social and religious conservatives, however. As a former attorney general with a reputation of being tough on crime, he did not yield any terrain to Republicans (or supporters of Alabama segregationist George Wallace) when talking about law and order. Plus, he was a spiritual and religious Catholic who expressed private moral reservations about abortion (though the issue had not fully ripened into a political controversy before his death).

He was sometimes rough, often described as "ruthless" when he ran his brother's campaign for president, but was seen by both left and right as blunt-speaking, passionate, and authentic. There is no doubt that in the closing months of his life and his campaign people across the spectrum were drawn to him. His followers ran the gamut, from culturally conservative blue collar workers—who became "Reagan Democrats" in the 1980s—to the poorest African Americans and Hispanics in America's underclass. The results of the May 1968 Indiana Democratic primary were a dramatic indication of this. He carried 9 of the 11 congressional districts, won 17 of the 25 rural southern counties, won more than 85 percent of the African American vote, and carried the seven backlash counties that segregationist George Wallace had won in the 1964 Democratic presidential primary.

So, although RFK is remembered as a liberal for his 1968 anti-war and anti-poverty presidential campaign, he is in fact the model that may best lead the way to the New Center in the twenty-first century. He represented someone who is neither left, nor right, but both; liked and disliked by both; pro-business but also pro-regulation; religious and even moralistic about family values and faith, but tolerant of dissent and committed to the separation of Church and State. Most importantly, Robert Kennedy connected with people who wanted their problems solved. This is a model that may hold the potential key to ending the cycle of hate and destructiveness in politics on both sides.

THE NEW REFORM ERA

I have a 72-hour rule. If I stay in Washington for more than 72 hours, I have to bathe myself in the same stuff I use when one of my dogs gets into a fight with a skunk—stuff to get the smell out.

—Democratic Montana Governor Brian Schweitzer,
May 23, 2005[4]

If we can once again find a leader like Theodore Roosevelt or Robert Kennedy, he or she must above all regain the trust of the American people. This leader must not only reject the hyper-partisanship that has alienated so many Americans but also stand for wholesale reform of the way business is conducted in Washington. Specifically, this means lobbying, money, and the special interests. To seize, hold, and build an enduring majority coalition in the New Center, there must be a broad, bi-partisan commitment to a program of *real* lobbying and political reform. Without this, it will be impossible to restore the people's trust, making effective democratic governance difficult, if not impossible.

Thus, one issue that could bring left, right, and center together is reform of the role money and lobbyists play in our political process. By 2006, we clearly have reached the critical mass for an angry center demanding real reform. The usual system for catching crooks is not working. Nor can we rely on congressionally imposed ethics rules that are self-enforced. Mechanisms currently in place for bi-partisan investigations and sanctions are helpful, but they are not enough.

Leaders of both parties have too often colluded in mutual bankruptcy, both literally and figuratively. Both sides have committed to borrowing and spending on pork and special interests with no end in sight; both have failed to produce any useful ideas for how government can serve the public interest, rather than special interests. The small government right and the big government left have both been discredited. Instead of government that worries about the common interest, we have government that more closely resembles a commercial transaction between donors and politicians. As Sebastian Mallaby wrote in the *Washington Post* in the fall of 2005, we have "a system dominated by . . . people who use interest groups to win control of government and government to win the loyalty of interest groups. . . . So long as voters regard elections as advance sales of stolen goods, corrupt and dysfunctional spending will discredit federal programs. Government has to be rescued from the me-me mindset."[5]

Democratic Montana Governor Brian Schweitzer may have summarized the current situation in Washington best: " . . . this has become almost legalized bribery. What is happening is, these lobbyists get special interests to hire them. And they give them large sums of money, 6, 10, 12, $15,000 a month. And then these lobbyists in turn give money to the leadership PACs that these folks in Washington, D.C. have. So, all it is is a way of moving the bag money to a new source."[6]

Governor Schweitzer used the right phrase: "legalized" bribery. Rarely are there clear-cut instances of lobbyists, legislators, and their staff caught taking bribes—defined as taking official action "because of" or "in return for" money or favors. The key element in a bribery case is causation. Both parties must have *intended* there to be a causally related exchange—money for action, action for money. The recent felony guilty pleas by lobbyist Jack Abramoff and former Congressman Duke Cunningham involved admissions by both that money had been used to obtain official actions. In the case of Abramoff, money had been paid (or trips financed) in order to obtain favorable official action on behalf of his clients. In Cunningham's case, he took money outright in return for helping the donor get government contracts and appropriations.

The worst-kept secret in Washington, however—what everyone knows, and what everyone knows that everyone knows—is that the system usually works on parallel tracks, not with clear causal relationships. There is nothing legally wrong or improper per se with a lobbyist making a financial contribution, meeting with the member of Congress shortly after, asking the member to vote favorably on legislation, and then having the congressman vote that way later on. However, it certainly does not look good. We all know that in politics, where appearances sometimes count more than reality, such correlations—or as they say in legal parlance, "temporally" related events—can lead to controversial headlines about "quid pro quo."

If we cannot depend on the criminal justice system to stop the buying of influence in Washington because of difficulty in proving actual bribery, it is clear from the 218 years since America's founding that we cannot depend on politicians to enforce rules against themselves, either. Current proposals before Congress in the aftermath of Abramoff and Cunningham would certainly be improvements over the current system. These proposals would limit the dollar amount of meals, gifts, or trips. Others would close all the loopholes left out of the McCain-Feingold campaign finance reform legislation, including a total ban on "soft money." However, the real issue remains, as Joe Lieberman said in the summer of 1996 during nationally televised hearings about Democratic fundraising practices, "It's not what's illegal that bothers me—it's what's legal."

There is really only one effective solution that would help restore the people's trust and actually deter conduct that has led to their distrust: Transparency. Translucent or "nearly transparent" will not make the grade. Full transparency is absolutely necessary. It means turning the lights on completely and letting everyone know what is happening behind closed doors when a lobbyist meets with a congressman. It means every lobbyist and every politician needs to come clean, or, reminiscent to Governor Schweitzer's ritual upon returning from Washington, they need to be hosed clean in full view.

There are several ways to accomplish this in the Internet age. First, every lobbyist should be required to instantly disclose all campaign contributions online. Checks would be electronically marked as campaign contributions, with an automatic link to Federal Election Commission records on the Internet. Then, every registered lobbyist and every congressional office should be required to keep an online diary—publicly available on a real time basis. The diary would disclose all lobbying activities each day, including all meetings, with whom, how long, what was discussed, materials left behind, "talking points," legislative language submitted, and telephone calls made by members and staff.

It sounds like a lot of work, and maybe it is. Electronic forms available on networked computers available in every senator and congressman's office, however, could help make it a routine procedure.

The technology exists for software to link campaign contributions to the diaries so that all are fully integrated in an easy to follow chronology available on a real-time basis on the Internet. That would enable anyone signing on to the appropriate member or lobbyist Web site to see that on January 10, Mr. Lobbyist gave $1,000. On January 15, he met with Congresswoman X. Then, on February 3, the staff member to Congresswoman X wrote a letter to the Secretary of Interior. Finally on March 5, the Interior Department granted a special energy lease to Mr. Lobbyist's client.

This does not resolve the issue of whether this transaction was a case of correlation or causation, but it is, at the very least, transparent. It puts all the facts out there and lets the voters decide whether there is causation (bribe) or correlation (ok). Save the investigative reporter the aggravation of trying to piece all these events into some "connect-the-dots" chronology attempting to suggest wrongdoing. Watch what happens if full transparency regime is actually enforced for all lobbying meetings and activities in Congress and in the administration. Members will have to consider that everything they do, everyone they talk to, every dollar they take in campaign contributions, will be fully understood and appreciated by the voters back home. The good lobbyists, the good public-spirited members of Congress, should not care. The bad ones with something to hide, well, when you turn the lights on in the kitchen, the cockroaches will run for cover. "Lights On"—that is the slogan for real reform from the New Center.

PURPLE NATION:
RED MEETS BLUE AND BLUE MEETS RED

A leader in the mold of Robert Kennedy, who supports policies drawn from both sides of the ideological spectrum, supports transparency reforms, and advocates for a focus on problem-solving in national government would surely accelerate the blurring of Red and Blue divisions in the country. In fact, there were signs in the 2000, 2002, and 2004 elections that this had already begun. You have to look beyond the presidential election results to find it.

For example in the same Red states that President Bush won by substantial margins in 2000 and 2004, many Democratic gubernatorial candidates also won. In addition, almost all of these candidates stood for New Center mixtures of fiscal conservatism, social liberalism, and cultural moderation described in this book.

For example, in 2004, Montana's Brian Schweitzer was elected governor by a margin of 50 percent to 46 percent while President Bush carried the state by a landslide 20 percent margin—a swing of 24 percent. Schweitzer reflects a particularly attractive Democratic candidate because he can talk about values of faith and respect for pro-life religious-based views in a respectful fashion. He is a fiscal conservative but sounds like an FDR New Dealer when he talks about social programs and the need for energy independence from Middle Eastern oil by taking advantage of massive quantities of coal to create synthetic and clean fossil fuel.[7]

Then North Carolina elected Democrat Mike Easley governor by a 10 percent margin while President Bush won the state by 12 percent—a 22 percent swing. West Virginia Democrat Joe Manchin succeeded Governor Wise by a 29 percent margin while President Bush carried the state by 13 percent—a 42 percent swing! Other Democratic senators and governors who won statewide elections in very Red states carried by President Bush in either 2000, 2004, or both by substantial margins include Kathleen Blanco of Louisiana, Dave Freudenthal of Wyoming, Bill Richardson of New Mexico, Mark Warner of Virginia and his lieutenant governor who succeeded him in 2005, Timothy Kaine, and the list goes on. Senator Hillary Rodham Clinton, in her successful campaign for the New York U.S. Senate seat in 2000, surprised many people by running stronger in upstate rural red counties of New York state than she had been expected to.

Indiana Democratic Senator Evan Bayh is another example of a mainstream Democrat who knows how to win among Red voters—in his case, very Red state Indiana has voted Republican, solidly, in the last ten presidential elections from 1968 through 2004. Yet, Evan Bayh carried Indiana by significant margins every time he ran statewide—for secretary of state, governor, and senator over the last 20 years. No one can doubt that his basic philosophy is in the mainstream of the Democratic Party. His voting record while a U.S. senator has been judged positively by the environmental, labor, and political organizations of the liberal wing of the Democratic party.

Senator Russ Feingold is another liberal who runs strongly in the Red rural areas of Wisconsin. For example, he carried Marathon County by 54 percent of the vote, the same percentage George Bush received, and won Taylor County by a narrow margin, while President Bush defeated John Kerry by nearly 20 percent.

Meanwhile, there are more than enough examples of Republicans, even conservative Republicans, who have managed to learn how to speak to Blue State voters. In one of the bluest states of all, New York, Republican Governor George Pataki, defeated liberal Democratic Governor Mario Cuomo in 1994 and was re-elected twice, in 1998 and 2002, by ever-increasing margins. In 2002, he carried the Hispanic vote and carried the counties in which the Democratic presidential candidates won by large margins. For example, in 2002, Pataki carried Long Island's multi-ethnic and heavily populated Nassau County by a margin of 51 percent, while two years later, President Bush carried only 47 percent. Ever since college, when he headed the Yale Political Union conservatives, Pataki has been an unapologetic fiscal conservative. However, he is also a moderate on social and cultural issues (including abortion and stem cell research) and that New Center mix is reflected by his ability to appeal to moderate Democrats, independents, and even some liberals in New York. Other examples include Republican Massachusetts Governor Mitt Romney, Pennsylvania Republican Senator Arlen Specter, Minnesota Republican Senator Norm Coleman, California Governor Arnold Schwarzenegger, and Rhode Island Senator Lincoln Chafee. John McCain, while an unapologetic pro-life conservative Republican, won 72.4 percent of Pima County, Arizona, while John Kerry defeated George Bush with 53 percent of the vote.

These state results simply re-emphasize that there is already a New Center operating in many of the so-called Red *and* Blue states. Both parties have a chance to campaign there and win. So, what is the common theme or pattern among all these successful elected officials who get elected in states that appear to be dominated by the opposite party? They fit the precise ideological mix of the New Center paradigm: fiscal conservatives, social liberals, cultural moderates, and (in the case of U.S. Senators) strong on national defense. That is where the growing center is in today's America. The center is anxious about the nation's cultural divisions, anxious about party ideologues who seek to destroy each other personally rather than solve our problems, anxious about the absence of national unity at a time the nation needs it most.

Here is the political paradox America faces at this unique moment in its history. On the one hand, there is an apparently deep political and cultural divide between Red and Blue America. Yet, at the same time, there is also a growing disaffection with the left and right and a growing consensus in the center. The answer to this paradox is simple: political leadership. What is needed is a political leader who can resist the purists from both parties and plant him or herself on principles and convictions.

Again, to return to Robert F. Kennedy, he penned a comment to his friend Allard Lowenstein in 1968, shortly before his death. Lowenstein regarded Robert Kennedy as his political hero. Despite this, he remained loyal to Minnesota Democratic Senator Eugene McCarthy, who had initially challenged incumbent President Lyndon B. Johnson for the Democratic Party nomination because of opposition to Johnson's Vietnam War policies. In 1967, Lowenstein had first approached Senator Kennedy to take on Johnson in the Democratic presidential primaries, but Kennedy had decided not to—angering Lowenstein and many other anti-war Kennedy friends.

Kennedy finally decided to enter the race after McCarthy had nearly beaten Johnson in the New Hampshire primary in February 1968, and it was clear Johnson was vulnerable on the War. Not long after, Kennedy and Lowenstein were on a long bus ride from an upstate New York Democratic Party evening reception. Kennedy spotted Lowenstein sitting alone, walked down the aisle, and sat next to him. Will you support my presidential candidacy, he is said to have asked. Lowenstein said no. "McCarthy was there when we asked him to run, and you weren't, and I'm sticking with him. It would be wrong to switch at this point."

Kennedy returned to his seat, glum, and scratched a note to Lowenstein on the back of an envelope and passed it up to him. The words aptly describe the kind of leadership that Americans need today more than ever: "For Al, who knew the lesson of Emerson and taught it to the rest of us. 'They did not yet see, and thousands of young men as hopeful, now crowding to the barriers of their careers, did not yet sec, if a single man plant himself on his convictions and then abide, the huge world will come round to him.'—From his friend, Bob Kennedy."[8]

IS A GRAND COALITION GOVERNMENT
NECESSARY—OR POSSIBLE?

"In Montana, we find ways to work together. Now people thought it was unusual that when I ran for governor I interviewed people

*from across the state and ended up picking a Republican state sen-
ator as my running mate. And people think that, well, that was
unusual. How are we going to work together? I say, well, simple,
we will. In fact, he and I've been roommates for the last six
months in the governor's mansion. We get along just fine."*

—*Montana Governor Brian Schweitzer, May 24, 2005*[9]

Just suppose we had leaders running in 2008 who are willing, as Robert
Kennedy said, to plant themselves on their convictions and then abide, waiting for the huge New Center to come round to them.

Imagine it is the late spring or early summer before the Democratic and
Republican Conventions. The two nominees are likely to be known by then.
The disgust with the food-fight politics and hyper-partisanship of the last
several decades will be even greater than it is today. The country is at once
divided, yet yearning to be united. The public mood demands change, not
just a change in leadership but a change in politics, even if just temporarily.
They are looking for a government led by political leaders who focus on solving problems, not destroying the political opposition. They are looking for a
government that rises above partisanship and actually unites the nation to defeat terrorism, achieve complete energy independence, fix our schools, rebuild our roads and bridges, pay our debts and deficits, is willing to pay for all
this with new *targeted taxes*, and create new hope and optimism for the future
of our children and grandchildren.

Imagine that one or both of the major party presidential nominees
seizes the moment. He or she announces before the party national convention that if nominated and elected, the president-elect will ask the vice-
president-elect to resign after the inauguration to accept a senior cabinet
position or become senior adviser to the president. Then using the 25th
Amendment, the new president will pledge to ask Congress to name as vice
president the defeated presidential nominee of the other party (or, if he or
she declines, the vice presidential candidate). The cabinet and subcabinet
would be divided as equally as possible between the two parties. A joint task
force composed of bi-partisan congressional leaders, the president, the vice
president, and their senior cabinet members would be formed to develop
legislation and solutions for the first 100 days addressing the nation's problems. An outside advisory panel composed of senior statespersons from
prior administrations of both parties would help develop those priorities and
those solutions. These will most likely cover winning the war against the
terrorists—wherever they are; achieving complete energy independence;

and rebuilding and investing in America's infrastructure—schools, roads, and human capital through education and training to help America keep its edge in the global economy.

All parties to this Grand Coalition will agree that it will last just four years, with both the president and vice president free to return to the traditional partisan system in the next election. Presumably, they will do so with the immense advantage of having learned how much more can be accomplished when debates focus on the issues rather than the politics of personal destruction.

Is this Grand Coalition government such an unrealistic dream? In all honesty, it probably is. Nevertheless, Theodore C. Sorensen, a brilliant adviser who served as John F. Kennedy's speechwriter and counselor when he was a U.S. senator and as president, proposed an idea similar to this in a book written in early 1984. The proposal above is actually one of four possibilities he advanced, all resulting with a president of one party and a vice president of the other.[10] He explained, in words that ring truer today after 30 years of gotcha politics than they did back then: "We must create through compromise a national consensus that reaches beyond partisan politics. . . . There need be no exclusively "Republican answer" or "Democratic answer." . . . [Our problems] require practical solutions not dependent upon ideology, personality, or political history. I believe the time has arrived in this country for a temporary bipartisan "grand coalition" of national unity."[11]

As Sovensen pointed out, as radical and seemingly unrealistic as the idea appears, it is not totally without precedent in democracies abroad and, on one occasion, in U.S. history. There are examples of coalition governments in foreign democracies in crisis. To name two examples: the Labor-Conservative British coalition government during World War II and the several Likud-Labor governments formed when Israel faced wars and crises from the Arab states and terrorists seeking to destroy them. There are also precedents for U.S. presidents inviting prominent members of the other party to serve in key cabinet positions. A recent example is President Clinton's Defense Secretary, Republican Bill Cohen.

The closest analogy cited by Sovensen in U.S. history, however, was the decision by Republican President Abraham Lincoln to select Southern Democrat Andrew Johnson to be his vice presidential nominee in 1864, replacing the faithful Republican vice president, Hannibal Hamlin of Maine. Andrew Johnson had served as Democratic congressman, governor, and senator from Tennessee. While he was a pro-union, anti-secession "War Democrat," he was not, as Sovensen pointed out, a "nominal or fallen-away" Democrat. He was still an important leader of the Democratic party and had supported Lincoln's Democratic opponent, John Breckenridge, in the 1860 presidential campaign.

Lincoln knew that he had received only 40 percent of the vote in 1860, and he also knew that with the nation facing its greatest crisis in its history, he needed something new and different to broaden his political base. Indeed, Lincoln faced the most extreme divisions in U.S. history at this time, where Americans were killing each other in the tens of thousands.

So, to the great displeasure of his Republican Party partisans, he reached out and asked Andrew Johnson to run with him as vice president. "Can't you get a candidate for Vice President without going down into a damned rebel province for one," griped the Republican partisan, Congressman Thad Stevens. But Lincoln, in the words of Robert Kennedy (and Emerson) planted himself on his convictions and there abided, held firm.

Lincoln did so because he believed the crisis facing the nation could not be solved through politics as usual. He knew that he faced a unique moment where bipartisan politics was needed—even if just temporarily. Andrew Johnson saw it the same way. Johnson explained his decision to accept Lincoln's invitation to his "old friends" in the Democratic party who were critical of his decision. His words could appropriately be used by the defeated presidential candidate in the 2008 elections who receives an invitation from the victor to become vice president in a Grand Coalition government: " . . . [T]he hour has now come when . . . the path of duty is patriotism and principle. Minor considerations and questions of administrative policy should give way to the higher duty of first preserving the Government; and then there will be time enough to wrangle over the men and measures pertaining to its administration."[12]

CONCLUSION

To repeat: There is nothing wrong with partisan politics. In fact, everything is right with partisan politics, but only if that means vigorous debate of the issues, not a machinery of character assassination, personal attacks, and the politics of personal destruction. Debating the issues informs and breathes life into our republic. Hate and sanctimony not only undermine our ability to solve our problems, but they also corrode the soul of the country as much as cancer destroys a human being.

There may be no way to break the gotcha cycle on the left and right and change the downward spiral of our current path without something as radical as the idea of a Grand Coalition government advanced by Ted Sovensen decades ago. Probably neither the Democratic nor the Republican nominee in 2008, will have the ability—or the desire—to take the risk of doing something new, so radical, and so uncertain, as this idea.

But perhaps—just perhaps—the people in the angry center will raise their voices so loudly, and they will be so numerous, that they will give one or both of the 2008 presidential nominees of both parties the courage. The great and angry center just might be willing and able to ask us all, partisans on all sides, to sit back and think about what is best for the country and how we can end the suffering and frustration of the scandal culture. The people might just lead us, convince us—left, right, and center, liberals and conservatives—to take a "time out" from partisanship, even if it is just a brief one-presidential term, to allow our nation to unite in common purpose for the common good to solve our problems at home and defeat the terrorist enemy abroad.

If one or both presidential nominees in 2008 can provide the leadership to reach out to the other party, and we as a nation can re-discover our common purpose and willingness to sacrifice for the public interest, then we can experience the vision of Thomas Macaulay in "Horatius at the Bridge":

> Then none was for a party—
>   Then all were for the state;
> Then the great man helped the poor,
>   And the poor man loved the great;
> Then lands were fairly portioned!
>   Then spoils were fairly sold:
> The Romans were like brothers
>   In the brave days of old.[13]

NOTES

PROLOGUE

1. All quotes for George W. Bush in this section are drawn from http://www. whitehouse.gov/news/releases/2004/06/20040614–2.html
2. Bill Clinton's comments are drawn from http://www.cbsnews.com/stories/ 2004/06/14/politics/main623087.shtml and http://www.command-post.org/ 2004/2_archives/2004_06.html

CHAPTER ONE

1. Ron Chernow, *Alexander Hamilton* (New York: Penguin Books, 2004), p. 391, citing Elkins and McKitrick.
2. Ibid., p. 391.
3. Ibid., p. 112
4. Ibid., p. 364.
5. Ibid., p. 366.
6. Ibid., p. 367.
7. Forrest McDonald, *Alexander Hamilton: A Biography* (New York: W.W. Norton, 1979), p. 229.
8. Chernow, p. 365.
9. Richard Brookhiser, *Alexander Hamilton, American* (New York: Touchstone, Simon & Schuster, 1999), p. 99; see generally pp. 97–100. Brookhiser called the affair "interesting but sordid." Ibid., p. 100.
10. Chernow, p. 370. See also, McDonald, pp. 243–44.
11. Ibid., p. 412.
12. Ibid., p. 409.
13. Ibid., pp. 409–10.
14. Ibid., p. 414.
15. Ibid., p. 416. See also, McDonald, p. 259.
16. Ibid., p. 417. (Emphasis added.)
17. Ibid.; for full account of the duel, see pp. 695–709.
18. Ibid., p. 531.
19. Ibid., p. 529.
20. Ibid., p. 530.
21. Stephen F. Knott, *Alexander Hamilton & the Persistence of Myth* (Lawrence: University Press of Kansas, 2002), pp. 12–13. The author indicates that Monroe "stumbled upon" the Reynolds affair, but there is considerable circumstantial evidence that Monroe, the future president who presided over the "era of good feelings," saw a sex scandal as a way to bring down the key political enemy of his icon and idol, Thomas Jefferson, and he intentionally facilitated

the disclosure of the correspondence with Maria Reynolds that Hamilton had shared with Monroe under an express understanding that it would remain confidential. In fact, the author points out, Hamilton himself was so convinced that Monroe had been behind the Callender published account that it almost led to a duel between them.

22. McDonald, p. 259. A poignant scene is described by Brookhiser regarding Monroe's visit to Mrs. Hamilton in the 1820s after Monroe had completed two terms as president. When the former President tried to speak of "forgiving and forgetting," Mrs. Hamilton would have none of it: "Mr. Monroe, if you have come to tell me that you repent, that you are sorry, very sorry, for the misrepresentations and the slanders, and the stories you circulated against my dear husband, if you have to say this, I understand it. But, otherwise, no lapse of time, no nearness to the grave, makes any difference." Chernow, pp. 727–28; Brookhiser, pp. 216–17, and see note 36 to text. Mrs. Hamilton died at the age of 97 on November 9, 1854.

23. Chernow, pp. 530–33.

24. McDonald, pp. 237–38.

25. Chernow, p. 534. See also, Knott p. 13. (Hamilton denied any public corruption but admitted that "my real crime was an amorous connection" with James Reynolds' wife.)

26. Chernow, p.533.

27. Ibid., p. 534.

28. Ibid., p. 537.

29. Quoted at Brookhiser, p. 134, concerning a correspondence with Henry Knox.

30. Chernow, p. 535.

31. Julian Boyd, a historian who had written in 1971 that Hamilton had assisted British intelligence, wrote a 78-page appendix to his volume, *The Papers of Thomas Jefferson*, arguing that Hamilton had used his position as Secretary of the Treasury for his "personal gain." According to Knott, Boyd argued that Hamilton was involved in speculation while serving as treasury secretary and had revealed his adultery with Maria Reynolds as a cover story to conceal serious financial misconduct. Boyd's conspiracy theory went so far as to suggest that Hamilton had "forged" the alleged extortion letters from the two Reynolds "as a cover story to conceal" his misconduct. They were "palpably contrived documents of a brilliant and daring man who . . . tried to imitate what he conceived to be the style of less literate persons." See Knott, p. 175 and note 64 for other anti-Hamilton historians who were sympathetic to Boyd's (mostly) speculations. See also, Brookhiser, p. 132, referencing Callender's speculations, that the affair was a "cover story" to divert attention from Hamilton's public corruption and McDonald, p. 335, referencing the near duel that occurred between Hamilton and Monroe over Monroe's refusal to contradict the innuendo in Monroe's writings that Hamilton had contrived the affair to hide his speculations in government securities.

32. Chernow, p. 542.

33. Ibid., p. 544.

34. Ibid., p. 315.

35. Ibid., p. 531.

36. Ibid., p. 663.

37. Jefferson's paternity of Hemings' seven children was ultimately demonstrated two centuries later by both strong circumstantial evidence as well as DNA

tests. Fawn M. Brodie documented that Jefferson and Hemings were at Monticello together nine months before the birth of each of Hemings' seven children, and no other children were conceived by Hemings when Jefferson was not at home nine months before. Jefferson freed only two slaves in his lifetime and another five in his will, and all belonged to Hemings. On her deathbed, Hemings told her son Madison that Jefferson was his and his siblings' father. And finally, in 1998, DNA tests confirmed that Jefferson (or a male in his family) fathered at least one of Hemings' children, Eston. Ibid., p. 512.

38. Ibid., p. 663.
39. Ibid., p. 664.
40. Ibid., p. 663.
41. Ibid., pp. 663–64.
42. Knott, pp. 205–06.
43. Ibid., p. 206, with Knott citing, for example, op-ed pieces in the conservative journals *National Review* and the *Weekly Standard*, with others accusing the Clinton defenders as engaging in a "smear" campaign against Hamilton.
44. William A. DeGregorio, *The Complete Book of U.S. Presidents* (New York: Random House, 1991), p. 271.
45. Ibid., citing Bailey, *The American Pageant: A History of the Republic* (New York: Heath, 1966), p. 493.
46. DeGregorio, p. 108.
47. Ibid., p. 322.
48. Ibid., p. 300.
49. Ibid., p. 325.
50. Ibid., pp. 325–26.
51. Ibid., p. 326.
52. Chernow, p. 326.
53. Suzanne Garment, *Scandal: The Crisis of Mistrust in American Politics* (New York: Times Books, 1991), p. 3.
54. DeGregorio, *Book of Presidents*, p. 271.
55. Garment, p. 3, DeGregorio, p. 439.
56. DeGregorio, p. 439.
57. Ibid., p. 435.
58. Ibid.
59. Ben Bradlee, *A Good Life* (New York: Simon & Schuster, 1995), pp. 407–09.
60. Ibid., pp. 230–31.
61. Ibid., pp. 216–17.
62. Ibid., p. 217.
63. Ibid., pp. 407–08.
64. Sergei Khrushchev, "How My Father and President Kennedy Saved the World," *American Heritage*; Naftali Fursenko, "The Scali-Feklisov Channel in the Cuban Missile Crisis," Cold War International History Project, Wilson Center.

CHAPTER TWO

1. Suzanne Garment, in her important, indeed seminal work, *Scandal: The Crisis of Mistrust in American Politics* (New York: New York Times Books, 1991), p. 30, writes that "[T]he assassination seemed a vast betrayal. Here was Kennedy, embodiment of the best impulses of the popular will, killed by a gunman

whose desires came to outweigh all the votes of the democracy. . . . Neither is it a surprise that [after the assassination] by the mid-1960s we began to hear political activists expressing the same mistrustful attitude toward American political life in general."

2. See http://www.chuckbaldwinlive.com/barry.html and http://www.buchanan.org/pa–98–0602.html.

3. From the end of chapter two, Goldwater, *Conscience of a Conservative*, quoted at http://www.virtuemag.org/articles/211.

4. Quoted at http://www.reaganfoundation.org/reagan/speeches/rendezvous.asp.

5. See http://www.pbs.org/wgbh/amex/rockefellers/peopleevents/e_1964.html and hear part of it at http://www.npr.org/templates/story/story.php?storyId=3613724.

6. Charles Peters, *Five Days in Philadelphia* (New York: Public Affairs, 2005), p. 16.

7. Mike Allen and Dana Priest, "Bush Administration Is Focus of Inquiry," *The Washington Post*, September 28, 2003, p. A1.

8. Johnson's win over Goldwater was the greatest landslide win up to then. Nixon's win in 1972 was greater, and Reagan's win in 1984 was the greatest landslide ever. In that year, Mondale won only Minnesota with ten electoral votes and McGovern won only Massachusetts with fourteen electoral votes.

9. But for an attempted assassination in May 1968 that almost killed Wallace and caused him to withdraw his candidacy, it is likely he would have carried even more states and drawn even more conservative voters away from the Nixon column. Had he not withdrawn, it is entirely possible that Vice President Humphrey (either by electoral votes or, by throwing the presidential contest into the Democratic-controlled House of Representatives) would have become president.

10. It wasn't until July 1995 (see http://web.utk.edu/~mfitzge1/docs/374/MDE1995.pdf), that President Bill Clinton attempted a final solution to the liberal conundrum of opposing quotas while favoring affirmative action. He accepted the phrase, "mend it, don't end it"—meaning maintaining using the goal of "affirmative action" to pressure companies doing government contracting and universities to reach out and look for qualified minorities; ensure that testing and other standards did not have inherent racial bias; and keep the pressure on to find, train, and increase minority participation in universities and the workplace. But the conundrum of affirmative action versus reverse discrimination has still not been solved completely.

11. "Abortion Law Development: A Brief Overview," by J. Lewis and Jon O. Shimabukuro, Congressional Research Service, updated January 28, 2001, p. 3.

12. 402 U.S. 62, 91 S.Ct. 1294 (April 21, 1971).

13. From timeline for 1972 published on website of National Right to Life Committee (www.NLRC.com).

14. 410 U.S. 113 at p. 153, 93 S. Ct. 705 (Jan. 22, 1973).

15. 410 U.S. at 153–54, 163–64 ("If the State is interested in protecting fetal life after viability, it may go so far as to proscribe abortion during that period, except when it is necessary to preserve the life *or health* of the mother.") (Emphasis added.)

16. Ibid., pp. 166–67 (setting forth the three trimester framework underlying *Roe*).

17. *Washington Post*, June 28, 1988, "This McGovern Democrat Business," by George McGovern, p. A15.

CHAPTER THREE

1. Jung Chang, *Wild Swans: Three Daughters of China* (New York: Touchstone Books, 1991), p. 323.
2. Thanks to the *University of Maryland Law Review* for their permission to use segments of my published article, "Spinning Out of Control: The Scandal Machine" (*Maryland Law Review*, V. 60, 2001, pp. 41–58).
3. Bob Woodward and Brian Duffy, "Chinese Embassy Role in Contributions Probed; Planning of Foreign Donations to DNC Indicated," *The Washington Post*, Feb. 13, 1997, p. A1.
4. Ibid. (alleging that contributions were planned and that efforts to implement a plan were suspected, but never fully substantiated).
5. Quoted in Edwin R. Bayley, *Joe McCarthy and the Press* (Madison: University of Wisconsin Press, 1981), p. 165.
6. Ibid., pp. 85–87 (explaining that Senator McCarthy took advantage of the media's long-standing policy of uncritically reporting charges, regardless of whether they were substantial or, in fact, true, and that the backlash from this policy prompted editors to allow journalists to begin interpreting the charges or even the facts that they reported).
7. "Information for Story Inaccurate, Source Says," *Dallas Morning News*, Jan. 27, 1998, p. 1A (acknowledging the inaccuracy of a source that caused the *Dallas Morning News* to report that a Secret Service agent was prepared to testify that "he saw President Clinton and Monica Lewinsky in a compromising situation"); see also, Bill Kovach and Tom Rosenstiel, *Warp Speed: America in the Age of Mixed Media* (Washington, DC: Century Foundation Press, 1999), pp. 20–21 (discussing the retracted *Dallas Morning News* story and noting that the press has a tendency to rely on unsubstantiated or secondhand information).

CHAPTER FOUR

1. U.S. Constitution, Article I, Section 5, which provides that a majority is a quorum sufficient for Congress to enact legislation; and Article II, Section 2, provides for the Senate to approve the President's judicial nominees by its "Advice and Consent."
2. Garment, chapters 4 and 5.
3. Peter W. Morgan and Glenn H. Reynolds, *The Appearance of Impropriety: How the Ethics Wars Have Undermined American Government, Business and Society* (New York: Free Press, 1997), pp. 1, 2, and 6.
4. Carter's quote comes from http://www.americanrhetoric.com/speeches/jimmycarter1976dnc.htm. See Garment, p. 42.
5. Bob Woodward, *Shadow: Five Presidents and the Legacy of Watergate* (New York: Simon & Schuster, 1999), p. 56.
6. Garment, pp. 43–44.
7. Woodward, p. 57.
8. Ibid., pp. 57–58.
9. Ibid., p. 58 (emphasis added).
10. Woodward, p. 58; Garment, pp. 44–45.
11. Garment, p. 45.
12. Ibid., p. 47.

13. Quoted in Woodward, p. 58 (emphasis added). As noted in the text below, the irony of Jordan jumping on the appearance bandwagon of the ethics apparat would soon become clear—at least to him and Jimmy Carter—when he shortly thereafter became another tragic victim of the scandal machine, in his case, as the first victim of the newly created legal instrument, the independent counsel.

14. Garment, p. 45.

15. Woodward, p. 60. In his book, Woodward seemed to blame Carter's high ethical standards for Lance's plight, more than the media and political reliance on innuendo and appearances rather than facts. "The incongruity in the face of Carter's clamorous rectitude was unsettling." Ibid. Woodward is certainly correct that Carter had set the trap by raising expectations of pure ethics in his administration. But the fact remains, this was a tragic moment foretelling many more such moments in the evolution of the scandal culture—where a man can be ruined and run out of town in disgrace because of the appearance of political "incongruity," as opposed to substantive proof of wrongdoing based on the facts.

16. Ibid.

17. Ibid.

18. Garment, p. 45.

19. The title changed with the 1983 reenactment of the statute. As previously stated, for simplicity, the term independent counsel will be used throughout this book.

20. The actual firing was done by someone named Robert Bork—then the solicitor general—after Attorney General Elliot Richardson and the Deputy Attorney General William Ruckleshaus refused and then resigned after Nixon's order to fire Cox over Cox's insistence on enforcing subpoenas to obtain copies of Nixon's tapes from the White House taping system.

21. Woodward, p. 65.

22. Ibid.

23. See, e.g., 28 U.S.C. 591(a), (d)(a)(2) [referring to information that is specific and "from a credible source"], and 592(2)(2)(b)(i) and (ii) [limiting discretion of attorney general *not* to appoint an independent counsel if there is no evidence of criminal intent] and 592(c) [requiring seeking appointment of an independent counsel if there are "reasonable grounds" to believe further investigation is warranted.]

24. Quoted in Woodward, p. 69.

25. For discussion of this Democratic (and Republican) double standard, see Garment, pp. 99–100.

26. Garment, pp. 52–56; Woodward, pp. 67–68; generally on the Jordan investigation, see pp. 67–82.

27. Woodward, p. 81.

28. Garment, p. 103.

29. Ibid., p. 104.

30. Woodward, p. 93.

31. Ibid.

32. Garment, p. 104.

33. Ibid., p. 105.

34. *Morrison v. Olson*, 838 F.2d 476 (D.C. Cir. 1988). Judge Silberman's decision is a masterpiece of scholarship as well as amazing clairvoyance. He wrote: "Authority to prosecute an individual is that government power which most

threatens liberty, for a prosecutor has the power to employ the full machinery of the State in scrutinizing any given individual even if a defendant is ultimately acquitted, . . . [the investigated individual is immersed] in a criminal investigation and adjudication is a wrenching disruption of everyday life. The Constitution therefore carefully distributes the various responsibilities for criminal prosecution among each of the three branches, so that citizens may not be endangered by one branch acting alone. . . ." 838 F.2d, pp. 487–88.

35. *Morrison v. Olson*, 487 U.S. 654, 108 S. Ct. 2597 (1988).
36. *Morrison v. Olson*, 487 U.S., pp. 701–02.
37. Cited in Garment, p. 106, p. 7 of Scalia dissent in Lexis/Nexis version.
38. 487 U.S., pp. 732–33. Quotations used by Woodward, pp. 94–95. Emphasis added.
39. 487 U.S. at 712.
40. Cited at Woodward, p. 95.
41. Garment, pp. 86–88.
42. Nofziger was prosecuted for a trivial alleged violation of regulations against post-government lobbying of the agency in which he had worked—in this case, the Reagan White House. While he was convicted at trial in 1988, the conviction was fortunately reversed on appeal. Again, it was only because of partisan Democratic pressures that McKay was appointed in the first place.
43. Wallach's prosecution by U.S. Attorney Rudy Giuliani, resulting in a single conviction that was reversed on appeal, is another example of what many at the time saw as a gross prosecutorial abuse by a politically ambitious prosecutor. Avital Sharansky, wife of the then-famous former Jewish Soviet prisoner, Natan Sharansky, who now was free living in Israel, was denied to the right to testify as a character witness because of opposition by one of Giuliani's prosecutors. Natan Sharansky left the courthouse and said on the courthouse steps "I have seen only one trial in the Soviet Union—my own. And now I have seen one in America." Garment, pp. 124–125. See *The American Lawyer*, "The Lynching of Bob Wallach," by Steven Brill (June 1988). For reasons that are still not apparent, Giuliani was never held accountable for his obvious poor judgment, if not abusive prosecutorial behavior, in this case.
44. Garment, pp. 90, 120–21.
45. Ibid., p. 88.
46. Cited in Garment, p. 120.
47. See generally, Garment, pp. 91–98; Michael Oreskes, "No Evidence Found to Back Charges Against Donovan," *New York Times*, June 29, 1982, p. A1; Philip Shabecoff, "F.B.I. Says It Can't Confirm Allegations on Donovan," *New York Times*, Jan. 28, 1981, p. A1. Based on this lack of evidence, the Senate confirmed Donovan over the objection of many Democrats. Philip Shabecoff, "Senate Approves Donovan, Rejecting Bribe Allegations," *New York Times*, Feb. 4, 1981, p. A17.
48. Seth S. King, "Donovan Calls for Special Prosecutor on His Case," *New York Times*, Dec. 22, 1981, p. A1; James Schwartz, "Independent Counsels: A Short History," *Washington Post*, Jan. 23, 1988, p. A8; Garment, pp. 93, 94, and 96, reporting on Silverman's three investigations; and Ralph Blumenthal, "Inquiry on Donovan Again Yields 'Insufficient Evidence' to Prosecute," *New York Times*, Sept. 14, 1982, p. A1. ("A special Federal prosecutor yesterday announced for the second time that he had found no prosecutable evidence of organized-crime connections involving Labor Secretary Raymond J. Donovan.")

49. See Stuart Taylor, Jr., "Donovan Indicted and Given a Leave to Defend Himself," *New York Times*, Oct. 2, 1984, p. A1; Garment, p. 94; and Kenneth B. Noble, "Donovan Resigns Labor Dept. Post; Must Stand Trial," *New York Times*, March 16, 1985, p. A1.

50. Selwyn Raab, "Donovan Cleared of Fraud Charges by Jury in Bronx," *New York Times*, May 26, 1987, p. A1.

CHAPTER FIVE

1. For a detailed account of this campaign, see Michael Pertschuk and Wendy Schaetzel, *People Rising: The Campaign Against the Bork Nomination* (St. Paul, MN: Thunder's Mouth Press, 1989).

2. Pertschuk and Schaetzel, p. 35.

3. This is clearly evidenced by the subtitle of the book narrating the campaign, *People Rising*, i.e., "The *Campaign* against the Bork Nomination." (Emphasis added).

4. Quoted in Pertschuk and Schaetzel, p. 263.

5. *Griswold v. Connecticut*, 381 U.S. 479 (1965). Robert Bork, *The Tempting of America* (New York: Free Press, 1990), pp. 95–100; Pertschuk and Schaetzel, p. 17, quoting Bork as describing *Griswold* as an "unprincipled decision."

6. Pertschuk and Schaetzel, p. 17.

7. 369 U.S. 186 (1962).

8. Pertschuk and Schaetzel, p. 16. *See also*, Bork, *Tempting*, pp. 84–90, especially pp. 84–85: "There is no better example of the [Warren] Court's egalitarianism and its disregard for the Constitution in whose name it spoke than the legislative apportionment cases, which created the principle of one person, one vote . . . it is not supported by the Constitution and is not, and cannot be, implemented consistently."

9. Bork, *Tempting*, pp. 251–261. ("All theories of constitutional law not based on the original understanding contain inherent and fatal flaws. . . . Just as it is possible to show that the invention of a perpetual motion machine will never occur, not because of the repeated failures to build one but because the laws of physics exclude the possibility of future success, so too can it be demonstrated that there is *no possibility* of a successful revisionist theory of constitutional adjudication in a constitutional republic [other than the original intent approach that I believe in].") Emphasis added.

10. Pertschuk and Schaetzel, *People Rising*, p. 265.

11. Ibid., p. 263.

12. 741 F. 2d 444 (D.C. Circ. 1984).

13. 741 F. 2d at 450.

14. Bork, *Tempting*, pp. 327–28. Bork writes that he was sure there was a "moral question whether the company should have made that choice known to the women. Perhaps it should have said that some were transferred, some were fired, and that it would not retain a woman even if she were sterilized. . . ."

15. 741 F.2d at 450, n. 1.

16. See Pertschuk and Schaetzel, *People Rising*, p. 269, quoting the late Congresswoman Barbara Jordan from Texas, who responded to Charles Krauthammer's charges of "mendacity" and "meanness" by replying that Bork had ruled "in favor of a company that gave its women employees the gruesome choice of getting sterilized or getting fired"—proving that even the good and truly great

leader for racial justice, Barbara Jordan, got swept up into the net of distortion and innuendo in the "campaign" to destroy Judge Bork.

17. Pertschuk/Schaetzel, *People Rising*, at 224–25.
18. The then FDIC director, L. William Seidman, had reportedly told a group of reporters that his predecessor, Edwin Gray, "would come weep on my shoulder about what he was being asked to do" by Wright. Seidman reportedly said that Wright's office had asked for "delays in legislation for the S&Ls and requests for changing supervisors" regulating Texas thrifts. Wright's spokesperson said the work he had done to communicate with the FDIC on behalf of Texas thrifts was "totally proper and consistent with the work done by members of Congress all the time." See Tom Kenworthy, "Wright's Book Was Different, Gingrich Says," *Washington Post*, March 21, 1989, p. A4.
19. Don Phillips, "Combative Wright Hits 'Flimsy' Case," *Washington Post*, June 13, 1988, p. A1, reporting on Wright's interviews on CBS's *Face the Nation* and ABC's *This Week with David Brinkley*.
20. John M. Barry, *The Ambition and the Power: The Fall of Jim Wright: A True Story of Washington* (New York: Viking, 1989).
21. Tom Kenworthy, "Democrats Give New Speaker Taste of Medicine He Prescribed for Wright," *Washington Post*, January 20, 1995, p. A11.
22. John E. Yang, *Washington Post*, "House Reprimands, Penalizes Speaker" (quoting Wright's May 31, 1989, resignation speech). Emphasis added.
23. Dan Balz, *Washington Post*, May 1, 1989, "Personal Drama Seen Reshaping Life in Congress," p. A11.
24. Scott Shepard, "Atmosphere of Roberts Hearings Thick with Politics," Cox News Service, September 16, 2005. ("Roberts . . . doing his best—like any presidential candidate—to avoid any gaffes. . . ."); Charles Babington and Joe Becker, "Alito Likely to Become Justice," *Washington Post*, January 13, 2006, p. A1 (" . . . liberal activists said their best hope was for Alito to commit a gaffe or lose his composure.")
25. *New York Times*, January 15, 2006, p. A17. (Emphasis added.)

CHAPTER SIX

1. As Suzanne Garment aptly put it: "Like Watergate, Iran-Contra grew out of a deep ideological fault line in American politics: the Vietnam-spawned struggle between ideologies, generations, classes, and institutions over the general direction and control of U.S. foreign policy." Garment, p. 199.
2. Garment, p. 201, quoting *Report of the Congressional Committees Investigating the Iran Contra Affair*, H-Report No.100–433, S. Report No. 100–216 (Washington: U.S. Government Printing Office, 1987), p. 398. See generally Garment, pp. 198–201 for the origins of the Iran-Contra struggle between the president and Congress.
3. Ibid., p. 221.
4. See generally, Woodward, pp. 189–209.
5. Woodward, p. 155.
6. Ibid., p. 156.
7. David Broder, "Bush Asserts Vindication in Iran Affair; Says Key Facts Were Denied Him," *Washington Post*, August 6, 1987, p. A1. Emphasis added.
8. Walsh's decision to indict Weinberger at all was criticized, even in the liberal Internet magazine Slate.com. Jacob Weisberg wrote on June 4, 1997: " . . .

Weinberger, like Shultz, was far from a black hat in the affair. He too had opposed the arms-for-hostages [Iran] deal. Indicting him was an exercise in prosecutorial pique, doomed to fail."

9. We know this thanks to the investigatory reporting of Bob Woodward in his book, *Shadow*, reporting on the conversations with unidentified Walsh prosecutors who opposed including this phrase in the indictment and senior Walsh deputies. The rest of this account, including the political ramifications on the presidential campaign, which relies on Woodward's conversations with the players involved, can be found in *Shadow*, pp. 200–205.

10. Ibid., pp. 201–202. Woodward uses the words that have been placed in quotes in this text—but they are not in quotes in Woodward's text. This probably means that Woodward was on "deep background," meaning he got these words from someone else or from Brosnahan, but not for direct attribution.

11. The words "nuclear bomb" are in direct quotes in Woodward's account. Ibid., p. 202.

12. Ibid., p. 201. Woodward's words, "not a big deal," are not in quotes. Woodward does quote Walsh as explaining why he believed this. Referencing Bush's claim that he was "out of the loop," Woodward quotes Walsh as telling Barrett: "'Nobody believes Bush when he says that,' Walsh said. He didn't consider the reference that 'VP favored' was a big deal. The congressional committees had long ago concluded that [the Vice President had favored the arms-for hostage deal]. Poindexter had testified about it publicly, and the Weinberger-Shultz opposition was all over the record despite Bush's denials." Ibid., p. 201. Note the lack of clarity here: the "nobody believes" reference is to Bush's claim of being "out of the loop"—not to him "favoring" the arms-for-hostage deal. Those are not the same things. Walsh might have confused the two—not thinking through that the note "VP favored" would be seen by the media and the public as evidence that Bush had lied in prior public statements—which could indeed be a decisive political issue in the closing days of a tight presidential campaign.

13. Robert Pear, *New York Times*, October 31, 1992, p. A1.

14. Walter Pincus and George Lardner, *Washington Post*, October 31, 1992, p. A1.

15. For these and other quotes and references to Walsh's announcement and quotes from the Clinton campaign, see Woodward, pp. 202–03.

16. Quoted in Woodward, p. 202.

17. With all respect to all the prosecutors involved in the decision both as to the timing of the re-indictment on the weekend before the election much less the decision to include the phrase, "VP favored," when it really was not legally necessary to do so, had Walsh or any of the prosecutors asked anyone with a shred of political experience whether that phrase could decisively turn the election against George Bush and would be played as major stories in all the nation's newspapers on the crucial last weekend before the election, it would have taken anyone about a nanosecond to say, "Duh—you have to be kidding. Of course it will have a great impact." How Walsh, a distinguished man with extensive political experience, and the many other distinguished attorneys who were part of the Iran-Contra team, missed such an obvious fact of political life, is a mystery to this day.

18. Quoted in Woodward, pp. 204–05.

19. Amitai Etzioni, "It's a Crime, the Way Politicians Go At It," *Washington Post*, August 5, 2001, Outlook Section, p. C1.

20. Jeffrey Rosen, "Trapped," *New York Times Magazine*, June 1, 1997.

21. See S. REP. NO. 103–100, at 20 (1994), reprinted in 1994 U.S.C.C.A.N. 748, 764 ("The [Justice] Department contends that it should have the authority to invoke the independent counsel process to investigate any *subject matter* raising conflict of interest concerns, without having to name specific individuals as targets.") Emphasis added.

22. 28 U.S.C. 591, Public L. 103–270, June 30, 1994.

23. Lawrence M. O'Rourke, "Many Lawmakers Targeting Independent Counsel Law," *Sacramento Bee*, Feb. 16, 1998, p. A17.

24. Sixty-Seventh Judicial Conference of the Fourth Circuit, "*The Independent Counsel Process*" (54 Wash. & Lee L. Rev. 1515, 1583 [1997]).

25. Only two other presidents in U.S. history had had the same experience: Harry S. Truman, who saw the Democratic House and Senate switch to the GOP in the fall 1946 elections; and Grover Cleveland, who saw the same takeover of both chambers by Republicans in the mid-term elections of 1894. Actually, after the 1952 elections, the Senate was divided—48 Democrats and 47 Republicans and one Independent (Senator Wayne Morse of Oregon). But Senator Morse chose to vote with the Republicans. With the Senate tied 48–48, Vice President Nixon broke the tie to give the GOP control. But in January 1955, Senator Morse switched to the Democrats and Democratic Senator Lyndon Johnson became Majority Leader. Doris Kearns Goodwin, *Lyndon Johnson and the American Dream* (New York: St. Martin's, 1976, 1991), p. 110.

26. Statement by Rep. Henry A. Waxman (D.-Cal) on October 7, 1998 ("The Price Tag of the Campaign Finance Investigation").

27. Juliet Eilperin, *Fight Club Politics: How Partisanship is Poisoning the House of Representatives* (Rauman and Littlefield, Maryland, 2006), pp. 6–8, 115–200.

28. Statement by Waxman, op. cit., October 7, 1998.

29. E. J. Dionne Jr., "Gary Hart: The Elusive Frontrunner," *New York Times Magazine*, May 3, 1987.

30. *Time Magazine*, May 18, 1987, pp. 16, 18. (Emphasis added.)

31. Gallup Poll, May 17–18, 1987 (Gallup.com). See also, Carl M. Cannon, "Politics as Nightmare," *National Journal*, February 13, 1999, pointing to the coincidence of the effects of liberal feminists and right-wing Christian evangelicals in making "private lives of politicians fair game." He quotes the *New Republic's* Peter Beinart as pointing to the "unacknowledged alliance" of feminists and the Christian right to "legitimize the exposure of politicians' private lives."

32. James R. Dickenson and Paul Taylor, "*Report on Female House Guest Called 'Character Assassination*,'" *Washington Post*, May 4, 1987, p. A1, Emphasis added.

33. Probably the most thorough treatment that slightly favors Ms. Hill over Mr. Thomas but still includes unexplained inconsistencies in her version of certain incidents is by two of the top journalists in America, Jill Abramson, then of the *Wall Street Journal* and now the managing editor of the *New York Times*, and Jane Mayer, then and now a highly regarded investigative reporter for *The New Yorker* magazine. See *Strange Justice* (New York: Houghton-Mifflin, 1994).

34. Michael Isikoff, *Uncovering Clinton: A Reporter's Story* (Three Rivers Press, New York, 1999, 2000 [Paperback version with new "Afterward"]), p. 351.

35. *Clinton v. Jones*, 520 U.S. 681, 117 S.Ct. 1636 (1997).

36. Michael Isikoff, in the afterword to the paperback version of his book, infers that Willey had confided in him off-the-record that the incident with President Clinton had occurred and that the advances were unwelcome. See Isikoff,

Uncovering Clinton (2000 paperback edition), pp. 362–368 and 378. But that account—even if true—still doesn't change the fact, as Isikoff would readily admit, that Willey's version of events was unsubstantiated by a third party, denied by President Clinton, contradicted in part by Linda Tripp. Moreover, Isikoff writes in his book that Ms. Willey had serious credibility issues. Finally, as indicated in the text, Isikoff seems to agree that the issue of whether sexual harassment took place was not really what drove *Newsweek*, in the final analysis, to publish the story—just as the "dare" was not apparently really what drove the Miami Herald to publish the story on Gary Hart. Clearly the rules of reporting on a president's private conduct, which previously had been seen as out of bounds by journalists, whether that be about Franklin D. Roosevelt, Dwight Eisenhower, or John Kennedy, had changed—or as Isikoff candidly admits in his book, as noted in the above text, had become "something of a blur." Ibid., p. 351.

CHAPTER SEVEN

1. Dan Balz, "Ready or Not?," *Washington Post Magazine*, October 25, 1998, p. 8.
2. Howard Kurtz, "The Big Sleazy: Is Clinton's Clan As Low Rent as Reagan's," *Washington Post Outlook*, March 26, 1995, p. 1.
3. *Washington Post*, August 20, 1995, "Dole or Gramm? Iowa GOP Says Yes," by Paul Taylor, p. A9.
4. The eight counsels and the nine Clinton Administration officials they investigated (in parentheses) are: Kenneth Starr and Robert W. Ray (Bill and Hillary Clinton, Webster Hubbell); Donald Smaltz (Secretary of Agriculture Mike Espy); David Barrett (HUD Secretary Henry Cisneros); Daniel Pearson (the late Secretary of Commerce Ron Brown); Curtis Von Kann (the late Eli Segal, Americorps CEO); Carol Elder Bruce (Interior Secretary Bruce Babbitt); and Ralph I. Lancaster, Jr. (Labor Secretary Alexis Herman).

    The estimated total cost of all independent counsel investigations during the Clinton Administration is derived from a *Washington Post* article published March 31, 2001 ("Clinton Probes Cost $60 Million, Total Counsel Costs for Administration Top $110 Million," by George Lardner, Jr., p. A10), based on totaling the GAO audit figures. The estimated total in the *Post* is in excess of $110.4 million. But the grand total in the text of "over $116 million" is used because by January 20, 2006, when Barrett issued his final 474-page report, he had spent a total of $21 million—an additional $6.4 million to what was quoted in the earlier *Post* article. Thus the total for all investigation during President Clinton's two terms was over $116 million for the eight independent counsels.

5. Paid as legal fees to the Arkansas Committee on Professional Conduct for costs of outside counsel and formally acknowledged a violation of one of the Arkansas Rules of Professional Conduct. Order of Special Division, In Re Madison Guaranty Savings & Loan, Civ. Order 2000–5677, effective as of January 19, 2001.
6. See, for example, Sidney Blumenthal *The Clinton Wars* (New York: Farrar, Straus and Giroux, 2003), p. 76.
7. Jeff Gerth, "Personal Finances: Clintons Joined S&L Operator in an Ozark Real-Estate Venture," *New York Times*, March 8, 1992, p. A1.
8. Time Magazine.Com, May 8–10, 1998, "Fool on the Hill." ("Dan Burton is so convinced Vince Foster was murdered that he brought a pistol into the back-

yard of his Indiana home and reenacted the crime—reportedly with a pumpkin standing in for Foster's head.") The DNC showed up at Rep. Burton's Congressional hearings investigating the Clinton White House, dressed as "Pumpkinperson"—but the report in the *Post* said the "large fruit" Burton shot could have been a "watermelon, honeydew *or* pumpkin.") See also, Al Kamen, *Washington Post*, Oct. 8, 1997, p. A19.

9. Ruth Marcus, "The Prosecutor: Following Leads or Digging Dirt,?" *Washington Post*, January 30, 1998.

10. *Clinton v. Jones*, 520 U.S. 681 (1997).

11. Appointing Order by the Special Division of the D.C. Court of Appeals, dated August 5, 1994. See discussion regarding that grant and the means of enlarging it both under the Independent Counsel Act and efforts by Judge Starr to bootstrap his mandate into what he regarded as related areas in *United States v. Webster L. Hubbell*, 11 F. Supp. 25, pp. 31–33. (D.C. D. Ct., July 1, 1998).

12. Starr was not obligated by virtue of his mandate to investigate Whitewater to undertake the Lewinsky investigation. He did this at his own volition. He could have, for example, simply referred the matter to the attorney general, recommending the appointment of another independent counsel to investigate the Lewinsky matter. In subsequent years, Judge Starr reportedly has told some associates that he made a mistake in not doing at least the latter—on one occasion in my presence he suggested he had second-guessed himself on this when we were invited together to discuss the Lewinsky investigation before a graduate school class.

13. 28 U.S.C. 594(h)(1)(B). Emphasis added. There is also a serious ethical question whether prosecutors should offer their opinions of the evidence or the probable guilt of a defendant after an investigation has been closed and no indictments are brought.

14. Robert L. Jackson and Eric Lichtblau, *Los Angeles Times*, September 21, 2000, p. A1.

15. *Washington Post*, editorial page, March 26, 2002.

16. *Los Angeles Times*, September 21, 2000.

17. In the Website release published by the "Office of Independent Counsel," as of April 4, 2001, there are 16 guilty pleas/convictions listed (two each involving two individuals, former Governor Jim Guy Tucker and Webster L. Hubbell): (1) David Hale, guilty plea, March 22, 1994; (2) Charles Matthews, guilty plea, June 23, 1994; (3) Eugene Fitzhugh, guilty plea, June 12, 1994; (4) Robert W. Palmer, guilty plea, December 6, 1994; (5) Webster Hubbell (billing fraud), guilty plea, December 6, 1994; (6) Neal T. Ainley, guilty plea, May 2, 1995; (7) Christopher V. Wade, guilty plea, March 21, 1995; (8) William J. Marks, Sr., guilty plea, August 28, 1997; (9) former Governor Jim Guy Tucker, guilty plea, February 20, 1998; (10) John Haley, guilty plea, February 20, 1998; (11) Stephen A. Smith, guilty plea, June 8, 1995; (12) Larry Kuca, guilty plea, July 13, 1995; (13) Jim Guy Tucker, convicted after trial, May 28, 1996; (14) James B. McDougal, convicted after trial, May 28, 1996; (15) Susan H. McDougal, convicted after trial May 28, 1996; (16) Webster L. Hubbell, plea on June 30, 1999, as part of plea to dismiss another indictment, to omission of material information to FDIC, $100 special assessment, no incarceration.

18. They are not exactly household names, most of whom pled guilty to mostly minor offenses: Charles Mathews, Eugene Fitzhugh, Robert W. Palmer, Neal

T. Ainley, Christopher V. Wade, William J. Marks, Sr., John Haley, Stephen A. Smith, and Larry Kuca.

19. Lanny Davis, *Truth to Tell: Tell It Early, Tell It All, Tell It Yourself: Notes from My White House Education* (New York: The Free Press, 1999). The full text of the Clinton memo can be found on p. 126.

20. The story of this network was broken by two of the best reporters in the business, Jill Abramson and Don van Natta, Jr., of the *New York Times* in a story published on October 4, 1998, on the front page under the headline, "The Testing of the President: The Investigation; Starr Said To Have Received Tip On Affair Before Call by Tripp." Another detailed exposition documenting the bridges between the Jones attorneys, Linda Tripp, and the Starr prosecutors leading up to the Clinton deposition was also documented by Pulitzer Prize–winning reporter Susan Schmidt of the *Washington Post* ("Tripp's Tapes: How They Got to Starr Is a Complex Tale," *Washington Post*, October 11, 1998, p. 1). Michael Isikoff in *Uncovering Clinton*, not exactly a book that is complimentary to Bill Clinton, also confirmed the Jones-Starr team's linkages through the network of right-wing attorneys and activists in additional first-person reporting. See, e.g., Isikoff, pp. 266–280. See also, Conason & Lyons, *The Hunting of the President*, pp. 338–365, especially pp. 349–51.

21. Cited in "A Chronology: Key Moments in the Clinton–Lewinsky Saga," "All Politics CNN with Time/CQ," cnn.com (covering June 1995–September 24, 1998).

22. *Jones v. Clinton*, 990 F. Supp. 657 (U.S. D.Ct. E.D.Ark., April 1, 1998).

23. See also Carl Cannon, "Politics as Nightmare," *National Journal*, February 19, 1989. ("Another underlying cause for the acrimonious tenor of the discussion in the House is the gerrymandering of so many of the nation's congressional districts. . . . The upshot is the creation of numerous House seats in which the Republican doesn't need to worry about Democratic votes—and vice versa.")

24. "Politics and People: Low Crimes and High Misdemeanors," by Albert R. Hunt, *Wall Street Journal*, p. A19, March 19, 1998.

25. *Clinton v. Jones*, 520 U.S. 681, 117 S.Ct. 1636 (1997).

26. 520 U.S. at 705–6: "We therefore hold that the doctrine of In sum it is settled law that the separation-of-powers doctrine does not bar every exercise of jurisdiction over the President of the United States."

27. Emphasis added. 520 U.S. at 865–66.

28. 520 U.S. at 965–66. The court earlier pointed out that "only three sitting Presidents have been defendants in civil litigation involving their actions prior to taking office. Complaints against Theodore Roosevelt and Harry Truman had been dismissed before they took office. Two companion cases arising out of an automobile accident were filed against John F. Kennedy in 1960 during the presidential campaign but were subsequently settled." (President Kennedy had unsuccessfully argued that his status as Commander in Chief gave him a right to a stay under the Soldiers' and Sailors Civil Relief Act of 1940, but the District Court denied the motion for stay, and the case was then settled.)

CHAPTER EIGHT

1. Cnn.com, June 30, 1999.

2. The final count of separate investigations originally requested by the attorney general and initiated by the "Special Division" panel of the U.S. D.C.

Court of Appeals was 20, not 21 (see listing to follow). But the subjects investigated were far more than 20 or 21. Twenty-five individual independent counsels either asked for expanded subject areas "related" to the original ones, or received brand new subjects to investigate on request of the U.S. attorney general, such as when Independent Counsel Kenneth Starr was asked to investigate, aside from Whitewater, the Travel Office, FBI files, and Vincent Foster suicide matters. Provisions of the independent counsel statute that allowed for such expanded mandates include 28 U.S.C. 593, e.g.,(b)(3), and 594(e).

The following is the list of the 25 independent counsels appointed, at least initially, to investigate 20 subjects or subject areas over 21 years—between 1978 and 1999 (only a partial list of those indicted and who pled guilty are provided) (Source: Frontline Chart, http://www.pbs.org/wgbh/pages/frontline/shows/counsel/office/chart.html):

   (1)   Arthur H. Christy, appointed November 29, 1979, investigating Hamilton Jordan, Chief of Staff to President Carter—no charges brought;

   (2)   Gerald Gallinghouse, appointed September 9, 1980, investigating Timothy Kraft, former Carter campaign manager—no charges brought;

   (3)   Leon Silverman, appointed first December 29, 1981, three separate investigations of Labor Secretary Raymond Donovan—no charges brought;

   (4)   Jacob Stein, appointed April 2, 1984, investigating Attorney General Edwin Meese—no charges brought;

(5), (6)   James McKay, appointed April 23, 1986, and Alexia Morrison, appointed May 29, 1986, investigating assistant attorney general, Office of Legal Counsel Theodore Olson—no charges brought;

   (7)   Whitney North Seymour, Jr., appointed May 29, 1986, investigating former Deputy Chief of Staff Michael Deaver—indictment and conviction after trial of falsely testifying before Congress and the Grand Jury that he failed to recall a conversation that had occurred many months before—3 years probation and $100,000 fine;

   (8)   Lawrence Walsh, appointed December 19, 1986. Fourteen persons were charged, eleven convicted, with two convictions overturned on appeal. These included NSC senior aide Oliver North, convicted but reversed on appeal; National Security Adviser John Poindexter, convicted but reversed on appeal; former Secretary of Defense Casper Weinberger (indicted, not tried, pardoned by President Bush I), and CIA official Claire George, tried and convicted of testifying falsely to Congress and subsequently pardoned by President Bush I; and guilty pleas: Robert L. McFarlane, who pled guilty to four misdemeanors; former State Department Latin Affairs official Elliot Abrams (pled guilty to two misdemeanor charges of withholding information from congress and pardoned by President Bush)—both McFarlane and Abrams subsequently pardoned by President Bush I; and guilty pleas from eight or more DOD or CIA-related officials, most involving false or misleading testimony to Congress or tax offenses. The only person to go to jail as a result of Walsh's prosecutions was Thomas Clines, a former CIA operative. See Outlook Section, *Washington Post*, May 28,

1995, "Special Prosecutors: What's the Point?" by Gerald E. Lynch and Philip K. Howard.

(9), (10)   Carl Rauh, appointed December 19, 1986, and James Harper, appointed August 17, 1987, investigating Assistant Attorney General Lawrence Wallace—no charges brought;

(11)   James McKay, appointed July 18, 1988, investigating White House Counsel Ed Meese and senior aide Lyn Nofziger; Meese—no charges brought; Nofziger, convicted, and conviction reversed;

(12), (13)   Arlin Adams, appointed March 1, 1990, and Larry Thompson, appointed July 3, 1995, investigating HUD Secretary Samuel Pierce and other assistants at HUD; Pierce—no charges brought; convictions for his top aide, Deborah Gore Dean, the former U.S. Treasurer, and two assistant HUD secretaries; (see *Washington Post*, March 26, 2005, "The Big Sleazy," by Howard Kurtz Outlook, p. C1).

(14)   Under seal, independent counsel appointed May 31, 1989—no information released;

(15)   Under seal, independent counsel appointed, April 19, 1991—no information released;

(16), (17)   Joseph diGenova, appointed December 14, 1992, and Michael Zeldin, appointed January 11, 1996, investigating Bush I State Department Officials—no charges brought;

(18), (19)   Kenneth W. Starr, appointed August 5, 1994 (predecessor Robert Fiske, Jr., appointed January 24, 1994, was not "independent counsel" since the act had expired, but rather was "special prosecutor" appointed by Attorney General Reno) and Robert W. Ray, appointed on October 18, 1999—investigations included Webster L. Hubbell, former associate attorney general (for actions at his law firm prior to 1992 and prior to his appointment at the Clinton Justice Department); the president and Mrs. Clinton; Whitewater and Madison Guaranty; the Vincent Foster suicide; the firing of certain White House Travel Office employees; the receipt of background FBI files by lower-level White House employees; whether White House Counsel Bernard Nussbaum committed perjury before a congressional committee; and the Monica Lewinsky matter.

(20)   Donald Smaltz, appointed September 9, 1994, investigating Agriculture Secretary Mike Espy—charged and acquitted on 30 counts by jury after five hours on December 2, 1998;

(21)   David Barrett, appointed May 24, 1995, investigating HUD Secretary Henry Cisneros—charged with 18 felony counts by Barrett, pled guilty to a single misdemeanor, paid $10,000 fine and later pardoned by President Bill Clinton;

(22)   Daniel Pearson, appointed July 6, 1995, investigating the late Commerce Secretary Ronald H. Brown—investigation terminated after Secretary Brown's death in plane crash;

(23)   Curtis Von Kann, appointed November 27, 1996, investigating the late Eli Segal, Director of Americorps—no charges brought;

(24)   Carol Elder Bruce, appointed March 19, 1998, investigating Interior Secretary Bruce Babbitt—no charges brought;

(25)   Ralph I. Lancaster, Jr., appointed May 26, 1998, investigating Labor Secretary Alexis Herman—no charges brought.

3. Regarding the source of this estimate of over $175 million in taxpayer costs for all the independent counsel investigations since its creation in 1978, that gross total is arrived at as follows: On June 30, 1999, the day the Independent Counsel Act expired, Cnn.com estimated that the 21 [*sic*—should have been 20] investigations had cost $166 million. One was still ongoing—the investigation of David M. Barrett of HUD Secretary Henry Cisneros. But the Barrett investigation went on another six years, at an estimated cost of an additional $11 million (for a total of over $21 million until he announced the end on January 20, 2006). Thus the total of over $175 million for all the independent counsel probes is conservative. Regarding the percentage constituting just the Starr–Ray probes of the Clinton Administration and the Clintons, these have varied in news reports between $60 million—$80 million—$60 million, *Washington Post*, March 31, 2001; $70 million, *Washington Post* editorial, March 26, 2002; $80 million, CNN.com, April 1, 1999 ("Independent probes of Clinton Administration cost nearly $80 million"). The variation is probably due to different definitions of what should be included in the total "probes" directly and indirectly related to the Clinton Administration, e.g., Webster Hubbell, Whitewater, and all the direct and indirect prosecutions in Arkansas that were at least related to the original investigation, Travel Office, FBI files disclosure, White House Counsel Bernard Nussbaum, Vincent Foster, Lewinsky, etc.

4. A former CIA operative named Thomas Clines. See note 2 (8), above.

5. The 14 dropped investigations were: Jordan, Kraft, Donovan, Meese (twice, by two independent counsels), Olson, Wallace, Pierce, State Department officials, Cisneros, Brown, Segal, Babbitt, and Herman. The three high-profile reversals were: Reagan National Security Council senior aide Oliver North, National Security Adviser John Poindexter, and Reagan senior aide, Lynn Nofziger. The one person who went to jail over Iran-Contra was CIA operative Thomas Clines, who pled guilty to tax-related offenses. (May 25, 1992, Clines serves 16 month jail sentence.) See Outlook Section, "The Big Sleazy: Is Clinton's Clan as Low-Rent as Reagan's," *Washington Post*, March 26, 1995, by Howard Kurtz for one of the best summations of the appearance of "sleaze" not having much substance behind it during the height of the scandal machine era.

6. This is the total reported by the Office of Independent Counsel after the final audit of Smaltz's total expenditures. See Final Report of the Independent Counsel, Donald Smaltz, published October 25, 2001. But the *Washington Post* reported on March 31, 2001, that the total cost of the Smaltz investigation was "29.3 million." George Lardner, Jr., "Clinton Probe Cost $60 Million; Total Counsel Costs for Administration Top $110 Million," *Washington Post*, p. A10. ("Donald G. Smaltz, whose investigation of former agriculture secretary Mike Espy ended on Espy's acquittal on gratuities charges, has spent $29.3 million.")

7. Jeffrey Rosen, "Stop, in the Name of the Law," *New York Times*, Dec. 6, 1998, p. D19 (quoting Donald Smaltz). Emphasis added.

8. John Mintz, "Espy Case Heightens Criticism of Independent Counsel Law," *Washington Post*, December 4, 1998, p. A16.

9. Dan Eggen and Albert B. Crenshaw, "Clinton-Era Cover-up is Alleged," *Washington Post*, January 20, 2006, p. A1.

10. Ibid., January 20, 2006. See also, 28 U.S.C. 598 (b).

11. Ruth Marcus, "The Prosecutor: Following Leads or Digging Dirt," *Washington Post*, January 30, 1998, p. A1.

12. Joe Conason and Gene Lyons, *The Hunting of the President* (St. Martin's Press, New York, 2000), p. 254.
13. Ibid.
14. Robert L. Jackson and Eric Lichtblau, "Whitewater Case Ends; Clintons Not Charged," *Los Angeles Times*, September 21, 2000, p. 1.
15. Susan Schmidt, "Hubbells Indicted on Tax Evasion, Fraud Charges," *Washington Post*, May 1, 1998, p. A1.
16. *U.S. v. Hubbell*, 11 F. Supp. 2d 25, 39 (U.S. D. Ct. July 1, 1998). On May 21, 1999, U.S. Court of Appeals for the D.C. Circuit vacated and remanded Judge Robinson's decision, but with instructions so unfavorable to Kenneth Starr's case that Starr filed an appeal of the Circuit Court decision to the U.S. Supreme Court. 334 U.S. App. D.C., 167 F. 3d 552 (1999). On June 5, 2000, the Supreme Court agreed with Judge Robertson and vacated the indictment. See *United States v. Hubbell*, 530 U.S. 27 (2000).
17. 11 F. Supp., p. 32.
18. Ibid., pp. 32–33.
19. Gerald E. Lynch and Philip K. Howard, "Special Prosecutors: What's the Point," *Washington Post*, May 28, 1994, Outlook Section, p. C7. See also Timothy Noah, "An Independent Counsel: Not Again!," *Slate Chatterbox*, September 30, 2003, who rejected the notion that independent counsels were needed to protect against political pressures that might compromise investigations by Justice Department career professionals.
20. Amitai Etzioni, "It's A Crime, the Way Politicians Go At It," *Washington Post*, August 5, 2001, Outlook Section, p. C1.
21. The Independent Counsel Act lapsed on June 30, 1999, pursuant to 28 U.S.C. § 599, which states that the act "shall cease to be effective five years after the date of the enactment of the Independent Counsel Reauthorization Act of 1994." 28 U.S.C. § 599 (1994); see also Roberto Suro, "As Special Counsel Law Expires, Power Will Shift to Reno," *Washington Post*, June 30, 1999, p. A6; and 28 C.F.R. § 600.1 (2000).
22. Suro, *Washington Post*, op. cit.
23. But that doesn't mean pressures won't continue to re-enact the independent counsel statute in the future. On September 30, 2003, after the disclosure of the name of a CIA employee's identity, Valerie Plame, apparently by the White House, Senator Joseph Lieberman (D.-Conn.), then running for President, called for re-enactment of the statute to investigate the Plame matter. Timothy Noah, "The Valerie Plame affair inspires a terrible idea," www.slate.com. September 30, 2003.
24. "Watt Pleads Guilty to Misdemeanor in HUD Case," *Washington Post*, January 3, 1996.
25. Ibid.

CHAPTER NINE

1. E. J. Dionne, Jr., "Revolution in Reverse," *Washington Post*, Nov. 19, 2004.
2. David Streifeld, "$4 Million Book Deal for Gingrich," *Washington Post*, December 22, 1994, p. A1.
3. Tom Kenworthy, "Democrats Give Speaker Taste of Medicine He Prescribed for Wright," *Washington Post*, January 20, 1995, p. A11.
4. Ibid.

5. John E. Yang, "House Reprimands, Penalizes Speaker," *Washington Post*, January 22, 1997, p. A1. Emphasis added.

6. Eric Pianin, December 19, 1998, "Livingston Rejected GOP Advice," *Washington Post*, p. A1.

7. Howard Kurtz, December 20, 1998, "Larry Flynt and the Barers of Bad News," *Washington Post*, p. F1.

CHAPTER TEN

1. PBS *NewsHour*, November 6, 2002, http://www.pbs.org/newshour/vote2002/races/ga_11-05-02.html

2. Richard Cohen, "American Politics Ad Nauseum," *Washington Post*, November 5, 2002, p. A25.

3. Charles Hunt, "NARAL To Pull Roberts TV Ad," *The Washington Times*, August 12, 2005.

4. Dana Milbank, "Democrats Conflicted on Playing Rough; Lack of Support for Roberts Ad Raises Questions of Tactics," *Washington Post*, August 13, 2005, p. A4.

5. "Carter: U.S. Presence Fuels Attacks," *Atlanta Journal-Constitution*, September 22, 2004, p. 12A.

6. In the first posting, on October 17, 2005, listing 21 "convicts" from the Reagan Administration, appeared in Daily Kos at www.dailykos.com/story/2005/10/17/194133/16, at 4:41 PM PDT, "lorelynn" wrote in the text of the list of 21 only that North's conviction had been overturned—not Poindexter's and Nofziger's. The second posting on April 6, 2006, appeared in Daily Kos at www.dailykos.com/story/2006/4/6/205317/9138, listed 19 "convicts" and in the text of that list, it is noted that Poindexter and Nofziger's convictions had been overturned. But it still did not alter "lorelynn" calling all 19 "convicts."

7. In the subsequent posting on April 6, 2006, "lorelynn" attributes this quote to the *Washington Post*'s Pulitzer Prize winning journalist, Haynes Johnson, apparently from his book, *Sleepwalking Through History*. See also, Haynes Johnson, "Strides Toward Higher Standards," *Washington Post*, February 3, 1989, p. A2. In the latter story, Johnson writes, "By last Election Day, 138 Reagan Administration officials had been the subject of official or criminal investigations, and 13 of them had been convicted. Never before under one administration have so many U.S. officials been involved in such cases. Even allowing for tighter guidelines and laws governing official conduct, the record is a sorry one." It is somewhat disturbing that a journalist of Johnson's integrity and reputation would get caught in adding the apples of "investigations" to the oranges of "convictions" and publish a total number of 138, which leads to a negative inference of unprecedented corruption due to a large number of "indictments" and "investigations" that never became "convictions."

8. Howard Kurtz, Outlook section, "The Big Sleazy: Is Clinton's Clan as Low-Rent as Reagan's?," *Washington Post*, March 26, 1995, p. C1. Kurtz pointed out that Democrats were first to randomly attributing "sleaze" and "corruption" to Republicans without hard evidence of convictions of crimes. "The Democrats were eager to use individual cases of scandal as a political weapon and they were perfectly positioned to do so [in the 1980s when they controlled the House of Representatives]." For example, Vice President Walter Mondale had campaigned in 1984 for president speaking vaguely about the "sleaze factor" in

the Reagan Administration and Gary Hart had called the level of Reagan Administration corruption "staggering." And former Congressman and Majority Whip Tony Coehlo, who later resigned over an ethics flap based mainly on appearances and no determination of wrongdoing, said during the Reagan years that the "sleaze factor" accusation "will work for us" politically, as if that made it okay. Obviously, Democrats paid dearly during the Clinton years for this careless use of the charge "corruption"—but seem to be repeating that gotcha error by doing the same thing in 2005–2006.

9. Notebook, *New Republic*, February 20, 2006, p. 8.
10. E. J. Dionne, Jr., "Tom DeLay and the Wright Stuff," *Washington Post*, April 15, 2005, p. A25.
11. Charles Babington, "Reid Apologizes for News Release on GOP," *Washington Post*, January 20, 2006, p. A4.
12. Author's emphasis.
13. Bill Press, *How the Republicans Stole Christmas*, (New York: Doubleday, 2005), pp. 71–72.
14. E. J. Dionne, Jr., "Revolution In Reverse," *Washington Post*, Nov. 19, 2004, p. A29.
15. Richard H. Davis, "The Anatomy of a Smear Campaign," *Boston Globe*, March 21, 2004. But see Jacob Weisberg, "The Pot and Kettle Primary," February 26, 2000, www.slate.com, in which the author describes Senator McCain's campaign's negative tactics and distortions against Governor Bush.
16. Paper written by Dr. Nancy Snow, assistant professor, Political Science, New England College, Henniker, N.H., February 21, 2000. http://www.commondreams.org/views/022100–106.htm <http://www.commondreams.org/views/022100–106.htm>.
17. Senator John C. Danforth, *New York Times*, June 17, 2005, editorial page. See also, Peter Slevin, "St. Jack and the Bullies in the Pulpit," *Washington Post Outlook*, February 2, 2006, p. C1.
18. Phillips, *American Theocracy* (Viking, New York, 2006), at 243, 368–69.
19. Ibid., p. 217. At the close of his book, Phillips quotes from Gary Wills in a 2005 article in the *New York Review of Books* who, referring to the Republican's various interest groups, wrote: "If religious extremism is only one large set of bodies in this fringe constellation [of Republican interest groups], it is a powerful one. That is why federal agencies reject scientific reports on ecological, stem cell, contraceptive, and abortion issues. They sponsor not only faith-based social relief, but faith-based war, faith based science, faith based education, and faith-based medicine." Ibid., p. 347.
20. Ibid., p. 369.
21. Alan Brinkley, "Clear and Present Dangers," *New York Times Book Review*, p. 11. (While reviewing Philips' book, *American Theocracy*, Brinkley writes that the power of these extremists within the Republican Party is "significant, but not conclusive.")
22. *Mayor v. Cooper*, 73 U.SA. 247, p. 251 (1868).
23. Paul Gewirtz, Chad Golder, "So Who Are they Activists?" 31 *Montana Lawyer* 20, 21 (2005).
24. Ibid.
25. Andres Martinez, "Paul O'Neill, Unplugged, or What Would Alexander Hamilton Have Done?" *New York Times*, January 14, 2004, "Editorial Observer," on editorial page.

26. Phillips, *American Theocracy*, p. 11.
27. Timothy Egan, "Built With Steel, Perhaps, but Greased With Pork," *New York Times*, April 10, 2004, p. A1.
28. Ibid.
29. Frank Rich, "In the Beginning, There Was Abramoff," *New York Times*, October 2, 2005.
30. Quoted from "Media Matters for America," http://mediamatters.org/items/200412200004, posting on December 20, 2004, which lists many other Limbaugh lies about all (not "some" or "certain") Democrats and liberals, e.g., liberals "would have sought out bin Laden and tried to make a deal with him" (8/16/05); of "hat[e] the military" (5/3/04); stating that "John Kerry really doesn't think 3,000 Americans dead in one day is that big a deal (10/12/04); for Democrats, "the more deaths in Iraq, the better" (12/10/04) and "probably have more fear of Christians than they do nuclear weapons being launched by North Korea" (6/09/05). Nor have Republican national leaders who have appeared on his program publicly denounced his overtly racist statements, such as on the day that Rev. Jesse Jackson joined the Kerry-Edwards campaign, Limbaugh said the "Kerry campaign has finally gotten a chocolate chip" (9/30/04).
31. *Hannity and Colmes*, Fox News Channel, October 4, 2004.
32. Broadcast, March 22, 2005.
33. The *New York Times*, January 20, 2006, p. A9. Included in its signatories were Ed Asner, Harry Belafonte, Susan Sarandon, Howard Zinn, and Jessica Lange.
34. "Outraged Liberals Find an Outlet and a Community Online," *Washington Post*, April 15, 2006, p. A1. The blogger, Maryscott O'Connor, not only seems to thrive on hate-Bush postings, she attracts ugly mirrors of Ann Coulter. As the expletive-filled hate words regarding George W. Bush poured in after one of her more vitriolic postings, she said: "I'm going to be proud of this."
35. Peter Baker, "A Bush Aide's Blunt Words," *Washington Post*, June 13, 2006, p. A19.

CHAPTER ELEVEN

1. Ron Chernow, *Alexander Hamilton* (New York: Penguin, 2004), p. 626.
2. Sebastian Mallaby, *Washington Post*, "A Time for McCain?" October 2, 2005, p. A17.
3. Ibid.
4. Michael Tomasky, "Party In Search Of a Nation," *American Prospect*, May 2006. While addressed to Democrats in search of a core, unifying message, the piece is equally applicable to Republicans (like former Senator John Danforth and other moderates) who see their party dominated by special interests on the religious right. Tomasky's much discussed article proposes the theme of the "common good" as the philosophical core for Democrats. He contrasts that brand of liberalism to the 1960s and post-1960s version, which focused too much on individual (or group) rights and interests rather than the broader public interest. He sees the need for a political philosophy that calls on all Americans "to contribute to a project larger than themselves . . . sacrificing for and participating in the creation of a common good." From the New Deal through the Great Society, Tomasky argues, "the Democrats practiced a brand of liberalism quite different from today's. Yes, it certainly sought to expand

rights and prosperity. But it did something more: That liberalism was built around the idea—the philosophical principle—that citizens should be called upon to look beyond their own self-interest and work for a greater common interest."

Tomasky is certainly right that what he calls "civic republicanism" is an important liberal value—just take John Kennedy's famous "ask not what your country can do for you" line in his inaugural speech or his creation of the Peace Corps as examples of this tradition. But Tomasky's article, however, failed to define the limited role of government—and, specifically, a government sympathetic to the private market and private sector as the engine of economic growth—that goes beyond the traditional notion of liberal government and that this chapter argues is now required—both on grounds of good policy as well as politically. Nor did he address the importance of conservative fiscal policy and moderation and tolerance on cultural issues and values (or, for that matter, foreign policy and national security issues) that are also required if an enduring new centrist majority is to be created by either political party. See also, Robin Toner, "Optimistic Democrats Debate Party's Vision," *New York Times*, May 9, 2006, p. A1.

5. Markos Moulitsas, "Problems on the Left: Hillary Clinton Too Much a Clinton Democrat?" *Washington Post*, May 7, 2006, p. B1; quote appears on p. B5. Emphasis added. Moulitsas also fails to address the fact that for five out of the last six presidential elections, until Bill Clinton ran and won in 1992, Republicans had won by landslide margins over traditional liberal Democratic nominees. Bill Clinton proved that a Democrat could run on a progressive platform, faithful to the party's FDR tradition, but still be able to win in many Red southern, border, and western states. As seen in his *Post* outlook piece, Moulitsas (and other bloggers on the purist left) are shifting their critique of the Clinton "third way" to his wife, Senator Hillary Rodham Clinton.

6. Alan Cassidy, "Talk of the Town," *New Yorker*, April 10, 2006.

7. William Saleton, "It's Time to Put Roe Behind Us," *Washington Post Outlook*, March 5, 2006, p. 1.

8. Ibid. The author points out that when *Roe* was decided in 1973, the average occurrence of abortions for women age 15–44 years old was approximately 16 per 1,000. That went up to almost 30 in 1981, but because of these improvements in contraception and public education, among other reasons, by 2006 the rate of abortions has dropped down almost to the level of when *Roe* was decided—to approximately 21 per 1,000.

9. *Newsweek*, November 29, 2004, back page.

10. War Powers Resolution of 1973. Public Law 93–148. 93rd Congress, H. J. Res. 542. November 7, 1973. For full text see http://www.policyalmanac.org/world/archive/war_powers_resolution.shtml

11. Leslie H. Gelb and Anne-Marie Slaughter, "No More Blank Check Wars," *Washington Post*, November 8, 2005, p. xx.; Gelb and Slaughter, "It's Time To Stop Slipping Into Armed Conflict," Atlantic Online, November 2005.

12. See Iowa Code, Section 42.1–42.6 (Coolice.Legis.State.ia.us) and "Legislative Guide to Redistricting" (Ed Cook, Legal Counsel, Iowa Legislative Service Bureau, 2000); Eilperin, *Fight Club Politics*, pp. 115–25.

13. Carl M. Cannon, "Enough To Make You Cry: Partisanship, Polarization and the State of Our (Dis)Union," *National Journal*, pp. 18–24, at p. 24. See also Cannon, "Politics as Nightmare," *National Journal*, February 13, 1999.

CHAPTER TWELVE

1. Jack Newfield, *Robert Kennedy: A Memoir* (New York: E. P. Dutton, 1969), pp. 97–98.

2. Lanny Davis, *The Emerging Democratic Majority: Lessons and Legacies From the New Politics* (New York: Stein & Day, 1973), p. 256.

3. Newfield, p. 98.

4. CNN, *Lou Dobbs Tonight*, May 23, 2005, http://transcripts.cnn.com, p. 13.

5. Sebastian Mallaby, "A Time For McCain?" *Washington Post*, October 3, 2005, p. A17. Mallaby captured the New Center message almost perfectly in this piece, as when he condemned what he described as the "transaction view of politics" that "holds that candidates must mobilize selected groups—farmers, small-business owners, minorities and so on—to support their campaigns, then repay them with government favors once they are in office."

6. "Lou Dobbs Tonight" broadcast May 24, 2005, http://transcripts.cnn.com, p. 13.

7. Brian Schweitzer, "The Other Black Gold," *New York Times*, October 11, 2005, op-ed page.

8. Newfield, p. 235. In 1972, when I was a coordinator of Al Lowenstein's unsuccessful congressional campaign in Brooklyn, NY, Lowenstein almost casually showed me that scrawled note, stuck in his side pocket, on the back of an envelope. I only hope his children preserved it after his tragic assassination in 1978.

9. "Lou Dobbs Tonight," May 24, 2005, http://transcripts.cnn.com, p. 13.

10. Theodore C. Sovensen, *A Different Kind of Presidency: A Proposal for Breaking the Political Deadlock* (New York: Harper & Row, 1984). The other three scenarios advanced by Sovenson being that the candidate make the proposal to run with a leading member of the other party and, if elected, serve only one term, (1) before the national convention, (2) at the convention, (3) after the election but before inauguration, or (4) after the inauguration using the 25th amendment, pp. 66–70. I have chosen the fourth because it permits a vigorous debate of the issues during a campaign where the outcome is uncertain but with the understanding that either presidential nominee (or his/her vice presidential nominee) will be serving as president or vice president.

11. Ibid., pp. 54–55.

12. Ibid., pp. 61–64.

13. Quoted by Sorensen at opening of *A Different Kind of Presidency*.

INDEX